Also by Denise Le Fay

The Temple of Master Hotei:

A Unique Past Life Memory

A LIGHTWORKER'S MISSION

The Journey Through

Polarity Resolution

Denise Le Fay

Illustrations by Yasmeen Harper

Printed in the United States of America.

Cover design by Todd Engel
Cover image by Ali Mazraie Shadi
istockphoto.com/Atropat

Interior illustrations by Yasmeen Harper

BookLocker.com, Inc.
2010

Dedication

This book is dedicated to all who have worked from both sides of the dimensional veil to bring about the greatest of transitions.

Contents

Illustrations ix

Gratitude... xi

Introduction.. xiii

PART ONE: Portals and Preparations 1972–1979 1

PART TWO: Interdimensional Lightwork 1980–1989 ... 43

PART THREE: ETs, Multidimensional Construction,
   Ascension, Polarity Battles, Polarity Resolution
   1990–2004 139

EPILOGUE: Completing Phase One 2004–2009 497

About The Author 511

About The Artist 512

Illustrations

PART ONE

Fig. 1.1.   *Eighteenth-Century Portal Encounter*

Fig. 1.2.   *Silver Portal Creatures*

Fig. 1.3.   *Earth Elemental Encounter*

PART TWO

Fig. 2.1.   *Yasmeen's Great Pyramid Sphere Memory*

Fig. 2.2.   *Sirius, Orion, Pleiades Star Glyphs*

Fig. 2.3.   *Egyptian Twins Polarity Arm Pose*

Fig. 2.4.   *Dance of the Ages Positions*

Fig. 2.5.   *Age of Leo through Aquarius Polarity Integration Poses*

Fig. 2.6.   *Throne Pose or Energy Stair Steps*

Fig. 2.7.   *Water Elemental Encounter*

PART THREE

Fig. 3.1.   *Great Pyramid Octahedron*

Fig. 3.2.   *ET Pineal and Pituitary Adjustments*

Fig. 3.3.   *Sixth Dimensional Geometric Blueprints*

Fig. 3.4.   *Ancient ET Lion Beings*

Fig. 3.5.   *Ancient ET Bird Beings*

Fig. 3.6.   *6D Blueprints or Morphogenetic Fields*

Fig. 3.7.   *Merkaba Craft and Being*

Fig. 3.8.   *Interdimensional Sky Tubes*

Fig. 3.9.   *A Reptilian Encounter*

Fig. 3.10. *Flat ET Face*

Fig. 3.11. *The 8D Orion*

Fig. 3.12. *The 6D Sirian*

Fig. 3.13. *The 5D Pleiadian*

Fig. 3.14. *The Demon*

Fig. 3.15. *Asian Man Lightshow Pose*

Gratitude

I want to thank my sister, Yasmeen Harper, for her wonderful illustrations of Starbeings, nonphysical creatures, and numerous other beings and objects characteristically unseen. It could not have been an easy task having to draw illustrations of nonphysical, other dimensional beings, Starbeings, creatures, a demon, interdimensional objects and energies for this book based only on my written descriptions of them. Between our numerous emails back and forth over seven months, we were able to adjust and fine-tune many of the drawings to get them as close as possible to what I have clairvoyantly seen.

Without your accurate intuitive senses, your ancient Egyptian past life memories, plus your patience with my insistence over having every illustration be as accurate to what I have seen as possible, this book would simply not be the same. Your drawings of nonphysical beings, entities and objects, brings the book to life in a very special way and bridges the dimensions, providing the reader with a rare and intimate glimpse of a handful of multidimensional residents. Thank you so for your time, energy, and dedication to this project.

Introduction

One unexpected afternoon thirty years ago, I had an important memory suddenly flood my consciousness. It was such an extreme vibrational reach for me in 1979 that I instantly broke into a sweat from head to toe because of it. I stood there shaking, with sweat rolling down my back and chest from the conscious reconnection with this beyond-ancient memory, as Mom and my sister Yasmeen watched and wondered what was happening to me. The three of us had been talking about something else when this memory event and clairvoyant vision abruptly surfaced like a perfect time-coded trigger.

In this clairvoyant vision memory, I saw a small group of Lightbeings standing in front of seven or so other identical Lightbeings. We were having an important discussion and very big decisions were about to be made by all of us. After listening to the smaller group propose their ideas to the rest of us, I raised my hand and stated, *"We'll go."* We all continued discussing this exciting new project a bit longer, then this small group of other nonphysical Lightbeings and I left. At this point, the vision ended but the memories and connections certainly have not.

As I stood in Mom's portal house in 1979, sweating, shaking, and panting from the energetic impact of making such a dramatic and conscious level shift at that time—back to the beginning of The Project—I knew something very important had just happened to me. Let me elaborate briefly about what this memory and vision were really about because it is directly related to this book, our current lives and rapidly transforming consciousness and reality.

This small group of spiritual beings were the *original US* as we existed when we were very close to Source. This new Project that was proposed was about creating certain worlds—the solar system, Earth, and much more. Eventually, we would begin slowly inserting other aspects of ourselves into these new and increasingly denser, lower vibrating dimensions, worlds, and realities. The Project—and this is by no means *the only* Project—was about our creating, and then intentionally devolving aspects of us vibrationally to insert into what we were creating. In this way, any of us who desired could directly experience and create further from within what we had originally created. There is an eternal desire for more creativity and experiencing, so we create and then enthusiastically insert different fragmented aspects of our Selves into what we have created at higher levels. We literally seed aspects of ourselves into our creations. That was what this Project was—creating new systems and worlds and then intentionally involuting vibrationally into them over incomprehensibly long periods.

From early childhood in this life, one of my most beloved simultaneous *"past life"* memories was of being an etheric merbeing (not yet polarized into either a female or male), that existed within the not-yet-physical element of water. I remember building things and creating waterways, rivers, lakes, freshwater streams and grottos for Lemuria when it was only etheric. As a child in this life, I remembered being this individual when Lemuria and its creators were not yet physical. I did not remember the name *Lemuria* as a child, just what parts I played in creating aspects of that world at a nonphysical level. It was a most beautiful, precious, and deeply loved creation of these others and mine, but to me as a child in this incarnation, they were simply my special fantasy-like memories that I ached to be within once again.

In the summer of 1965, my parents drove us from where we lived in southern California, upstate to see the great Sequoias or Redwood forests for the first time. I was thirteen at the time, and the very first moment I saw the Redwood trees I knew we were within a little pocket of my beloved ancient Lemuria that still exists today in physicality. I was ecstatic seeing, feeling, and smelling the Redwoods, the ferns, the rich soil and being in those ancient Lemurian forests once again. I was blissfully contented and horribly homesick all at the same time, which is a common sensation Wanderers and Lightworkers often have on physical earth.

On the trip home, Dad drove south along the Pacific Coast Highway and I saw Monterey California for the first time. It also looked and felt like portions of my beloved Lemuria and I wondered how much of the original Motherland still exists physically in pockets like this along certain areas of California and elsewhere. Years later, I went to La Jolla in SoCal and instantly recognized more remnants of original and very ancient Lemuria there as well.

I felt it necessary to include my memories concerning how and why this particular Project originated, primarily because this book deals with the completion phase of it. When we, as great unified spiritual beings existing next to Source first discussed this Project, we knew we would create The Project within the structure of a timeline—a beginning phase, middle, and an end phase. There has to be an endpoint, a shift-point, a completion and graduation point within The Project and that is what this book is about. The original few vibrationally devolved into many so we could experience and further learn from deep within our creations. However, there always comes the point when you vibrationally stop, turn around, and intentionally begin evolving energetically back out of the Project because it has expanded as far as the original creators desired. It and so many of us have journeyed as far away from Source as was originally planned. When all has been created and experienced—usually multiple times in many different incarnations, bodies, personalities, and time periods—the few know when it is time to wrap things up and graduate into something new. In our current lives, that is what we have been living through. We stopped, turned around and began evolving vibrationally. The Project has served us all very well, and now we—in our numerous and diverse forms and levels—are ready for a new Project elsewhere. However, before we could complete and exit this Plan we had some serious personal, planetary, and collective tidying up to do first. There is a rule about No Cosmic Littering while on the road!

I suspect *A Lightworker's Mission: The Journey Through Polarity Resolution* may be a bit different from some of the current Ascension or Lightworker related books. It most definitely is not is a book about *new age* knowledge merely dressed up in old Piscean Age religious, spiritual, or occult teachings for the exiting world, its old systems and astrological Age. Neither is it channeled material from a higher dimensional being or group of beings, Archangel, Starbeing or group of ETs. Nor is it a spiritual How-To book, or an intellectual instructional manual that defines reality for you step-by-step. It is not Eastern or Western wisdom teachings from the past Piscean Age or any others before it. What this book is about is my journey—as a First Wave Lightworker Wanderer—living and interdimensionally working through the alchemical ascension, polarity resolution, and dimensional shifting process. *A Lightworker's Mission* is about what it looked like, how it felt, the interdimensional joys and marvels, the dangers and darkness, confusions, doubts, pain and tremendous struggles of being a First Wave Lightworker within a profoundly dark, polarized world and energetically transmuting portions of residual lower vibrating energies. This is of course strictly from my personal perspective and developmental levels and consciousness at the times each of these events and transitional phases happened to me over the decades.

Since my past life at the beginning of the Age of Leo, I have remembered that I was on a mission on Earth, and that one important aspect of that mission was to take the place of my ancient and greatly loved Starbeing friends who have been my teachers and guides while I was learning here. I knew I had reached the point in this current life where I would graduate or shift energetically into something similar to what they had been for me. I sensed I remained behind on earth long ago to accomplish a lengthy mission of personal and ongoing development—to get my hands and soul dirty working that mission from within the physical third dimension. The Wanderer usually requires plenty of personal experiences *within* the dimension and world that she/he has come to assist shift or ascend when that time arrives. This current life and time is that time for humanity and earth, as well as for the many Lightworkers and Wanderers.

A Lightworker's Mission is about my personal experiences from the perspective of polluted and often dark and ugly polarized *ground zero.* It is about my personal and extremely unglamorous, unromantic, First Wave Lightworker passage through Phase One of the tremendously difficult, alchemical ascension and polarity resolution process. If it educates, it does so by *firsthand experience*—the good, the bad, and the ugly of it.

Many people have a wildly distorted impression of what *Lightworkers* are, what they do, and why. I feel one big reason for this and other confusions about the current ascension and planetary dimensional shifting process, has to do with the fact that certain new astrological Age teachers, channelers, writers, lecturers, and global sacred site activators are all doing something highly specialized. They all are doing these different things, yet obviously all for the same end result. They are different teachers doing very different things for many different people during everyone's different stages of remembering and awakening around the planet. Because of this, numerous voices and different personalities have been needed to all say the same things basically, but in their unique individual ways, so as many people as possible receive the overall ascension and dimensional shifting message around the planet.

These known and unknown Lightworkers, Wanderers, Starpeople and Indigo's need different public teachers, writers, lectures and channelers to help *them* further wakeup and remember—plus explain why they are back on Earth now going through all they are via the evolutionary ascension process. The many Planetary Servers need each other to help us all better remember what our individual spiritual and energetic gifts and talents are within this unfolding, planetary ascension and dimensional shifting process.

There is still the important need however, to be able to discern information or read energies being dispersed by so many people around the planet. Sometimes the information or channeled message becomes slightly distorted for a number of reasons, and it is extremely important to be able to energetically discern information and sift through it all *on your own*. Energies, consciousness, DNA and reality are changing so rapidly now, that things and information I enjoyed and could relate to months ago, are nearly meaningless and boring to me today. I suspect this is only going to increase for all of us as we continue with our compressed transformations, so discern your way through these intense and rapid changes and the information provided by so many about it all.

I know there are many seemingly average people across the planet that have been living and doing serious Lightwork for years; resolving polarity within themselves, plus transmuting massive amounts of residual lower dense, dark, or negative vibrating energies on Earth and the astral (Collective) created by billions of people over the past 12,500-some years. The majority of these Lightworkers will never write a book about what they have personally suffered through, struggled with, and learned doing this intense transformational energetic work for self and All. They will never fly to another country to direct or even participate in the activation of some ancient sacred site. They will never be interviewed, go on the *new age* lecture circuit, or have videos of themselves on YouTube sharing their astonishing, mind-blowing and heart-wrenching personal spiritual Lightworker experiences. Many of them will never even attend a workshop or lecture conducted by another Lightworker. Nevertheless, I know they are out there and that they are magnificent, resolute beings; that they are the brilliant, unsung heroes, the Light Warriors, the real living Alchemists of our time.

Just because these many nameless and invisible Lightworkers across the planet will never become publically known or famous, certainly does not mean they have not energetically done all they have over the past decade or longer. All of you unknown Lightworkers out there *are* known and are deeply and greatly valued.

Terms I have used such as 3D, 4D, and 5D are to communicate complex concepts within the incomprehensibly great vastness that we create, learn, and express within as spiritual beings. If I did not use terms like this to try to describe different frequencies and consciousness locations within this interdimensional vastness, we would all become momentarily lost. Therefore, until telepathy is everyone's native tongue again, we will have to use definitions and terms like this to describe the levels and layers within different dimensions and locals.

Over the decades I've had people ask me how I can know so much about certain things, yet not know about other things. Believe me when I say that I have been frustrated by this myself. I have also been asked how I can be psychic yet still become physically sick, when to them I should have seen or known what was coming and been able to prevent it. In addition, if I can communicate with certain ETs, then why don't I see UFOs all over the place? That last one is easy—because all the ETs I have known never needed any type of UFO craft to get from one place to another.

My point is that one can be a very old soul, a Lightworker, a Wanderer, and reincarnate with either total or partial amnesia as to their personal mission and higher dimensional identity during their life/lives on Earth. Because of this, it must often look and sound to certain people as if we Lightworkers/Wanderers are tripping all over ourselves trying to remember more of the Big Picture, and that is usually the case. Other times we sound like we know exactly what is going on and what is most likely going to manifest, and that too is often correct. There are important reasons why Lightworkers and Wanderers do not have full access to their higher dimensional identities and knowledge from within their 3D incarnations from the beginning; sanity and safety are the two main reasons. Over the years and decades, we remember more when we can safely cope and carry higher dimensional knowledge and energies in a lower frequency body and world.

A Lightworker's Mission covers over three decades of multidimensional experiences I have lived through in relation to my spiritual journey and undertaking as a Lightworker. This book is about what it looked and felt like living through the different decades, stages, and levels of what I will refer to as *Phase One* of the ascension, polarity resolution, and dimensional shifting process.

Far more Lightworkers and Wanderers reincarnate during the time of the great astrological Age changes or transitional cusp periods than during the many long years during each mid-Age. We do this to assist humanity in casting off the old exiting Age's energies, consciousness, belief systems and physical systems, and by carrying within our bodies and consciousness the new incoming astrological Age energies. However, this Age change into Aquarius and our current lives in it are far different because so much more is happening than simply an astrological Age change. It is the completion of an incomprehensibly long cycle of creativity and learning within much more than just astrological Ages, but also other cosmic and Galactic orbits and cycles within this cosmic neighborhood. We are doing much more now than exiting the Age of Pisces and entering the astrological Age of Aquarius; we are completing a massive multi-layered cycle within numerous other cycles and the Mayan calendar end date of Winter Solstice 2012 reflects this evolutionary process.

I chose to begin this account in 1972 because that was an important and obvious transition point for my whole family. Much was ended, and much begun for us in 1972. Mom was intuitively led to the portal property, which she bought in early spring of 1972. My son Chris was born in late spring of 1972, so I decided to have this book begin at that point. I could have gone back even earlier in my life because I have always been a Lightworker Wanderer and was in nearly constant contact with higher dimensional beings from very early childhood. However, I chose 1972 as the starting point in this incarnation to what I will call *Phase One* of the compressed ascension or evolutionary, polarity integration and resolution process.

When Mom bought the portal property in early 1972, and six months later placed her new house on it, that home became the hub of thirty-two years of highly unusual phenomena, interdimensional work and energy transfers, intense Lightwork, and often-difficult polarity integration and resolution work for me. It also became my important and much needed retreat for when my extremely severe physical ascension process started in early 1999. Decades earlier Mom sensed this particular home would be terribly important for me at some point in the future, and that most certainly turned out to be true.

Denise Le Fay

December 2009

A LIGHTWORKER'S MISSION

The Journey Through

Polarity Resolution

PART ONE

Portals and Preparations
1972–1979

In November 1972, my recently divorced mother placed her new mobile home on a quarter acre of land she had bought six months earlier. This little plot of land was located in a very rural and unpopulated area in southern California. She and my younger sister Yasmeen moved in and began the process of slowly making the bare and isolated place a real home.

At that time I was married and living in another county in southern California and didn't see Mom or Yasmeen much. In June of 1972 I had my only child—a wonderful healthy son. My marriage did not last long and when my son was only two our divorce became legal and we each went our separate ways. Some marriages are to bring in certain souls and that is about it. By 1975, I moved to the same rural town my mother and sister were living in and rented a small house a few blocks away. It was a time for all of us to heal the wounds from our marriages and divorces and adjust to our new lives and being single parents.

It was good living so physically close to my mother and sister as I learned to grow up quickly myself and did my best to help my young son feel safe and stable without a father. I would often go over to Mom's house to visit and we would work on planting pine trees on her bare quarter acre or any number of other things that a new house on empty land requires. The creativity and hard physical work helped all of us as we moved through our newly divorced transitions and adapted to single life again.

40☺At that time, Mom was forty to forty-one years old and living through her Uranus Opposition transit hence, her life changing divorce, house selling, moving and property buying during that time. I was only twenty-two to twenty-three at the time but knew very certainly that I would never remarry. I discovered how necessary freedom and independence was for me and that I desired to be on my own, in charge, and fully responsible. A husband and a litter of kids was never my idea of a wonderful happy life. My soul had another important and well-planned agenda carefully laid out, and within an amazingly tight timeline, I discovered years later. Of course I wasn't fully conscious of all this at that time, only that I could easily clairvoyantly see and feel numerous snapshots of my life up until age forty. There is that potent Uranus Opposition transit again! I could psychically see and sense portions of my life up until age forty, but from that point on, it was totally black and empty to my inner clairvoyant vision.

I knew this meant I would not die at age forty or shortly thereafter, but that my life, my reality and I would change so dramatically at age forty that I simply could not relate. Starting at age forty my life would be much more on the other side of the Veil, and because of this, it was a blank, black, nothingness to my current psychic vision. I didn't worry or focus on this at all but lived my life prior to turning forty as I was supposed to—as all of us are supposed to. I lived and matured, played with, taught, and deeply loved my special old-soul friend who was within the body of my son in this incarnation. I had boyfriends and I lived, loved, and learned. The two decades of the 1970s and 1980s—my twenties and thirties—were my time to be as *"normal"* as I was capable of within society and reality at that time.

From what I now know, from birth through age thirty-nine was my period in this life to fulfill certain pre-incarnational agreements, important karmic plans, and to birth my only child. I had those first thirty-nine years to complete personal karmic plans with many people for many reasons. My turning thirty-nine in late December 1990 would usher in a profoundly different energy and phase of Lightworking for me personally. I believe many Baby Boomer aged Lightworkers were triggered into vastly higher energetic levels of personal awareness and planetary service at the beginning of their individual Uranus Opposition transits at age thirty-nine. Ignorance *is* bliss as they say, and I thoroughly used and enjoyed my thirty-eight years prior to that very intense and life changing astrological transit activation at age thirty-nine.

During those early years in the 1970s when I lived in the same small rural town as Mom and my sister Yasmeen, we all began having abnormally unusual experiences at her house and land. At that time none of us really focused on what a portal was or all that was energetically building year-by-year in that location and why. I do know our Higher Self often deliberately keeps the lower ego aspects of us in the dark during certain phases and stages of our lives. This is done because the ego simply is not designed or equipped to handle higher-level soul plans and infinitely higher energies and consciousness. In most cases it helps the ego aspect of us to NOT know what we are about to get ourselves into! In the early stages, it is both safer and easier for us to not consciously remember many of the pre-planned life initiations, stages of intense soul growth, not to mention the difficult Lightworker missions many of us will be living through during that incarnation. In most cases, this type of safeguard or deliberate higher awareness amnesia is created by our Higher Selves to protect us until it is time to consciously carry a little more.

Mom's plot of land was literally out in the middle of a huge empty field. There was a paved two-lane road in front of her property to the north with a row of large, tall eucalyptus trees between it and the road. To the east was a twenty-plus acre field used to grow crops of potatoes, wheat, and millet. Other years the soil would be ploughed under to rest and recuperate for a couple of years. This was great for us because it meant we had no neighbors, barking dogs, kids, vehicles or anything else next door to us on that entire east side—just a huge field that buffered us from other neighbors to the east.

The property to the south of Mom's lot was also empty land owned by an elderly husband and wife. Their house was located near the front of their acreage facing an unpaved street, but the back empty half of their land was positioned directly behind Mom's lot. He had two horses on those back few acres for a couple years, which I enjoyed being a horse lover. The majority of the time though it was empty land to the south of Mom's lot.

The *only* property next to us that had people living on it was to the west, and unfortunately, the two lot lines were side-by-side with nothing like a tall solid fence, bulletproof brick wall, prison razor-ribbon barbwire barricade, or a deep and wide castle moat separating them. During the three months Mom was shopping for a new mobile home after having already bought her land, a young man bought this lot next to hers on the west and moved his mobile home, wife, and baby son onto the property. This seemingly benign action and coincidental timing will make more sense later. Keep it in mind however because it is important and symbolic to what happened repeatedly over the decades. When Mom bought her lot, she desperately wanted to buy this west adjoining lot also but simply could not afford to do so.

The surrounding areas were very rural in the 1970s and 1980s and there was little traffic past Mom's house during those decades. There were no streetlights, no sidewalks, and there was no mail delivery so one had to have a Post Office box to receive mail. At that point, there were no sewer or gas lines either as is often the case with small rural towns outside the city limits. There were very few other houses nearby as well, which was something we enjoyed actually. There were rows of huge and endlessly messy eucalyptus trees all around this small rural town however. I never liked them because their energies always felt rather negative and menacing to me, not to mention how endlessly messy they were all year.

Mom was intuitively drawn to this particular rural town after looking at numerous other small towns on the outskirts of larger cities in southern California. She was immediately attracted to the location from an energy standpoint. Years later, she told me she felt quite compelled to buy that particular land and put her home on it so my sister and I would have a place to live in the future. That sounds like something most parents would consider for their children—especially a mother for her divorced daughter and grandson. It was always a strong intuitive pull for Mom with that weird property, plus sensing it would be a much needed home for me a couple decades later. That certainly turned out to be the case.

One of the early anomalies Mom experienced on her new property (I experienced it numerous times when I moved in years later), was what sounded like a tiny horse galloping insanely fast counterclockwise around the house outside. It was, and still is, a mystery. I remember Mom telling me about hearing a sound at night of wee hoofs galloping at supersonic speed around her house. Many nights she lay in bed listening for a half-hour while trying to imagine what in the world could make that sound at that speed. She said she had gone outside many nights to investigate, but the energy usually felt intensely "*uncomfortable*" so she promptly went back inside the house.

This was another of the many weird phenomena that happened repeatedly on and around Mom's property. It was a strange anomaly that would make you giddy at first, like too much of one Elemental energy will often do, but then later, a little spooked and overly sensitive because things felt rather *dark, wild, and otherworldly* when this particular phenomenon would happen. Years later when I was living there with Mom, I heard these tiny running hoofs speeding around the outside of the house and started paying attention to what phase the Moon was in when we heard this. Often, but not always it was on or near the New Moon which just added to the overall mystery of the event.

∞ Another anomaly that happened on Mom's property after she planted a backyard lawn was the overnight appearance of *Fairy rings*. She would discover rings in her backyard lawn that were about five or six feet in diameter and they had not been there only hours before. I saw those many times myself, along with the infinity symbol many times over the years. These two shapes would just appear in the backyard lawn overnight and would last for months before they finally disappeared. There were no trees, bushes, or anything planted in the lawn area, only the grass. This may be a natural phenomena that happens in lawns due to bugs or something the soil does or doesn't do, I don't know, only that we had them show up in the backyard lawn throughout the decade of the Seventies.

A year after the one and only neighbor to the west had moved into his new mobile home, he sold it to a woman close to my mother's age. Evidently, he was having money problems and suddenly left town owing unpaid utility bills and who knows what else. Within a couple months, this new owner moved in with her teenage son, daughter, and alcoholic husband. I have changed everyone's names in this book who are not family members. Therefore, I will call her Tessie, her repulsive husband Stan, and their deranged teenage son Johnny. Her daughter got pregnant and disappeared very quickly, but the other three remained living next-door to Mom for many long and profoundly miserable years. The situation deteriorated as the months and years past and Stan was drunk most of the time and repeatedly beat the hell out of Tessie and his son. Johnny of course grew up to be a perfect imbalanced replica of his drunken, violent, cruel, and incredibly lowly evolved father and mother.

Mom had multiple problems with these west side neighbors from the very beginning and it only escalated over the years. All the family members, including Johnny's numerous male friends, were negative, violent, alcoholic and/or drug addicted imbalanced people. Mom's house and land was literally an island of higher frequency energies and Light amidst a massive sea of lower consciousness and negative energy people. It was a dangerous and highly uncomfortable physical, psychic, emotional, and energetic position for us. The multidimensional and multifaceted reasons for all this and much more would not be fully realized by me until nearly three decades had passed however.

It wasn't until about 1977 that Mom was financially able to have a six-foot tall wooden fence installed along the front north street-side of her property line, and much more importantly, along the horrible west side. At least with a solid six-foot tall wooden fence between the west neighbors yard and ours, Mom and the rest of us felt slightly more protected from their insane violence, constant drunken bouts, noise, and endless negativity that was often directed at us for the simple reason we weren't like them. To people like this, tribe and clan is everything, and anyone who exudes a different energy than they do instantly becomes *The Enemy* and is perpetually on their hate radar. So finally getting a solid physical barrier between Mom's house and property and theirs, was a very important symbol for both sides of this growing polarity war.

My sister graduated a year early from high school in 1975, and shortly thereafter spent six months back east with relatives. This left Mom alone for much of the time during these early years living in the portal house. However, she occasionally had to babysit for me while I was at work, which gave her more time to get to know her only grandchild.

Two prominent events happened during the latter half of the 1970s at Mom's place that informed us something atypical was indeed happening on her property and the large field to the east of her lot. The first anomaly was something very powerful that Mom experienced one afternoon while outside watering her plants. It was the middle of the day, the sun was shining, and everything was as it usually was—until this vivid and fully conscious anomaly happened. As she stood there watering her plants on the east end of her house with a garden hose, she suddenly heard and then saw a man come running around a corner from her backyard. As he came dashing in around her carport area, he saw her standing there watering and stopped dead in his tracks. The two of them stood silently staring at each other in great confusion and shock for half a minute or so.

Mom described this man as wearing black knee-pants, white stockings and black shoes, and an oversized white shirt with long baggy sleeves. He was not wearing a hat and his long brown hair was pulled back into a ponytail. She could easily see his hair was a mess and his shirt was only partially tucked in. She said he was breathing hard because he had been running away from something. Behind him, she saw the image of an old wagon, a small stone building with a window and a very large tree. These objects were not physically on Mom's property or anywhere around it however.

Fig. 1.1. Eighteenth-Century Portal Encounter

This eighteenth-century-looking man and Mom stood about eight feet apart and stared in shocked disbelief at each other. She said he looked and felt as if he had literally stepped out of eighteenth-century

England and right into her 1970s southern California backyard. By the shock and confused look on his face, Mom could clearly see he was just as mystified and perplexed by running into her as she was of seeing him. She said he eyed her up and down too and then glanced wide-eyed at the garden hose she was using to water her yard plants. She told me the look on his face over the water coming out of her garden hose was even more confused than the look he gave her when seeing the type of dress she was wearing.

This whole experience lasted about three minutes before it completely vanished. However, three minutes of profound shocking anomalies like this often feels like two days, and the event changes the people who experienced it. While Mom was staring at him she was also psychically picking up what was happening with this strange man from another time and country and why. She said she psychically knew he had been in bed with some young married woman when another man—probably her husband—had accidently discovered them. He had collected more men and was now chasing this vile adulterer. That was why he had been running, was disheveled and out of breath. She sensed he had been running away from the angry men chasing him, rounded a corner in his county and timeline, and suddenly ran straight into Mom in her 1977 North American backyard! Can you imagine how shocked and confused they both must have felt seeing each other like that?

Near the end of this portal encounter and time bleed through, the man glanced back over his shoulder at the men chasing him, then back at Mom for the last time, then took off running again and disappeared from her sight. She said the rest of the scene remained for another minute, and as she continued watching, a tan dog came trotting into the scene following the same path the fleeing adulterer had traveled. A few seconds after watching the dog, the whole scene—including the wagon and large tree next to it—disappeared and Mom's normal physical yard and timeline reappeared.

Mom carefully described her experience to me but because we are able to clairvoyantly see images each other intensely focuses on, I could clairvoyantly see and feel what she had actually seen even though I hadn't been there physically. This is a very handy psychic tool when one wants to exchange important experiences visually and empathically with another person. My family has always been able to do this with other family members, which made these type encounters easier to share with each other. What we did not realize then was that the whole area was a huge portal, which was why so many weird things came and went on that area of land. She and I experienced numerous anomalies over the decades at her house, but it would take time and increased awareness before I was able to connect so many strange metaphysical dots that spanned more than three decades. It would take more time to better understand my current Lightworker mission, what Mom's

14

portal house and land was really about and why we were living there.

It was a couple years later when another impressive anomaly and clue helped me begin to grasp what was most likely happening on Mom's land. It was around 1978 or 1979, but this particular event happened to a husband and wife who were simply driving home one evening. As they approached Mom's house they both saw something very unusual.

It was around 10 PM when this couple was driving home. As they approached Mom's house they both saw something clearly illuminated in their headlights slowly crossing the road in front of them. Obviously, neither Mom nor I were present when these people saw what they did. Thankfully the two of them came back the next day around noon, parked their car in front of Mom's house, got out and were looking along her east side property line in the empty field. Mom heard these strangers and went outside to investigate. When she discovered them out there obviously looking for something, she inquired about what they were doing. That was how we even heard about this particular anomaly. What was so great about this event was that it was not us that experienced it, but two strangers who happened to be driving past at the right moment to see something very strange walking out of Mom's driveway.

Standing out in the yard they both told Mom about what they had seen the night before. It was so outrageous sounding that Mom asked if they had been drinking. Very seriously, they claimed they had not had a drop and she believed them due to how serious and emotionally upset they seemed to be over what they had witnessed.

Mom told me later that they looked to be in their late sixties and seemed to be honest, sincere, intelligent people. They drove a nice car and were well groomed and dressed decently, so she felt they were not deranged people trying to deceive her for some mysterious reason. After they described to her what they had seen, Mom knew they were serious because people would not openly share something as wildly paranormal as that experience was back in the late 1970s. It was a different world back then and there was much more ridicule than today over someone experiencing phenomena like this.

Mom watched the couple slowly and meticulously combing through the dirt and broken dried weeds as if they were at a crime scene. She asked them what exactly they hoped to find out there and they excitedly replied in unison, *"Footprints!"*

The story the couple related to Mom was that they had been driving home the night before when, at the same time, both of them saw two small, hairless, silver

Fig. 1.2. Silver Portal Creature

creatures with long tails coming out from Mom's property and walking slowly across the road. They both saw them very clearly because the two creatures were directly in front of them and fully illuminated in their headlights for nearly half a minute. The husband had been driving at the time and said he immediately slowed the car and asked his wife if she was seeing the two creatures also. She informed him she was and asked what they were. From their personal descriptions, the two creatures were about three and a half feet tall, hairless, silver skinned with long thick tails that just reached the ground, and round eyes that glowed pale yellow in the cars headlights. The two creatures walked upright and side-by-side slowly as they came out from Mom's driveway and continued across the paved road.

After an hour of searching our gravel driveway and dirt planter areas, the whole backyard, the east side property and the edge of the empty field to the east, the couple found nothing. No footprints, no animal tracks, no human tracks, no broken branches, absolutely nothing. As we progress with this multidimensional story, this will make more sense because people, beings, creatures, and animals could come and go at our portal house and land and never leave any physical signs of anything. It was another aspect of the portal and portal house and evidently a very *normal* one at that.

The couple's lack of physical evidence did nothing to diminish their personal and powerful encounter experience with those two silver-tailed bipedal creatures. The couple knew what they had seen the night before and told Mom that nothing would alter that fact for them. Mom and I well knew exactly what the couple meant, how they felt about it, and why. It is really great when you get some type of physical evidence to share with other people, but even if you don't, it does not change what you yourself lived through and how it permanently alters your psyche, belief systems, your consciousness and reality. After a few blatant reality expanding personal experiences like this, one could care less about proving (or trying to prove) anything to narrow-minded disbelievers. It is more than enough that you have repeatedly encountered things that exist beyond physical reality and your ego doesn't need to prove anything to anyone for any reason.

The husband and wife got back into their car and happily drove off into the early evening sunset that day with their unique paranormal encounter permanently etched onto their hearts and souls. Mom waved goodbye to them and wished them well on their journeys. In that moment, Mom's attitude about the constant anomalies occurring on her property and the property east of it, shifted slightly thanks to the elderly couple who had seen two silver skinned, tailed, hairless bipedal creatures walk out from her property the night before.

It is one thing having unusual paranormal experiences yourself, but it is another thing having strangers experience them at the same location you have. That simple fact did much to assist Mom in emotionally and psychologically dealing with what our family had been experiencing over the seven and a half years she had owned that house and land. Events like the husband and wife's experience just driving past her property became an irrefutable backdrop to the otherworldly anomalies Mom and I repeatedly experienced there. This event, along with other experiences and energies that both friends and strangers felt the second they stepped behind our six-foot fence barricade, helped validate for she and I that something else was most certainly going on with that house, land, and the surrounding acres as well. It really is amazing how quickly we adapt to very bizarre and/or negative energies and phenomena as a way of psychologically coping with a reality that constantly colors far outside the accepted lines of so-called *normal.* The real test is how we deal and cope with the highly bizarre that repeatedly intrudes into our daily reality trying to crack it open.

Don't misunderstand me however. As a lifelong psychic, clairvoyant, clairaudient, claircognizant, empath and one who has remembered multiple past lives from early childhood, the paranormal has always been my normal. It is all I have ever known. At age five, I was painfully aware I was back on Earth again and felt there must have been some terrible mistake. I had very serious and frustrated talks with the *Sky* at age five and told them—up there—about how I wanted to go back Home and the sooner the better! I did not want to be back in polarized, dangerous, dark, cruel and insensitive earth physicality again with its scary natives, and I let the *Sky* know all about my great displeasure with the current setup.

The *Sky* talked back telepathically inside my five-year-old head (as it did for many decades) and reminded me that everything was exactly as we had all carefully planned long before I reincarnated as Denise this time around. These voices inside my head reminded me of some of the soul reasons why I was back in 3D physicality again at this particular time, and about how very important it really was. The *Sky* told me to relax and deal with it, and that I would once again adapt to living within this lower vibrating, dense, polarized dimension and reality just as I always had. There were important reasons why I was back here again and I would remember more when I was capable of housing that higher Light and be able to deal with the repercussions of it. *Glowing in the Dark* is exactly what Lightworkers/Wanderers/Starseeds do whenever they have reincarnated in lower frequency 3D throughout the past 12,500 years, and doing so typically produces difficult and oftentimes dangerous and deadly consequences.

I am very familiar with reality being greatly more than what so-called normal people experience and emphatically claim exists. In fact, I used to become concerned if four or five days passed and I had not perceived some anomaly or had a higher dimensional meeting or telepathic conversation with some marvelous nonphysical Starbeing. That was my *normal*. As I mentioned earlier, there are usually different events, people, experiences, energies and phenomena throughout our lives that we are deaf, dumb, and blind to no matter how great a clairvoyant seer one is. Our Higher Self simply reveals more to us when we are capable of physically housing and psychologically coping with higher energies and consciousness or Light without harming any aspect of our minds, bodies, or psyches. The majority of these types of things are pre-planned and carefully time-coded by our Higher Selves.

I learned many years later that my Higher Self and other nonphysical, higher dimensional Starbeings/ET family and friends from Home were all functioning within a well-known Plan and cosmic, galactic, and astrological timeline. Despite my being a very sensitive psychic, it was not time for me to remember everything about why I—as a Lightworker—was reincarnate on Earth again. It was dangerous and difficult enough without me consciously remembering so much more, plus what lay ahead energetically. Knowing that would have caused me to run screaming in the opposite direction! Our ego selves are often deliberately kept unaware of certain situations and future events as a form of protection for ourselves, others and The Plan itself.

The primary thing I have been deeply interested in from very early in this life, was what I have called, *being conscious of process.* Translated, that means I have always felt it very important for me in this incarnation and timeline to be as fully conscious as I could of some current *process* so I could share my slightly different perspective about certain events to other people. To me it was not enough to live through potent life-lessons and learning's; I wanted to be more consciously aware of moving through them at the time. I wanted to be consciously aware of much more of the Big Picture and I have been focused on this from childhood. Much of my life has been trying to *back engineer* it and what I have seen and experienced because it is unfolding along multiple timelines and dimensions simultaneously.

While I was living in my small two-bedroom rented house a couple blocks away from Mom's place, I had an interesting awake experience one day. I didn't own a clothes dryer at that time so I always hung my laundry outside on a large clotheslines at the back of the house and property. This area was another open and overgrown field with dry waist-high weeds and grass. There was a large weed free area surrounding the clothesline however so I could stand and hang my laundry easily.

That particular morning it was a sunny and cloudless warm day and I was out there hanging my laundry around 10 AM. I was about halfway through hanging up my laundry when I physically heard, and then saw, the dry weeds and grass moving near one side of this small field. I stopped what I was doing and stood watching the waist-high dry grass moving for a good half minute. I assumed it was some dog in there that I couldn't see yet, but, was ready to flee back to my house if the dog emerged and became aggressive discovering me standing right there.

As the crunching sounds and moving, parting dry weeds and grass neared the cleared area of the field right in front of me, I stood waiting and watching, ready to run if needed. What stepped out into the light of day and the bare dirt was not any dog however. It was a male Earth Elemental or a typical Earth Fairy.

He emerged out from the dried weeds and grass that were taller than he and his hat were. As he took a few more steps towards me standing there, he first spotted my feet, and instantly his head jerked up to look at whatever was attached to them. He was as profoundly shocked at running into me as I was of running into him. We both proceeded to stand there in the open weed-free dirt and brazenly check each other out. This close viewing of each other lasted for at least a minute and a half before he finally winked-out and vanished from my vision.

He was about three-foot tall, wore dark brown baggy pants covered in dry powdery dirt, and black leather cuffed boots that came up to his mid-calf. They too were covered in caked mud and powdery dirt. In fact, every inch of him was covered in this powdery dirt. He was dirty but not in a repulsive way, but in a lusty and sensual *earthy* way. It looked perfectly normal all over him—and being an Earth sign myself—I liked him immensely. I believe my being a Capricorn is another reason why I was able to see him so easily.

He wore an oversized off-white shirt, and like everything else, it too was covered in powdery dust. On top of his shirt, he wore a dark brick-red colored vest with tiny bird and rodent bones and other bits and pieces of prized trinkets that were carefully sewn onto the front of it. These trinkets and tiny bones swayed and clinked slightly when he walked or moved. In addition, he wore a dirty and crumpled pointed hat that had long ago folded over to one side where it now hung permanently and perfectly.

His thick and wavy dark brown hair hung just to his shoulders, but it was his long graying brown beard that caught my eye. It was impressive hanging down on his chest and completely covered the neckline of his shirt and vest. I was surprised actually by how typically elfish-looking he was.

Fig. 1.3. Earth Elemental Encounter

He was proportioned like a typical human male but was only about three-foot tall. I also didn't psychically sense any negative, devious, or dangerous energies or attitude from him. I had the feeling that he had been in his dimension walking along staring at the ground in front of him when suddenly, there were my feet, my very physical human feet. He felt like he was as shocked at seeing me show up in his world as I was of seeing him in mine. I did get the impression that he gave me time to stand there and take him in visually and energetically. I had the feeling he could have winked out and vanished the split-second he first saw my feet, but he didn't. He and I stood there and stared at each other for a good minute to a minute and a half. If you are a psychic and used to seeing things at what feels like near light speed, then a minute and a half is a very long time indeed.

As I looked him over carefully, I had the strong impression that his clothing did not come off—ever. I had the definite sense that his clothes, hat and boots were exactly like an animal's coat of fur; they were actual aspects of him and not separate objects as human clothing is. And of course, he was extremely *Earth earthy*. He was an energetic aspect of the Earth, but from below its surface. He was an Earth Elemental that lived within the second dimension—the frequency range just below the one we exist within—and for whatever the reasons we met each other face-to-face that special day. I telepathed to him how very grateful

27

and happy I was to have been able to see him and he seemed surprised that I knew how to communicate that way. He did not reply telepathically or in any other way, but just stared intently at me. Within a few seconds of my telepathically talking to him, he winked out and was permanently gone.

While I lived in this same rented house a couple blocks from Mom's portal house, I had many lucid dreams that were rather interesting. This particular dream happened around 1976, which means I was about twenty-four or twenty-five years old. In this lucid dream, I suddenly found myself standing in some enormous hallway inside the White House. I am not a political person and this dream was not about politics but something else entirely—something that I needed to see and know absolutely for myself back in 1976.

Standing there in this hallway inside the White House, I saw many other people who were astrally projected there also. They were all adults and looked as if they were hiding and trying to not be perceived by the physical awake people moving about inside the White House. I could tell that the majority of these astral men and women I was seeing were not Americans and that was the real point to this lucid dream experience. I needed to witness, for myself, that this type of foreign astral spying was happening within the White House exclusively to eavesdrop on conversations in different rooms there.

I was merely a psychic witness to this foreign astral spying and could personally care less about what was going on in there. Nevertheless, I needed to know for myself that certain people did intentionally astral project with the intent to spy and gather information, and not only in the White House, but in many different places too at that time. After witnessing this in a few different hallways and rooms within the White House, I woke myself up because I did not even want to be there. I had learned what I was supposed to, which was that certain people and countries did this and did it very well, so I got my astral backside out of there fast and never returned.

Another lucid dream I had around 1976 was scientific. Like politics, I was not interested in what was exciting and new within the scientific communities either but that did not seem to matter. I sometimes clairvoyantly see or witness different events like this going on in other parts of the world. This time it was scientific as opposed to political or military.

In the dream I am suddenly viewing, from up in the air as if I was hovering near the ceiling, different men in white lab coats working below me. They had large magnets and mirrors set up and were doing repeated testing of turning on some light that looked like a line of light and sending it through magnets, bouncing it off of a mirror, and so on. Of course, I didn't understand what I was seeing in 1976, but years later I realized what I had seen were scientists developing laser light. I only saw them experimenting with laser lights through magnetic fields and reflecting beams off mirrors. Again, this seemed to be more about me just witnessing certain actual events than much of anything else. In many of these lucid dreams, it wouldn't be until years later that I would realize what I had seen originally. Such is the nature of being a psychic or clairvoyant. The clairvoyant visions, precognitive tragedies, and political or military events are usually not what the lesson is about; they are often only about my witnessing certain things so that I know *other* things and *other* truths.

During mid-1977, I had been working on some drawings and text for a local metaphysical newsletter when another scene from my ancient Egyptian male past life suddenly surfaced. Evidently, the drawing I had been doing was close enough to this particular Egyptian past life scene that it functioned as the deep level trigger between the two lives and events.

In my mind's eye I suddenly saw my past life male self in ancient Egypt using a small, handheld device to cut into rock surfaces and carve beautiful hieroglyphs and colored artwork. The ancient device looked somewhat like a silver-colored metal penlight, or a small laser pointer, however, it emitted a tightly focused white laser beam of light. It was a small tool used to easily and quickly cut and carve stone in 12,600 B.C. Egypt. The real uniqueness of this ancient Egyptian laser tool was that it was entirely directed and controlled by the operator's mental focus and emotions. There were no other buttons on it to operate other than an on/off button. The tool functioned exclusively through the artist's directed thoughts and emotions. The image you held in your mind's eye was your model; the emotions you intentionally created at certain times controlled the different colors that the tool emitted and instantly imbedded or *painted* on the stone.

This may sound like a fun tool to use, but it was highly intense work and there was absolutely no room for the artist to mentally or emotionally wander! The tool itself was directed exclusively by your thoughts, your intent, desires, and emotions. Did I mention this small handheld tool quickly and easily cut into stone as if it was room temperature butter? It was quite amazing really.

With practice, an artist could quickly turn on and off specific emotions within him or herself, which automatically triggered a specific color to be emitted. I remember intensity caused the color black to turn on, and a peaceful, loving feeling caused different skin tone colors to activate. Feeling joy trigged blue, and gratitude caused green shades to be activated within the tool. From our perspective today, this tool is amazing, but in that past life, it was merely another of many such common everyday tools.

✝✡☪☸ This next experience has nothing directly to do with the portal house, but I want to add it for perspective. When I psychically sense, see, feel, and know some approaching physical event, I usually perceive it three weeks or more before it actually manifests physically. Three weeks or so just seems to be my precognitive psychic window.

One day while living in the rental house a couple blocks from Mom's portal house, I had another precognitive clairvoyant vision of something big and unpleasant coming. I clearly clairvoyantly saw many hundreds of American men, women, and children lying dead on hard bare dirt in some foreign country. Dead bodies of endless numbers of people and children were all I could see, but what confused me the most about this vision was that I could not see any external reasons for why they were dead. There was no blood, no chaos, no mess, no explosions, no broken bodies or crushed heads, no torn or damaged clothes, no weapons, no fires or floods, no gunfire or bullet holes—just dead people carefully lined up in endless rows everywhere. It was horrific and incredibly confusing.

In psychic situations like this I usually scan the surrounding area I am clairvoyantly seeing to collect more information about the location, year, time of year, country, and so on. In this case, my consciousness was in this physical location viewing the colossal slaughter and I needed to figure out where this location was on the planet. I saw what looked to be large banana tree leaves and heavy jungle at the outer edges of this encampment where all the dead people lay. Seeing the foreign trees and jungle told me it was most likely somewhere in South America. I took in as much visual information as I could from the main clairvoyant perspective I was seeing the scene from. Part of me did not want to move around psychically too much because it was a fresh kill zone and still heavily populated with the recently dead. Great fear, anger, and traumatic energies hung thick in place around the large encampment and dead bodies. It was a dark and terrible mess physically and astrally as all events like this are.

It looked to be late morning or early afternoon and was hot with plenty of sunlight burning down. I could see long tables and benches under roofs in open-air buildings and large communal eating areas. I also saw what looked like loudspeakers attached to the wood support beams of these crude buildings. This told me that messages were frequently transmitted to the people as they ate, worked, or walked about the place. Certain areas had large masses of dense black energy hanging in place and I did not even turn fully to clairvoyantly view it because I knew it was lower energies remaining around the numerous and recently vacated dead bodies.

A few days after I had this clairvoyant vision Mom came over and I told her about it as I always did whenever I clairvoyantly saw some major future event. Often she was my only psychic witness. As it turned out, a bit over three weeks later Mom and I heard on the TV news one evening, that something called *The Jonestown Massacre* had happened on November 18, 1978 in Guyana South America. As I watched the news report from the actual physical location, I was seeing on TV exactly what I had clairvoyantly seen three weeks earlier. When I heard that 909 people had been murdered, or convinced to committed suicide, I understood why I would not clairvoyantly wander around the location much psychically. Thankfully, I did not see all 909 dead bodies or souls that day. I saw two large groups of probably a hundred each that were laid out in long rows side-by-side. Sick people and religions...

⊕ From about the age of seven I had a nonphysical Guide who taught me how to function in my astral body while out of my physical body and/or asleep. He was always there in his dark brown hooded Monk's robe with a blacked-out face area under the hood, standing behind my bedroom curtains waiting for me to go to bed and get out-of-body. Poor Mom and Dad had to listen to my fears and concerns about the *strange man standing behind my curtains* when they tucked me into bed each night.

I could clairvoyantly see him hiding and waiting for me behind my floor length curtains, only because the toes of his shoes were visible and the curtains were moving. Once I was out-of-body I could see all of him in his hooded Monk's robe, but the face area was always blacked out. Why you may be wondering? So I would not become overly emotionally attached to a face or personality, or become infatuated with him. This is a common tactic nonphysical beings use with many of us reincarnated here who are being taught (reminded) by higher dimensional Guides and teachers.

Many years later as a young adult, he was still showing up occasionally in my dreams to teach me other important things. This particular dream happened sometime during 1975 or 1976, and he wanted to teach me about my physical body, its death, Elemental beings, and the different dimensions. I found myself lucid in this dream and we were standing underneath a large beautiful tree outdoors somewhere. He and I stood side-by-side gazing down at my dead physical Denise body lying on the ground before us. It was a very unemotional situation to both of us, and he, my dear old trusted guide and friend, stood viewing my dead body as he taught me this valuable lesson.

As he and I stood viewing my dead physical body, different Elemental beings began joyfully exiting it and celebrating that they were finally free and now able to return to their individual 2D homes. My nonphysical guide continued teaching me that the four Elemental energies are required to make a seeming sacrifice, to leave their homes and dimension so I can have a physical body vehicle to function within during my 3D incarnation. It was amazing actually seeing this truth play out in this manner.

I was embarrassed by the Elementals great glee and rejoicing over being free of my body at first but that was quickly followed by the greatest respect and gratitude you can imagine. I would not have had a physical body to live and learn within if it were not for those Elemental beings leaving their home dimension and hang together uncomfortably in 3D with me for however many years I needed a physical body. It was amazing to realize these Elemental beings were going through a similar evolutionary learning process to what I, as a nonphysical spiritual being was by incarnating into a dimension that was physical. In third dimensional physicality, we all were literally *out of our natural element.* I, as a nonphysical spiritual being, and they, as nonphysical second dimension Elemental beings, all could experience living for a while within 3D physicality if we came together in this dimension for a time. That was the lesson my astral guide wanted me to remember.

As soon as I understood, or more accurately remembered that this is what was required when using a physical body within a physical dimension, I became profoundly grateful to every one of these celebrating Elemental beings jumping and singing and carrying on around my dead physical body. They did not seem to care at all about my moment of understanding, love, and deep gratitude towards them, they were just celebrating that they were free and could finally *go home.* My guide stood there and witnessed me having yet another mini revelation and larger insight into some of what it takes to have a physical body vehicle to use. He has done his job well once again. I only had a couple more dreams with him after this one and then he retired from being my guide. I will always be extremely grateful for him and all he taught me over the years.

In 1979, I discovered an older man and his wonderful wife who gave lectures and informal meetings about all things spiritual and paranormal. We quickly became good friends, and Mom, my sister and I often attended his lectures and weekly Wednesday evening meetings. He would discuss different spiritual and metaphysical topics and belief systems, and sometimes he would lead the group through guided meditations, which was my first experience with this. Samuel also did past life regressions, and in 1981 I had him regress me once because I wanted to see if I could collect any further information about an already remembered past life.

Sometime in late 1979 Samuel constructed copper divining or dowsing rods for any of us who wanted to experiment using them. Mom and I both got a pair of divining rods from him and had instant and impressive results considering we had never used them before. The two rods where shaped like capital L's and you held the shorter part in each hand with the longer part of the rod facing away from your body and parallel to the ground. Samuel had placed two slightly wider diameter copper tubes over the small grip parts of the rods so they would move freely without your hands even touching them. It made it easy to hold both of the slightly larger copper tubes in each hand lightly and slowly walk along, watching how the long ends of the rods swung open, crossed each other, or completely rotated in large sweeping circles.

Mom called me a week or so later and wanted me to try the divining rods at her house so I drove out there to see what was up. Once there, Mom and I started walking up and down her driveway and along the east side of her property. It did not make any difference if she held the rods or if I did because they swung completely around in full circles every couple of steps we took.

We both walked the entire backyard area with the divining rods and they would swing wildly open at one step forward, then they would swing closed or tightly cross each other in front of you with the next step forward. It was as if Mom's entire property was a potent energetic grid of invisible three-foot squares. When Mom held the copper rods, they would swing in full circles in her hands with every step she took. It did not matter where on her property she walked either because the rods would just make full circles in both directions in her hands. The copper divining rods would open widely and then cross widely for me, and sometimes swing in full circles, but only along the driveway and eastern side of the property.

Because that whole area was so rural there were no electric or phone lines buried underground. The only thing buried in the backyard was the septic tank and leach line and we knew exactly where they were. There were no overhead or underground lines of anything in the driveway or the backyard. There was an electric and phone line that ran from one front west corner of the house, to the front street where a large electric pole was planted. There was the incoming water line that ran along the edge of the driveway to the back east corner of the house, and we assumed that was probably what was causing the divining rods to be so active in that particular area. There was nothing else buried on the property or the surrounding field next door or behind Mom's property.

As with so many of the strange anomalies that happened on her land and the large field to the east, it would take a few more years worth of strange experiences before we could look back on the divining rods episodes with more insight and understanding as to why they behaved so extremely.

The decade of the Seventies ended with me moving ten miles to a small nearby city where I rented an apartment for my son and I. Mom and my only sibling remained at her weird portal house just outside of this small city, but we visited each other frequently. I would go back out to Mom's house and spend a few hours talking and sharing about what I had been up to, and sometimes Mom would stop by to visit her grandson and me at our apartment when she came to the city to do her shopping. We stayed in close contact with each other despite my move and we continued to experience anomalies in both locations.

PART TWO

Interdimensional Lightwork

1980–1989

The decade of the 1980s arrived and I had just turned twenty-nine years old. My Saturn Return arrived along with the start of 1980, and I began the astrological process of becoming an *adult* adult. The first Saturn Return is something everyone lives through from age twenty-nine through thirty-one and is often a tough transition time for many people. Because I am a Capricorn, which is ruled by Saturn, it wasn't that much of a energetic stretch for me. I was familiar with Saturn anyway, so this major life transit and Initiation wasn't too horrible or intense for me. Other later planetary transits most definitely would be, but not this first Saturn Return.

I had recently moved my 8-year-old son and myself into a small city a few miles from Mom's house and rural property where I remained the entire decade of the 1980s—my thirties. It was a fun, intense, and extremely creative decade for me. It was my decade to grow and establish myself as a member of humanity within society, as much as I wanted to, that is. I did enjoy my highly creative decade of learning, loving, creating, performing and teaching.

The first apartment I rented in this small city was a cute little two-bedroom place across the street and a down a block from the Elementary school I enrolled my son in. It was a great setup for both my son and I with his school being so close to our apartment.

Around 1976 my sister discovered a local woman who taught Belly Dance classes. Yasmeen told me about them, we both took her beginner class, and I was instantly in *Seventh Heaven!* The very first time I ever heard Belly Dance music and saw this middle-aged woman dancing to it and playing brass finger cymbals, I was hooked. It was as if I already knew it, knew how to do all the complex movements and recognized the foreign rhythms and remembered how to play the finger cymbals. It was all very natural to me from the first moment I saw her dance and heard the music. I absolutely loved that style of dance and its earthy, heavy drumming.

I stuck with it, eventually became a professional Belly Dancer, and performed all over southern California during that time. I also taught Belly Dance classes for the seventeen years I performed, which I truly enjoyed. During the 1980s I also gave psychic readings, I erected astrological natal charts (by hand) and did natal chart interpretations as well. I occasionally lectured about metaphysical topics and did public group psychometry readings also. Yasmeen and I both gave classes at a local metaphysical book and quartz crystal store, plus astrology classes at a local College. It was a busy but highly creative decade for me and I thoroughly enjoyed it and all the hard work.

For a short period during the 1980s, I worked with the local police department as a psychic. I helped them with a couple of missing person's cases and a couple of local robberies. Understand that this was between 1982 and 1984 and everything I did for them was unofficial and probably unknown by the rest of the police department. It was very different back then and I know they tired my abilities only because they saw a fast and easy way to possibly close some confusing cases. I didn't assist them for long because it simply was not my desire or calling to work with the police. It was however, an interesting experience and one I am grateful for having.

One of the first strange events I remember happening at this new apartment began in 1980. At first this may all sound like it is completely unrelated to the events and energies at Mom's portal house, but it is all connected. As I mentioned earlier, my life has been a process of learning to back engineer certain events to discover there was indeed a constant otherworldly thread running through everything in it. The unfolding and continuing awakening process was slow and steady for two decades so Mom and I could build a strong foundation energetically on multiple levels and dimensions. We however, did not fully realize that was what was happening at the time.

One evening at my new apartment, I had been practicing to new Belly Dance music I had recently bought. I needed to be intimately familiar with it before I could use it publically to perform to, therefore lots of listening and practicing had to happen first. This particular night I had been dancing to this new music and had an abnormally enjoyable time doing so. When I was done, I got my young son ready for bed—bathed, pajamas on, teeth brushed, hair brushed and so on. In other words, it was a very normal night for us.

I got him kissed and safely tucked into bed in his bedroom and then I got myself ready for bed. I smoked back then and would always have a cigarette in bed before I curled up to go to sleep. I was in my bed having my usual cigarette when I noticed some strange shadow anomaly happening near the ceiling where the corner walls meet with it. There was always a natural shadow in that area anyway, but as I lay there in bed smoking, I could clearly see the shadow growing in size. I watched it carefully for many minutes then noticed the same anomaly happening at the opposite corner in the same location near the ceiling. Both growing shadows were quickly spreading out horizontally along that wall near the ceiling.

Laying there smoking and watching this new phenomena, I did what I always do, which was to discerned psychically what was happening as best as I could. I didn't sense any negative or dangerous energies or sensations at all but it sure was a weird sight. Then, all of the sudden, I started to pass out! I had been laying there smoking a cigarette, watching, wondering, and carefully analyzing the new anomaly spreading across one wall in my bedroom, when I suddenly started to go unconscious. As hard as I fought against it, I could not remain awake or conscious. It was all I could do to lift my arm enough to drop my burning cigarette into the ashtray on the bedside nightstand. As I dropped it into the ashtray, I passed out! In a matter of seconds, I went from being wide-awake and highly focused on the spreading dark shadow anomalies on my wall, to suddenly being unable to remain conscious.

The next moment, I discovered I could not move my body from the waist down. I was suddenly paralyzed and quickly panicked over the fact that I could not move my lower body. I could move my upper body and arms fine, but everything was paralyzed deadweight from my waist down. My next thought was to get to the only phone in the kitchen as fast as I could. I didn't have a phone in my bedroom so I had to pull and drag my paralyzed bottom half out of bed and then slowly, and with great effort, pull myself towards the kitchen to call for help. It was a long, difficult, and exhausting process. I struggled to pull my entire bodyweight using only my hands, arms, and shoulders and I would only move forward a foot at a time. It seemed to take me forever to get out of bed and then a few feet towards my bedroom door. I was quickly becoming weaker as my arms and shoulder muscles fatigued and I was sweating from the extreme exertion.

A second later, I was awake in my bed and could only physically move my eyes! What in the hell was going on? I struggled to move any body part physically but could not. I strained to see the anomalous dark shadows on the wall again and saw they were larger and darker than before I had first passed out. The problem at that moment—as I saw it—was that I did not remember going to sleep or dreaming. I had been wide-awake one minute, and then the next I was going unconscious. The next second I was paralyzed from the waist down and trying to drag myself to the kitchen.

Then suddenly I am back in my bed again and awake, but still cannot move anything except my physical eyes. With much confusion, I suddenly realized that all my effort and struggle to get out of bed and to the kitchen phone did not happen physically as I believed it had.

As I lay there in my bed, frantically trying to figure out what in the world was going on and why, I stared to pass out again. This time I was more *conscious of process* and seriously tried to understand what was happening to me. The thing that was the most confusing during this entire horrible process was that I honestly believed I was fully awake and struggling physically each time I tried to move my body. There was never any difference in my consciousness or awareness from being physically awake and conscious, to being unconscious and seemingly paralyzed from the waist down. My awareness was absolutely the same from one state of consciousness into the other state, and it took me going through this transition numerous times to even begin to realize it.

I passed out again and began the same process of struggling to get my (what I absolutely believed was my physical body) into the kitchen to call for help. This time I had gotten almost to my bedroom door when I heard my young son scream from his bedroom. Deep maternal panic and fight flooded my being and I turned my direction to his room instead of the phone in the kitchen. Panicked before, now I was frantic over hearing him scream. Why was my eight-year-old son screaming in fear? Why was he calling out to his Mommy for help in the middle of the night? Why in the hell am I paralyzed? Why can't I pull my body faster so I can get into his bedroom and just see what is going on in there?

In the next second, I was back in my bed wide-awake but could only move my physical eyes again. Either I am physically awake and paralyzed throughout my physical body, or, I am out-of-body and struggling to drag my half-paralyzed astral body around the apartment, doing it believing that I am actually awake and that it is happening physically. I am in my bed again, flat on my back, and cannot move anything but my eyes. I cannot even scream out to my son to wake him or to hear if he is even in his bedroom, which at this point, I am starting to sense he is not. Not astrally that is.

My next awareness is of me struggling to drag my half-paralyzed body out of my bed again, and this time, I am hell-bent on getting to the only phone in the kitchen to call for help. I have forgotten again that I am in my astral body and that this is not happening physically. I must add at this point that I was well familiar with being out-of-body astrally at night because I'd had trainings with this from early childhood with one of my Guides. I was an old pro at being able to deliberately get out-of-body and around astrally and consciously remember everything I did (at night).

Therefore, having this type of weird experience was highly unusual for me and I did not recognize what was happening for most of that long and very difficult night.

This time I made it all the way into the kitchen, but because I was paralyzed from the waist down, I could not reach the phone up on the wall! I spent a lot of time there struggling to pull myself up far enough to grab the wall phone. In the next second I would be back in my bed, flat on my back again and only able to move my eyes. On and on it went for six full horrible and exhausting hours that entire night. It was the rising sun seven hours later that finally seemed to break the spell of paralysis. As soon as I saw the first rays of sunlight coming in through those curtains on the east wall where this phenomenon started, I could finally physically move and I ran straight into my son's bedroom to see if he was in his bed. He was laying there sound asleep as if nothing had happened over the past seven terrifying hours.

Once I saw he was indeed physically in his physical bed and looked to be fine, I started crying over the hours of struggle and trauma I had gone through. I got my black eyebrow pencil and drew a large pentagram on my belly (over my solar plexus) because I was so exhausted. As silly as it was, doing this was the only thing I could think to do at that moment. That morning must have been a weekend because I remember my son did not have to go to school that morning. Hours later Mom showed up without my ever calling her over any of this. My young son Chris met her at the back patio gate and informed her that I had drawn a pentagram on my tummy, so something *must* be wrong.

I told her everything I had experienced the night before and that I had the feeling my son had been taken from the astral plane. Despite how horrible the whole event was from my maternal perspective, and despite having heard my son scream out for my help from the astral, I believed that whomever the ETs were that took him that night were not negative lower frequency beings. There was a feeling to this whole event as if it were something that had to happen for his sake and it was not a negative ET astral abduction. I believe that because I was quiet capable of consciously astrally maneuvering myself—and my positive ETs friends and stellar kin knew this—that was why they kept me physically and astrally immobilized while my son was with them for those six hours. They must have known I would not let my only child go easily, and so they somehow put me on astral *hold* all night long. Chris had no memory of anything happening that night nor any dreams or feelings at all. In the end, I think that because he was only eight he was not supposed to consciously remember this particular astral ET meeting.

I should backtrack a bit so this next experience makes more sense. When I was fifteen years old (1966), I had a conscious clairvoyant, telepathic meeting with an ancient and dearly beloved ET friend. He and a couple others had often been energetically near me that I was consciously aware of from the age of three. He was a youthful, very attractive blond male with sky-blue eyes who was a higher dimensional Pleiadian being. I didn't know the word *Pleiadian* or what that entailed for decades in this life however. From the age of three, I did know he was nonphysical and existed elsewhere at a higher energy location. He, and a few others I have known and loved, have all worked together for many thousands of years, which is normal at higher dimensional levels of being.

The day this clairvoyant meeting took place, I had been sitting in my bedroom listening to music on my little AM radio while doing my school homework. Suddenly, there he clairvoyantly was in my mind's eye. As is typical of many of these higher dimensional beings, they just get right to the point with no formal introductions or anything. From their perspective, it is like picking up the phone and calling someone to inform or remind them about something important.

The Pleiadian telepathed the image of a fifteen-year-old boy with straight blond hair and sky-blue eyes. He telepathically added that this boy was going to *"be *my son in the future"*. I immediately responded telepathically that I was not interested in getting married or having any children. He informed me that it did not matter and repeated that the mental image he was showing me was indeed my son, as he would look when he would be fifteen years old. After a few moments he told me that, *"I am his real Father."* Hearing that declaration, I was more confused than ever because I always knew he was not a physical human man. So how could he be my future son's *real father?* The mental image the Pleiadian male showed me of this fifteen-year-old boy did indeed look very much like him so I was confused to be sure.

After the Pleiadian was certain I had correctly received his entire clairvoyant and telepathic message and would consciously remember it, he faded out and disappeared once again. I was then left alone with great 1960s music playing on my AM radio and a horde of questions running wild in my fifteen-year-old mind.

To bring you all the way with this particular multidimensional situation I will add that I did get married years later and had only one child—a son who has straight blond hair and sky-blue eyes just like his *real* stellar higher dimensional Pleiadian *father.* My mother, father, sister, my son and myself are all what some people call Wanderers or Starpeople. (That is not as amazing or outlandish as it may sound believe me.) From age three, I have consciously remembered more than most Wanderers usually do. Incarnating with psychic abilities made it that much easier for me to remain in conscious contact with some of these higher dimensional Starbeings/ETs throughout this life. Wanderers/Starseeds/Lightworkers usually do for reasons that will become increasingly apparent through the many seemingly unrelated and unusual events and anomalies within the pages of this book.

Decades later, I would understand exactly what my ancient Pleiadian friend was trying to convey that day in 1966 when I was fifteen. He was trying to remind me about the complex concept of Wanderers by showing me my future son, who physically looks very much like that particular nonphysical male Pleiadian. He was not my son's physical or energetic father, but my son carries a lot of Pleiadian energies and 5D High Heart consciousness, and *that* was the real meaning behind my Pleiadian friend's telepathic message. My son is a Wanderer with strong 5D Pleiadian energies and Heart.

The different physical and nonphysical experiences and events in this book are about many of the encounters my family and I have had over the decades and the interdimensional reasons for much of it. I certainly realize how confusing and seemingly unrelated some of these experiences may sound because they unfolded slowly and deliberately over the decades. It took me a couple decades to understand many of these issues at deeper levels myself. Even with constant clairvoyant, etheric, telepathic, dream, and other dimensional memories, abilities, and conscious contacts I still wasn't able or ready to understand numerous aspects of what was happening to me and why. Because of this, you too are going to need to connect the many interdimensional dots that literally cover just over three decades as you read these pages. Do not think your way through it, just feel and unfold as you go along, and some of your personal interdimensional dots may make more sense to you as well.

Another anomaly that began within a couple years of moving into the portal house, were what looked like people in shadow walking back and forth on the covered backyard deck. Remember, this was back in the late 1970s and the term *shadow people* would not become a commonly known name for this anomaly for another twenty-some years. Nevertheless, very early on, Mom first saw these dark shadows of men and women walking past the kitchen window that looked out on the back covered deck attached to her house. We all saw them repeatedly over the decades but this phenomenon seemed to increase and decrease of its own accord. I was never able to figure out or discern what the unseen tides where, if any, that seemed to either cause more activity or allowed us to more frequently see the shadow people at certain times and less so at other times.

They were often much easier to see using one's physical peripheral vision. Often, if you turned your head to look at them (or many other nonphysical beings) directly, they instantly vanish. If you can train yourself to not look directly but be content with viewing, feeling, and discerning from this indirect peripheral point of view, you can rather easily see and sense many of these nonphysical, other dimensional beings for many seconds; long enough to get a good look at them and intuitively feel them and the whole interdimensional situation.

They never seemed to see or sense us, at least not that I could tell, which made this phenomena seem like it was some type of bleed through from elsewhere. As we learned over the years this was very much what the portal house and land was all about; strange things, animals, people, ET beings, elementals, physical people and events from other countries and time periods would easily and suddenly pop-up inside the house and outside on Mom's property or the acreage around it. This phenomenon was so common that eventually we adapted to it and didn't take all the weird encounters as anything too terribly out of the ordinary.

You could stand at the kitchen sink while doing the dishes and carefully watch the parade of nonphysical, silhouetted shadow people on the back deck as long as you used your peripheral vision and did not look at them directly. It certainly made the unpleasant job of washing the dishes pass much more quickly.

However, many times you would be walking towards the kitchen, round the corner, and automatically loose a little squeal of shock because the back deck was full of shadow people milling around out there like they were having a cocktail party or something. It would oftentimes catch you off guard and make you jump and squeal when you suddenly caught sight of seven or more shadow people standing only four to ten feet away from your kitchen window and backdoor. Thankfully, we never saw them inside the house but only on this backyard deck or porch area.

I want to add that none of them looked at all like any of us so this phenomenon was not some type of residual energy coming from us. Mom, my sister and I are all rather short people and there were no men at her house at all. These shadow people were all much taller than we were and there were always many males in the group as well. Keep in mind also that Mom was the first Caucasian to live in that area so these shadow people were not previous residents who had owned that land and physically lived on it prior to my mother buying the property. This was a different phenomenon entirely than residual etheric energetic imprinting. These shadow people on Mom's back deck looked like very well dressed modern men and women.

Third dimensional portal areas allow many different beings to intentionally, and sometimes unintentionally, slip through from one dimension, timeline and location, into another dimension, timeline and location. These things and beings can be both from this Earth reality and dimension, but they can also be from completely different nonphysical dimensions as well. The shadow people on Mom's back deck were beings from elsewhere that appeared to us like watching some strange event happening in another reality, and they never saw or felt us watching them that we could tell. It was like having a muted TV playing in another room yet you can still easily see the program that is playing on that particular station.

Around 1982 I moved my son and me to another apartment in this same small city. Being a divorced single parent meant I had to find decent apartments with a monthly rent I alone could afford. We moved again into another two-bedroom apartment where we remained for over five years. It was an upstairs apartment that felt a bit more removed from some of the less wonderful people and energies residing in a couple of the ground floor apartments. It certainly was not the absolute best of places for us to live, but it was what I could afford at that time. I did my best to keep us safe from some of the other neighbors who preferred to party long and hard and as often as they could.

One of the first things I remember happening at this new upstairs apartment was the beginning of a series of unusual lucid dream meetings with a male who I called *my crazy twin brother.* He didn't look like me at all as he had rich brown skin and I'm Caucasian. My very first impression of him was that he was a Mayan. I did not know anything about the Mayans or the Mayan calendar at that time in early 1982 however. Nothing had happened at that point concerning the Mayan calendar and all that it entails (that I was consciously aware of), so these recurring dreams with my Mayan *crazy twin brother* were yet another unusual interdimensional connection.

The first lucid dream I had with him he came rushing in excitedly wanting to ask me something deeply important. I instantly viewed him up and down and was highly intrigued. He had beautiful light brown skin, brown eyes, a very angular face, and long straight black hair. He wore clothes I was not familiar with as they weren't anything I had seen before. I didn't pay all that much attention to his clothes actually, only because he was so exuberant, playful, so energized and excited that he easily pulled you right into him and what he was doing.

Back in the mid-Seventies, I dyed my hair black. It is naturally straight and was very long back then. The fact that our hair looked so much alike made me really happy because I had remembered many of my past lives when I had beautiful brown, cinnamon, red, or yellow skin and all of them with long black hair. I dyed my straight brown hair black because of these remembered past lives. A few years later when I started Belly Dancing, having very dark hair was a plus, so I kept it that way for many years.

My etheric Mayan *crazy twin brother* told me in this first dream that he desperately needed my help. He claimed he needed me to help him build a bridge. He said he would work building it from his side but that he needed me to help build the other end of it here from my side. In other words, he asked me to help him build an energy bridge that would connect his higher dimensional world with the physical third dimension and timeline I was living in.

For some reason his dream request sounded to me like the most normal thing I had heard in a long time. The proposed nonphysical bridge building project made perfect sense to me the second the words fell from his lips in this first dream meeting. I somehow instantly knew exactly what he meant and why this energy bridge was so vitally important at that time in late 1982. I knew and yet I did not know all the complex reasons for it.

I told him I did not know what I could do here in physicality, but that I would happily do whatever I could to help build his interdimensional energy bridge from my side of the Veil. He was ecstatic. He was so happy, so relieved, so excited that I had instantly agreed to help him build this bridge, that he started running in circles, jumping, and howling like a *crazy* person. I just stood watching and deeply loving him and feeling very happy for him that his interdimensional bridge building project was now officially a *GO*. I grinned warmly and lovingly at him acting like a handsome nutcase as he ran around doing flips and yelling weird yelps and foreign words. It was all somehow perfectly normal and happily wonderful to me.

Three or four months later came the second lucid dream encounter with my Mayan *crazy twin brother*. In this second dream, he was overflowing with higher energy, joy, excitement, and pure enthusiasm. He didn't seem to need to be doing anything to be this way either.

He was running a lot of much higher energy through himself it seemed. He always made me smile, made my heart sing, and made me miss Home terribly.

He informed me that the energy bridge building was coming along better and faster than he ever thought it could. He was giddy with excitement and joy over what he and I were doing and how easily we both were building this nonphysical, interdimensional bridge from our respective dimensions. I told him I honestly did not feel I was doing much at all from my physical side of the Veil. He instantly informed me that I was very wrong and each of us was indeed constructing the energy bridge from both of our dimensional sides. He was profoundly happy and grateful I had done all I had here in 3D physicality as that was making the entire bridge building happen so much faster. I repeated yet again that I felt I was not doing that much from my dimensional side with this bridge building business, but he would not hear it. He tried many times to convince and reassure me that I was continuing to do my part in this huge, interdimensional bridge building project even though I did not feel I was contributing nearly enough.

Four more months would pass before he returned in another dream to let me know where we stood with our interdimensional bridge building project. Every time he showed up in a dream, he was always so energetic and full of joy and wonderful silliness. He always made me feel such hope and strength with my seemingly being stranded here in polarized physicality. He knew far more than I remembered at that time, and I now believe that was why he was so proud of what I was able to do working from this much denser side of the dimensional Veil or border.

The next dream arrived a few months later and he did a lot of running around, jumping, twirling and singing like a crazy fool—and I thoroughly enjoyed every second of it. In this dream meeting, he was wearing numerous brightly colored tropical bird feathers in his long black hair. He wore a scant leather loincloth, but it was his red, blue, yellow, purple and teal colored feathers that had him wild with joy it seemed. I remember just watching the show and loving my *crazy twin brother* more than I even did before. He yelped, jumped, danced, flipped and howled with total abandon and I relished every delightful gesture he made and happy emotion he radiated. He seemed to be celebrating something special for us both. There wasn't much dialogue between us in this dream meeting, just this Mayan celebration party, or whatever it was. He frolicked, I watched, and I fell in love with him totally.

It was another four months or so after this dream meeting before he showed up again. In this next dream, he had shaved his long beautiful black hair all off and looked so different I was shocked. He acted very differently too which emotionally shook me considerably. I remember thinking in my lucid dream that he possibly was "crazy" after all. I yelled angrily at him for cutting off all his gorgeous long hair and demanded to know why he had done such a seemingly crazy thing. He was literally bouncing all over the place with his high energy and did not acknowledge me much at all. He never responded to my questions about why he had cut his very long beautiful hair all off. It seemed to be a silly non-issue to him.

As I watched him, I slowly realized that our interdimensional bridge building project must be very close to being finished. That realization was terribly bittersweet. I was extremely happy we had completed our interdimensional project, but I was also deeply saddened to have my beloved Mayan *crazy twin brother* leave me on Earth alone again. I sensed that once this bridge building project was finished, we would not see each other in dreamtime meetings like this ever again.

Having to say goodbye *again* to yet another beloved higher dimensional extended family member cut deep. I had not completely healed my ancient Egyptian emotional wounds from having remained on Earth in 12,600 B.C. when the three ancient ET kin exited physicality and returned to their different dimensional homes. Now it was happening again with my beloved Mayan *crazy twin brother*. It was another bittersweet parting where they left while I kept returning to Earth.

Nevertheless, this is how it works with Wanderers/Lightworkers functioning within a physical incarnation on Earth. They often have many higher dimensional ET family members, friends, assistants and guides who remain within their higher home dimensions to assist the reincarnated Lightworker/Wanderer within physicality. We work from both sides of the Veil or dimensional boarders to accomplish different things within different phases of the planetary and dimensional shifting ascension process. It certainly is emotionally difficult however when they leave because certain energy projects are finished, yet you are still here in the dark with the volatile masses in 3D functioning in a trance. This is much like being a spy in a foreign land, and when your home contacts have to leave you for awhile, it is emotionally painful and lonely being in that foreign country, or planet, or dimension without them.

This was the last dream meeting I had with him in late 1983, which told me our invisible multidimensional energy bridge had indeed been completed. I was very happy and proud about that, but I did miss him terribly for quite awhile. I wondered if some of his actions in those last two dreams were his way of trying to make our upcoming disconnection a bit easier for me emotionally in physicality. I believe that was the case at any rate.

It was around 1983 that Mom's next door neighbors—the lowly and violent alcoholic husband and wife team—moved out and left their son Johnny alone there. Evidently, they moved into the same city that I had a couple of years earlier. I could not believe how much more dangerous and miserable it would now become for Mom living alone there with lowly Johnny and his male partners in crime right next-door with no parents. Yes his parents were drunk all the time, but at least they kept Johnny somewhat under control only because *they* did not want any problems or expense with the police or lawsuits. Now even that small positive protection was gone.

Mom told me about the many horrific things Johnny and his male friends did now that they lived there alone. There was a constant flow of beer and drugs, stolen properties, violence and guns, which always makes things tense when combined with deranged lowly idiots and plenty of alcohol and drugs. These types of lower vibrating people and activities are not good combinations and easily attract lower or negatively focused nonphysical entities.

Another aspect of this that is rather interesting is that Mom had begun her menopause around this time. Johnny and Co. were her personal tormentors, but also her very difficult and painful teachers. I am sure from their perspective Mom was just the *"old bitch next door"* that was to be harassed as much as they could get away with. It was a very difficult, dangerous, dark and frustrating time for her.

Some of the things she experienced at their hands were animal abuse and outright torture, physical and emotional abuse of girlfriends they brought to the house, destruction of old vehicles parked on their property, urinating and vomiting outside and general drunken insanity, excessive noise, violence, filth and constant negativity.

Johnny and Co. lived there alone for one year, one very dangerous and miserably long year. During that year, Mom learned about when to get involved physically, and when not to. She also learned how to intervene psychically and energetically when necessary. One day after listening to them get stupid-drunk and pound the hell out of some non-operational car stored over there for hours, they then turned their attention to a dog and started pounding on it with metal pipes and whatever else they could find amongst the trash over there. It was a dog that belonged to one of Johnny's insane male friends.

It was when they brought out a couple of guns and were aiming at the already beat up, tied up dog, that Mom quickly learned how to intend her menopausal ass off! She said she stood for hours at her window that faced their property and watched the insanity and violence escalate all day. When she saw the guns come out, she knew they were going to play target practice with the dog. At that point, she focused on both of the males that had guns and kept mentally sending them the message that they were tired and hungry. She continued sending them the message and energy that they should go get something to eat *right now!*

Within a half-hour, they put the guns back in the house and left to get something to eat. For the moment, the dog was safe. When they returned a short time later, their focus was on something other than killing the poor dog. This horrible day, and so very many others exactly like it, taught Mom that she could indeed affect reality when needed and at least temporarily deflect extreme negative energies. Not bad for an *"old bitch"* amidst a flurry of imbalanced and changing hormonal levels and constant intense hot flashes is it? Menopause is so much more than what we have been told it is, but more about that later when mine started.

As is often the case with people like Tessie, Stan, and Johnny and Co., through their already low consciousness, low energies and subsequent stupid and dangerous physical actions and addictions, they usually energetically attract the attention of one or more negative nonphysical entities. By entities I mean similar low frequency, nonphysical, nonhuman beings, entities, or demons. Do not be troubled by the word *demon* please as it is just another term to describe certain nonphysical, nonhuman, negatively focused beings or entities. We could call them dark repulsive little shits or highly dedicated and professional monsters if you prefer. They are nonphysical, nonhuman, other dimensional beings that thrive on attaching themselves to the multiple millions of Johnny's around the planet. Violence, fear, hate, bloodlust, alcoholism, drug addiction, lowly sexual energies and perversions, emotional problems, mental problems, living in physical (and emotional) filth and trash all vibrate within a much low range of frequencies that the majority of these beings and entities resonate with.

Think of this like shark hunters throwing out chum to attract the biggest and most dangerous sharks out at sea. When low vibrating people do low vibrating things, it is just like throwing out *energetic chum* for the biggest and most dangerous demons and other negatively charged entities out in that huge, nonphysical sea. It is as simple as that. *Like attracts like* is a cosmic Law and not just a fluffy, new age term. Within polarized physicality negative lower vibrating nonphysical, nonhuman entities usually feed off like-frequency humans—plus they use, manipulate, direct and control them also. In many cases these entities, beings, or demons attach themselves to certain humans who, on their own, produce many lower negative energies anyway. They and their addictions and actions are the energetic chum and they do not realize any of this. They do not recognize when they have become puppets that regularly execute the desires of the demon or negative entities that overshadow and now control them, their friends, and often anyone else within their extended group who vibrates similarly.

The other side of this polarized 3D situation is that if there are any abnormally high vibrating, light-filled people nearby who literally glow in the Dark, then they too often become targets of the demon or negative entities attached to the lower vibrating, lower consciousness humans. This polarized energy battle suddenly quadruples and you now have much more to deal with than just lowly ignorant, alcoholic or drug addicted, negatively polarized physical humans. You now also have to do battle with whatever negative nonphysical entity or entities that have attached itself to any of them. Suddenly it has become the polarity battle of Dark verses Light in very real physical and nonphysical ways.

The next important event that happened with me was many months later in September of 1984. My sister Yasmeen was temporarily living with my son and I in this same upstairs apartment. She camped out on the living room couch during the time we lived together there and somehow it worked out just fine for all of us. It was a highly creative, exciting, and intense time for both of us and obviously, we needed to be living together to better connect more of those invisible, multidimensional dots in a shorter period.

I will never forget this day and event because it instantly changed everything and propelled us into the next level of this unfolding interdimensional Lightworker mission and greater awakening process. It happened quite unexpectedly one sunny and very normal afternoon. My sister was sitting on the couch reading some book set back in Egypt that she had checked out from the local library. I was in the kitchen doing the dishes. Suddenly she hollered at me to come out and listen to something special in the book. She wanted to read it to me so I shut off the water, dried my hands, and went out to the living room and sat down on the coffee table opposite her on the couch to listen.

She began reading a paragraph from this book when this monumental memory suddenly exploded in my consciousness. In that split-second the memory of another of my past lives erupted up into my consciousness, my physical body, my heart and my being. I immediately interrupted her and started talking quickly about what I had just remembered and was continuing to feel and see as I talked about it. She could tell by how I was acting that this was strong and important, so she laid her book down and gave me her full attention. As if having the memory of a very ancient past life suddenly spill out into your consciousness is not enough, what happened next really put the whole thing well over-the-top.

As I was excitedly and urgently describing everything I was remembering and still seeing and feeling, in mid-sentence Yasmeen interrupted me and completed the last half of my sentence. I stared at her wide-eyed with my mouth hanging open and she at me. In those few moments of my describing the first few scenes and memories from this past life, that information triggered her memories of having been in that same past life too. In fact, it turned out that we had been twin brother and sister in it; I was the first-born twin brother and she the twin sister.

Yasmeen and I were astonished over this important and distinctive past life memory we both now were having. Unknown to us that day was the fact that this was only the beginning of so very much more in relation to our ancient Egyptian past lives together. It not only was a day of ancient past life memories, it was also a conscious and energetic connection back to that past life and timeline, but also to the three higher dimensional Extraterrestrial Beings (ETs) or Starbeings that had been there as well.

Remembering a past life is usually rather intense and certainly highly emotional because you do not just intellectually remember your past life or lives—you relive it and feel it emotionally and physically. You will often also remember, emotionally and sometimes physically feel and relive your physical dying and death in it as well, which is always profoundly revealing. Obviously, that is a lot to receive, remember, relive and integrate back into your current personality, awareness, physical and nonphysical bodies in a matter of seconds or minutes. Remembering one of your so-called *past* lives is always highly emotional and usually rather intense. However, this particular past life memory made the others I had previously remembered, pale in comparison.

This particular past life happened in 12,600 B.C. on the cusp of an astrological Age change. The Age of Virgo was ending, and the new astrological Age of Leo was beginning. This past life in truly ancient Egypt happened at the exact opposite point on the great 26,000-yearlong precessional wheel from this current life. There were deliberate reasons for this which will be revealed as we go further into these interdimensional events, past and present lives, Photonic light energies, and astrological Ages and timelines.

Our lives today sit on the exact opposite cusp point of the ending Age of Pisces and the beginning of the new astrological Age of Aquarius. Pisces and Virgo are opposite signs as are Aquarius and Leo. It is no accident my family and I (and the majority of you reading this) had past lives at the beginning of the Age of Leo and are reincarnate now as we enter the Age of Aquarius. Our Higher Selves deliberately designed this for multiple reasons. There are direct energetic connections and harmonics between many of us reincarnate now, with our past life selves who lived so long ago at the beginning of the opposite Age of Leo.

Many of us reincarnate now had past lives in 12,600 B.C. Egypt, in Atlantis, or lived in other important locations on earth during the transition from the Age of Virgo into the Age of Leo. Lightworkers usually reincarnate in much greater numbers during the turbulent transitional periods when astrological Ages are changing. They do this to help breakup the exiting Age's energies, consciousness, and belief systems, by carrying within themselves and their bodies the incoming new Age's energies and consciousness. Age after Age the natives are never happy about this, but it is another aspect of what Lightworkers do.

Opposite astrological Ages have strong energy connections with each other, and the Ages of Leo and Aquarius even more so because they both exist within the space of the Photo Band of higher dimensional light. This book is not about the Photon Band, but about some of the things that happen while we are in it. I don't remember earlier earth cycles within the photonic light, only living in 12,600 B.C. Egypt as it simultaneously entered the Age of Leo and the photonic light, and now, in this current life and time as we enter the Age of Aquarius and this higher frequency photonic light again. I bring this subject up because Leo and Aquarius are the only two astrological signs/Ages that orbit into and exist within this higher dimensional photonic light for a couple thousand years or an astrological Age. These periods are referred to as the Age of Light, the Age of Peace, or the Age of Enlightenment.

This particular ancient Egyptian past life was slightly different from others I had previously remembered due to the great length of time between my life today and it—halfway around the great 26,000-yearlong wheel. Secondly, that my current life sister and other (current) family members and son were all there as well. Lastly and most interestingly, that there were three amazing ET beings there—one from 8D Orion, 6D Sirius, and one from 5D Pleiades.

I do not mean these ET beings existed *physically* on those three star systems as we physically exist on third dimensional Earth. These three higher dimensional beings intentionally down-stepped their individual energies enough so they could exist within denser, slower frequency bodies, and function in lower frequency physical 3D Earth even way back in 12,600 B.C.

The energies and consciousness on Earth around 12,600 B.C. were infinitely more evolved than what they have been ever since. Humanity was exceedingly advanced spiritually back then in comparison to current time and consciousness. The reasons for this were because this 12,600 B.C. Egyptian past life happened about 1,100 years *before* the great planetary disaster that caused so much physical damage to earth, and even greater damage and trauma to the collective psyche of humanity. This mid-Age of Leo damage and fear due to that planetary disaster around 11,500 B.C. has remained within the planetary collective all this time like a huge, unresolved Post Traumatic Stress Disorder.

Even though humanities consciousness was much more advanced during this ancient Egyptian past life period and prior, these three Starbeings still had to make substantial vibrational changes to their energy bodies so they could even exist within and directly interact with those advanced humans and 3D Earth back then. Evidently, they knew some sweeping planetary disaster and enormous changes were forthcoming in about a thousand years, so they made the necessary energy changes to their bodies to be able to physically manifest on Earth prior to that global catastrophe. I remember the Great Pyramid being built during my past life there in 12,600 B.C. as something that would help humanity much later in multiple ways and on multiple levels. It would help humanity through the dark, incomprehensibly horrible times after the planetary disaster and fracture of Earth and humanities consciousness. I do not recall all of the ways the Great Pyramid did this for humanity, but I do remember it held certain higher energies and light in place within itself and the entire Earth grid system during the very dark and fractured Ages after this planetary shattering of 11,500 B.C.

Once these three Starbeings had physically manifested in 3D Earth reality around 12,600 B.C., they created a way to seed others from their three different frequency stellar systems and dimensions. They made it easy for many to quickly step into 3D physicality at that time. In other words, they helped seed numerous Starseeds on Earth just prior to the planetary disaster. I and my sister (and so many others) were some of these beginning Age of Leo Starseeds in ancient Egypt. My past life twin sister and I were seeded through the Orion being, and other of my current family members were seeded through the Sirian and the Pleiadian then as well. There are many of us reincarnate today that were seeded from those three different dimensions and star systems at that time.

So there we were, my current life younger sister and I sitting in my apartment in September 1984, suddenly having this very ancient past life memory flood back up into my consciousness, and then hers as well. It was an interesting experience having another person in this life know what you are going to say about a past life of yours from 12,600 years ago! I would begin telling her about what I was seeing and remembering, and in mid-sentence, she would complete my description before I had a chance to. We would then stare at each other with silly, amazed, and excited grins on our faces for a couple of seconds, then continue verbally sharing what we both were remembering from our ancient Egyptian past lives. It was an amazing day for many reasons and things only became more remarkable from that day forward.

Only a couple of days after our ancient Egyptian past life memory surfaced, I discovered an anomaly had appeared in the living room of this apartment. Again, up near the ceiling where the two walls met, there was another portal starting to manifest. Over a period of about four or five days it grew from a one-foot wide shadow, to a large three and a half foot wide very dark shadow. It also seemed to warp and distort the straight lines and angles of the two corner walls and ceiling where they all met. This portal was exactly like the one that opened in my bedroom at the other apartment the night I was physically and astrally paralyzed for seven hours while my son was evidently taken elsewhere.

This portal was so large and potent that people without any clairvoyant abilities physically saw it every time they came into my apartment. Numerous times my young son and his group of school buddies would all come tearing into the apartment from playing outside— usually to get something to eat—and they would all have to stop for five seconds to check out the strange dark shadow *thing* up in the corner near the ceiling. My sister and I never told my son or any of the kids what was going on then, but would just laugh and make jokes right along with them about why that one corner of the living room looked so crooked, dark, and strange. Being young children was more than enough for them to cope with; they had young boy things that were vastly more appropriate than weird interdimensional ET portals manifesting in my apartment. I was very relieved actually that the kids all thought it was just a fun and weird silly *thing* and didn't think much more about it. It saved me from having to explain things I was not about to explain in 1984 to much of anyone, and certainly not nine-year-old boys.

Another difference between this portal and the earlier one was that it remained in that living room location for well over a year. My mother saw it every time she came to visit and so did some other adults I knew well enough to know I could reveal it to them and not have them panic or turn it into something negative. Over the length of that year many children and adults physically, not clairvoyantly, saw this long-lasting interdimensional ET portal in my apartment living room. That made this strange business all that much more real and important to me because I was used to being the only one clairvoyantly seeing nonphysical, other dimensional beings and energies. Mom often saw them too at her portal house and property, but this portal at my upstairs apartment in the city was a very new layer to this complex interdimensional unfolding process.

Each day my sister and I would have more images and memories from our ancient Egyptian past life float up into our consciousness. We would always share every new and exciting scene with each other because it was like putting pieces of an ancient interdimensional jigsaw puzzle together. Every few days this past life was increasingly coming to life within this life because two people were remembering what they individually experienced in it, but also, that we both lived together as twin star seeded brother and sister. While our 12,600 B.C. Egyptian past life memories were expanding, the shadowy portal distortion in the living room was growing larger, stronger, and darker. I sensed there was a direct connection between the two events, but it took a couple weeks before more of the ancient and multidimensional puzzle pieces connected and more questions were answered.

The more I remembered of this past life in Egypt of 12,600 B.C. with these three amazing ET beings from different dimensions and star systems, the more I realized those three Starbeings had made deliberate contact with me and then my sister Yasmeen in our current lives and time through this ancient Egyptian past life. They wanted us both to make a fully conscious connection between ourselves in this current timeline, and, our ancient past life selves and timeline in Egypt

12,600 years ago. The real question was why, and that took some more time and additional discoveries to grasp and integrate into my current self and life however.

Eventually I realized the living room anomaly was indeed a portal and that these three multidimensional Starbeings were using it as an anchor-point into 3D to make a fully conscious reconnection to us, in this timeline. Something else unique was happening well beyond my sister and I remembering our ancient past lives in Egypt together however. Only a day or two after that first day I remembered my past life in 12,600 B.C. Egypt with these Starbeings, our mother had a very interesting lucid dream contact back at her portal house.

I called her a few days after the first day I had remembered this past life and we set up a day and time for my sister and I to go out to her house and share what we had remembered with her. She didn't tell us about her dream until after we told her about our ancient Egyptian past life memories, the three Starbeings in it, and also about the newly manifested portal in my apartment living room. After I had shared much of my past life memories, Mom shared her lucid dream, that we calculated happened only about twelve hours later.

In Mom's dream, she heard some noises outside and went out her backdoor to investigate. She walked down the carport and immediately noticed large four or five-foot tall smoky quartz gemstone points the size of large fence posts planted upright in the ground along her east property line. She walked out there (in her dream) to get a closer look at them and try to figure out what they were and why they were in her yard. She told us the smoky quarts points had been buried every few feet down the east side of her property, like fence posts, and that they ran all the way down to the paved street on the front north side of her lot.

These smoky quartz fence posts ran from the back edge of her house at the east property line, down her driveway, across the paved street to the north side of the street where there was a triangular formation of three telephone pole-sized smoky quartz points buried in the ground. In her dream, she walked down her driveway carefully looking over each four to five-foot tall smoky quartz points. Then she walked across the street to view the cluster of three extra tall telephone pole-sized smoky quartz poles or points that were standing there. After looking the three of them over carefully, she decided to get in her car and drive down the road heading east, following these much larger and taller smoky quartz poles along the side of the road.

About half a mile down the road from her house she saw what looked like a UFO hovering silently near the top of one of these smoky quartz points or telephone poles. She said this was not much different from coming across a work crew of human males repairing electric lines and poles using one of those large trucks with an attached bucket to get all the way to the top of the poles.

She drove her car up, parked, and got out to get a closer look at the large UFO floating silently there in the air. She told my sister and me that she saw some humanoid beings inside this UFO, but that they were all wearing some type of space suits with helmets. The helmets she said, all had smoky quarts colored visors on them but she could easily see the male's faces through them. They looked down at her standing on the ground below them, but then went back to working on finishing their work with that particular smoky quartz point or pole. They were installing numerous smoky quartz points or poles from her east side property line all the way on down to the small local airport a couple miles away. (There is an actual small physical airport there.)

She got back into her car (in her dream) and continued driving east, following these many huge smoky quartz poles. They made a turn north following the paved road just like actual telephone and electric poles do, and then crossed the road again heading east towards the small airport. She drove her car all the way to the last smoky quartz point/pole where one worker dressed in more earthly looking work clothes was working on the ground. There was another UFO hovering silently there too, working on completing this row of gemstone poles. The same type ET males were in it in suits and helmets with smoky quartz visors as she had seen a half mile or so earlier. She said one of those workers looked down at her standing there below the UFO or etheric work vehicle, and she sensed he was very glad she was there and able to see him and the others and what they were doing. She smiled back at him and they had a brief and silent moment of acknowledgement between them.

Immediately after this, the one and only man working on the ground walked up to her. He was not wearing the same type of space suit and helmet that the other males in the two UFOs had been. He was driving a typical work truck and wearing standard construction work clothes. He walked up to her, smiled warmly and said, *"Don't worry, everything will be Okay."* Mom's dream ended after this statement and she woke up wondering numerous things.

When Mom finished telling us about her dream, I asked her to describe what the one worker at the end who talked to her looked like. I already knew who he was but wanted to hear her describe him without her knowing who he was. She said he had extremely white flawless skin, deep sapphire-blue eyes and blue-black hair. She had almost perfectly described the Orion ET being from my ancient Egyptian past life memory, minus the twentieth-century North American work clothes and truck.

The three of us sat there around Mom's dining room table pondering much that day. When combined, my sister and my recent Egyptian past life memories, Mom's extraordinary ET work crew dream, my newly developed living room portal, and the three ancient interdimensional Starbeings connecting with all three of us that afternoon suddenly made more sense. First me, then my younger sister, and less than twenty-four hours later our mother had each been triggered by these same three stellar beings to consciously remember more about who we were at deeper levels and why we were reincarnate on Earth now. All three of us had cleared the first big hurdle it seemed, and now it would be an ongoing, unfolding process of understanding a bit more each week, month, year and decade.

Another very positive bit of information Mom shared with Yasmeen and I that day was that the horrible insane neighbors next-door had moved out and were now renting their house. Mr. Damaged Goods Johnny and Co. was finally gone, and another woman with two school-aged daughters had rented the place and recently moved in. It was a very happy day indeed and one that brought much relief and sense of safety finally. Anyone other than Tessie, Stan, Johnny, or Johnny and Co. had to be infinitely better than what Mom had endured during the years they lived next-door.

Thankfully, Mom's new neighbor was a vast improvement and she only had to endure noisy children playing outside occasionally which was preferable any day to an alcoholic husband and wife team beating each other unconscious, an emotionally deranged and violent, alcoholic, drug using teenage son, plus all of Johnny's lowly alcoholic male buddies doing what they did. This new (renter) neighbor—Rosa and her two young daughters— were a breath of fresh air for Mom and a welcomed relief from the insanity, violence, repeated thefts and constant drunken brawls and threats that Johnny and Co. produced every few days. Mom and her property were usually the focal point of Johnny and his drunken friends, so to see all that go away after so many years of abuse at their hands was a minor miracle. The three of us found the timing of these two events rather interesting as well.

It was around this time Mom began her daily mind's eye visualization ritual of creating a huge etheric pyramid of light that covered her entire property and house. She did this every day for years, and over time, you could easily feel and even see a pale golden light energy that completely filled her property outside and inside her house.

(Many years later in late 1991, my son and I moved in with her and I too began this daily practice of building a pyramidal structure of higher vibrating light energy around her property and house. From the mid-1990s on, this golden light energy became so strong and established that even workmen and other strangers instantly saw and felt it and commented to us about how amazingly good it felt and looked visually when they stepped through the front gates and onto our higher vibrating portal property.)

A few weeks after first remembering my ancient Egyptian past life with the three different dimensional ET beings, Yasmeen started remembering strange blueprints and diagrams of the Great Pyramid from that past life. These blueprints did not look like blueprints of today however. What she was remembering was an enormous spherical object that levitated up off from the top of the Great Pyramid when certain energies where running within it. This large sphere would rise up and hover a few feet above the very top of the pyramid as if the whole thing was some

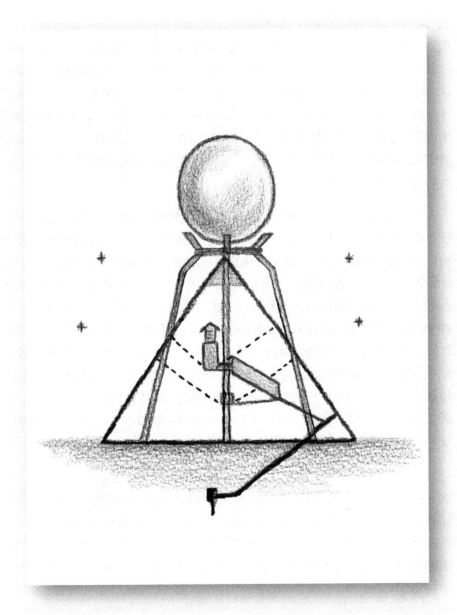

Fig. 2.1. Yasmeen's Great Pyramid Sphere Memory

type of immense machine at one level. We never did completely figure out all that she was remembering then but we both kept telepathically picking up messages and images from the three ET Starbeings about the Great Pyramid and much more. Something big and important was up—something much more than us just remembering our beginning Age of Leo past lives in Egypt with them.

Yasmeen drew sketches, drawings and graphs, took notes and drew more sketches and drawings and we discussed what it could be and possibly mean, both back in 12,600 B.C., but also why we were being given this information in 1984 and 1985. Much of it was a mystery to us and we certainly could not physically build the strange device she had been seeing in her mind's eye and remembering from our ancient Egyptian past life. Maybe that information was just some higher light for us to integrate at that point and not necessarily reconstruct or do anything with physically.

There was often a very strong sense of an alien presence within my apartment that manifested through the portal the three Starbeings had created. It never felt bad or negative, just very alien and otherworldly. It was intense, silent, deep, vacuum-packed and stellar feeling and so vast it was overwhelming at times. In physicality, we can psychically see and sense the energetic dimensional boarders and cutoff points to this dense 3D realm. The dimensions that exist above it vibrationally are each so much larger, lighter, faster and far-reaching than the others that it makes you feel very small indeed. The higher dimensional energies that poured through the living room portal into my apartment were familiar and comforting but rather difficult to cope with in a lower frequency 1984–85 body. Those higher dimensional energies made me miss Home, but at the same time, they sometimes made my dense physical body feel overwhelmed by the profound vastness, purity, and massive size of those particular three higher dimensions. 3D physicality is minuscule in comparison to the progressively higher vibrating, substantially larger and increasingly less dense dimensions and realms vibrating much faster above it.

In my past life of 12,600 B.C. Egypt with these three Starbeings, they seeded many of us as I mentioned earlier. They also interdimensionally created and built the Great Pyramid in what seemed to me to be a *very* short time span during that life. I also remember being a boy of eight or nine and standing with my twin sister, gazing respectfully at the lion-headed Sphinx. The Sphinx was there well before the Great Pyramid was created in this 12,600 B.C. past life. The Sphinx was in excellent condition in this past life, but had been built earlier by others to anchor and greet the approaching new Age of Leo and the entrance into the Photon light during that astrological Age.

There was only one physical entrance point into the Sphinx. Many stone steps led up between the great huge paws to the Lion's heart or chest area where this single doorway existed. One entered the Sphinx through the only *physical* entrance that was at the Lion's chest—through its Heart—that lay connected to the Earth between the outstretched front legs and massive paws. Astrologers will easily recognize the different symbols for the sign of Leo the Lion and it ruling both the physical heart and the creative High Heart.

In this same Egyptian past life I remember training as a young teenager within, what we today would call, a UFO. These particular UFOs were small, two passenger physical flying vehicles that most of the Starseeds trained within to fly and navigate up and down the Nile. The river Nile was a very easily seen landmark from the air and we all used it to not get lost as we flew back and forth between Upper and Lower Egypt delivering supplies.

We were like modern-day teenagers learning how to drive the family car, except in this case the family car was what we would call a small two-seater UFO. The reason the young Starseeds had to learn to pilot them was really about learning mental and emotional focus and how to maintain it no matter what. The UFO vehicles were controlled by the pilot's mental focus, thoughts, and deliberate emotional output. Once you had that difficult learning mastered, if needed, the driver could then place the UFO vehicle on *autopilot* and take a break, rest, or do something else for a bit. Nevertheless, the real lesson was about learning to focus mentally and emotionally, maintain that focus, and not become exhausted by it. The pilot attempted to fly the UFO craft from what we would today call a comfortable meditational state. You mentally and emotionally focused on where you wanted to go and that was programming your flight plan. You sat there comfortably focused on the Nile River below as your landmark and guide to another city many hundreds of miles away. Your mental focus, reinforced by your emotional desire, was the tools and fuel that directed the UFOs from one location to another.

There were also vastly larger UFOs in this past life but I do not recall ever piloting any of them, only these small two-seaters. I have an extremely clear memory of a few of these very large UFOs parked inside a massive cutout area high within a stone cliff face. You could easily see these large parking areas or UFO parking lots high within the sides of cliff faces as you traveled up and down the Nile between the large main cities.

Months later, my sister and I both were giving classes at a local metaphysical and quartz crystal

93

shop in town owned by dear elder friends of ours. It was January 1985 when this particular event took place at one of my sisters evening classes there. I had gone along that evening because I wanted to participate as one of her students. It was fun for me being able to take part that evening instead of teaching some class myself. My sister led the students into a meditational state for fifteen minutes or so, and then afterwards we were to draw whatever we had perceived while in that mildly altered meditational state. She had previously supplied all of us with art paper and crayons to do our drawing, so there we were on the floor like kids in kindergarten school excitedly ready to draw whatever we perceived.

The three Starbeings saw this as a great opportunity to make clairvoyant and telepathic contact with me, or, they were behind the whole class anyway. Before that evenings class, I had only felt and seen the three of them together through my ancient Egyptian past life memories. The three of them had not made a fully conscious reconnection with either of us clairvoyantly or telepathically in this life; two of them yes, but not all three together at the same time. Evidently, they had been slowly reintroducing me energetically to them via our 12,600 B.C. past life memories. This is often how these types of higher positive ET situations unfold; a slow reintroduction to what exists elsewhere in other timelines and locations to not energetically or psychologically overwhelm the current personality, energy system and physical body.

Because these three ET beings most likely were behind our giving these afternoon and evening spiritual/metaphysical/astrological classes, I should have sensed this higher dimensional setup by them prior but I didn't. They had done the invisible preparation work so that I would be participating in this particular class led by my sister. I only knew I wanted to be one of the students at that evening's class, participate, and play with crayons instead of having to teach. I was sitting on the floor of the metaphysical crystal shop along with her other students that evening with art paper and crayons at the ready.

I did not usually meditate only because I was used to simply accessing higher information through my psychic abilities. It was a normal, fast, accurate and easy way for me to tap into information that I needed. As my sister guided her class into a meditative state I was down and out in seconds and guess who was there waiting for me? The same three majestic Starbeings from three different dimensions and stellar systems I knew from my past life in ancient Egypt! There were all three of them together in *this* life and timeline—not from my past life from 12,600 years ago. It was so wonderful, so amazing, so heart wrenchingly special to see the three of them together again in my current timeline as Denise. It was a mini interdimensional family reunion and I was ecstatic being face-to-face with the three of them once again.

I do not know how much physical time passed during this meditational meeting, but it seemed from my perspective to have been a good forty-five minutes at least. I am sure it was only minutes physically, but at this other nonphysical level, linear time does not exist as we are used to in physicality. The four of us had a very potent, fully conscious, current time meeting and exchange of information, energies, love, respect and gifts. I would not be the same after this current life reunion with the three of them, and that was exactly part of their higher and larger plan I later realized.

The three of them stood with the Sirian male to my left, the Orion male directly in front of me and a bit closer, and the Pleiadian male to my right and even closer to me. They stood in place like this as if they were deliberately holding something unseen and geometric that they very much wanted me to be aware of. They did not stand exactly should to shoulder with each other, but at a diagonal line facing me with a couple of feet between each of them. This was so strong and obvious a message coming from them despite it not being telepathically spoken. It was another important message and one I got loud and clear even though I did not fully understand it that evening.

In my mind's eye I stood there before the three of them again as I had so many times in my past life in Egypt. They were a remarkable sight and my heart filled with joy just being with them once again after such a long absence. They each stood unmoving and telepathically silent, giving me the time to take it all in and make comparisons and adjustments with my ancient Egyptian past life memories. I was profoundly grateful for them giving me those moments to just absorb and radiate love and joy all over the place before them. They stood on their energetic diagonal line, waited for me to emotionally integrate all this and get up-to-speed and rebalanced again.

The Pleiadian male was the only one who telepathically spoke with me that night. The other two did not move or psychically leak one word and I had to respect that and not telepathically assail them with piles of questions. They seemed to be energetically holding the meeting and energetic space in place for all of us that night. The handsome blond Pleiadian did the telepathic talking but I also sensed other things and energies emanating from the Sirian and Orion beings. None of it was in the form of deliberately telepathed words however.

The Pleiadian telepathed about how a great deal of change was coming for me, and later, for humanity and the world. He stressed the need to *"gather the people together so they all would see, know, and understand what is going to be starting soon."* He told me that more of them—meaning higher dimensional Starbeings— would be reconnecting to many other Wanderers and Lightworkers much like the three of them were currently doing with me, my sister, my mother, and even my son but in a less conscious way. The Pleiadian stressed how very important it was (at that time in January 1985) for as many people as possible to be consciously aware that (positive) higher dimensional Starbeings would be making increasing etheric, clairvoyant and telepathic contact with many reincarnated Wanderers and Lightworkers to help them, and then we in turn would help others wake up much faster. Evidently, the time for this new event was right around the corner from January 1985. There was a definite timeline with all of this strange business, but I was only beginning to understand that it really covered my entire lifetime in this incarnation. Fully understanding all the different aspects and layers of what was ready to begin was not what was important; increasingly awakening and remembering who you were at higher levels within this complex and interdimensional unfolding process was.

The Pleiadian stressed how important it was to "*build and prepare*", but exactly what he did not explain. According to what he told me that night in 1985, if the like-others and I did *build and prepare,* then everything else would slowly and automatically return to our conscious awareness naturally and when it was suppose to, just like a masterfully created and carefully measured interdimensional time-released capsule.

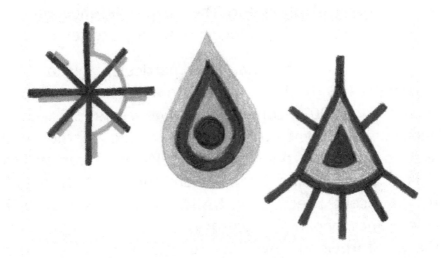

Fig. 2.2. Sirius, Orion, Pleiades Star Glyphs

The next interesting occurrence that happened during this interdimensional meeting was that they revealed three stunning symbols or glyphs representing their individual star systems. Each glyph symbol was rather complex, but this message or download of information was so strong that I was able to consciously remember each stellar glyph with no distortions. I drew them exactly as the Sirian, Orion, and Pleiadian transmitted them to me clairvoyantly, even down to the deep blue and yellow-gold colors along with that distinctive diagonal line.

(For those of you familiar with Barbara Hand Clow's Pleiadian model and drawing entitled *The Canopy Of Light* from her 1995 book *The Pleiadian Agenda*, you will easily see the close similarities between my 1985

Pleiadian star glyph and it. The main difference between these two Pleiadian symbols is that they are reversed.)

Keep in mind that this particular exchange of information with them happened in January 1985. It wasn't until 2007—some twenty-two years later—that I discovered current NASA photos online of the Sirian system, beautiful photos of the Pleiadian star system, plus all that is in the Orion system and the Orion nebula. It was recently seeing the NASA photos that proved the significance and high accuracy of the three star glyphs these Starbeings revealed to me twenty-two years earlier.

The Pleiadian stepped out of that invisible but clearly sensed diagonal line with the Sirian and Orion, and stood close enough to me to hand me something. He bent forward from the waist slightly and handed me a large gold antique key. I took it from him and stared at it closely trying to figure out what I was supposed to do with it. He waited for me to ask him telepathically what it was and what I should do with it. Once I finally did, he smiled softly and replied, *"The Key is in the Heart."* He said I could place this key in my heart and later use it any time I needed. I did as he suggested and placed the large symbolic antique gold key to my etheric chest and deposited it inside my energy heart.

This key was not *the* answer nor was it some mystical or magical etheric tool. The Pleiadian was simply trying to express complex concepts to me then with as few words as possible. Higher vibrating beings often resort to this type of symbolic communication with those of us within polarized physicality, bodies and brains, simply to bypass our intellects and egos and reach the deeper levels within us that do understand. The Pleiadian was trying to stress that the *Key is in the Heart* and not the human egoic left brain intellect. He was trying to remind and prepare me for what was coming years later (1998–1999 onward) about much higher frequency 5D Heart consciousness. That was why he was stressing, *"The Key is in the Heart"* and not in our lower, polarized, and limited third dimensional left brain consciousness. In 1985, the Pleiadian Starbeing was reminding me about an entirely different and vastly higher way—a fifth dimensional way of being via the High Heart or higher dimensional Heart consciousness.

Telepathic communication with higher dimensional Starbeings consisted of clairvoyant images, corresponding emotions, some telepathed words, and instantaneous deeper level knowing all rolled up into one large chunk of information/perception at the same time.

Telepathy is not strictly linear words like physical speech or even reading this linear sentence. It is also a much more complex, spherical, multi-sensory quantum form of perceiving and communicating great chunks of information or light within only a couple of seconds. In other words, it is the new higher method (2009 and beyond) ascended humanity will begin to perceive, communicate and transmit information compared to the lower and very slow, limited and strictly linear 3D consciousness and communication. The more typical lower type of telepathy is nothing more than unspoken linear words and sentences, which many higher dimensional ETs find profoundly boring and painfully slow—like drawing in the dirt with sticks! Higher forms of perception and interdimensional communication are well beyond simple linear telepathy, and obviously a bit more difficult to describe using linear words and language strung together in a single linear line. Our evolving/ascending consciousness means that ESP and telepathy are automatically evolving as well.

As the end of this etheric clairvoyant meeting with my three much-loved ancient Starbeings, I told each of them how much I loved them and how grateful I was to see them again. The Pleiadian smiled gently at me and the other two remained silent, radiating higher Home energies for me. I thanked them all repeatedly for everything they had just given me, and with that, the meeting ended and I was back in normal awareness in the metaphysical bookstore and crystal shop.

I instantly grabbed a few crayons and frantically began drawing the three star glyphs first, then the large antique gold key, and lastly the ancient Egyptian crook and flail. My sister could tell by how quickly I was drawing that I was trying to reproduce everything I had just perceived. She waited for all her students to finish their drawings before she spoke again. Thankfully, I had gotten all of what I had been shown by the three Starbeings down accurately on my art paper. I had never drawn anything that fast in my life, and I now understood why I had wanted to go to my sister's class that night and be another of her students. This was yet another of many cleverly designed learning events created by higher dimensional hearts.

Once her class was finished and she and I drove back home to my apartment, I could not wait to play Show and Tell with her. I described everything the three Starbeings had shown and told me during her meditation and drawing session. We both were amazed at the three beautiful star glyphs and how they seemed so *perfect* despite the fact that we didn't understand or recognize them at that time. Of course, the message about the *Key being in the Heart* was deeply special and we both had trouble even verbalizing our feelings about all of it. It was another night of high energies, excitement, and creativity, and the living room portal remained extra active and strong from that night on. It seemed to have gotten a bit larger, a bit stronger, a bit more anchored into 3D physicality because of that evening's clairvoyant interdimensional meeting. I had no doubt that this too was another deliberate creation and deepening connection between the 8D Orion, 6D Sirian, the 5D Pleiadian and myself within this life and timeline.

It was a couple months after this event that I even thought to ask Yasmeen where Sirius, Orion, and the Pleiades actually where in the night sky. We were outside one evening when I thought to ask and she knew exactly where they all where. She first pointed out Sirius way off to our left in the eastern night sky. Next, she slowly traced out a long diagonal line in the night sky up to Orion, which was almost directly overhead then. She continued tracing this invisible diagonal line in the sky farther to our right, and sure enough, there were the cluster of the Pleiades stars.

I was stunned, I was giddy, and I was blown-away because the three physical star systems were positioned *exactly* as the three Starbeings had shown me in their stellar glyphs. I also immediately understood why each of them stood so perfectly positioned on that weird invisible diagonal line throughout our clairvoyant meeting in January. The three of them were showing me—on multiple levels and in multiple ways—where each one of them energetically came from and the interconnections between those three star systems with humanity and Earth. Evidently, they needed me to be very aware of this and not forget it once I returned to so-called normal consciousness. With their intense posing and holding of their higher Home dimensional energies in such a seemingly unusual diagonal line, they were able to anchor this important information into my conscious mind.

The other aspect of this clairvoyant message that was and still is rather complex, was seeing the Crook and Flail from our past life in ancient Egypt with these same three Starbeings. That night in January 1985 when I received this information and drew it with crayons at my sister's class, this part of the message was very large and complex. At the top of the drawing were the three star glyph symbols on that invisible diagonal line. In the middle of the paper was the large antique gold Key the Pleiadian had handed to me to keep in my heart. At the bottom, I drew a square encircled with pink heart energy and then that surrounded with Orion energies. The reason for this was that my current life sister Yasmeen and I were both seeded by the Orion Starbeing in that Egyptian past life. It was because of my past energetic connection with the Orion Starbeing in ancient Egypt that I surrounded this center object with symbolic Orion energies. This center object at the bottom of my drawing represented me in this current incarnation and timeline. To the right side of this, I drew the symbol of the Crook, and to the left side, the Flail. To better explain I will have to backtrack a bit again to that past life in 12,600 B.C. Egypt.

☥ As mentioned previously, I was a male in this ancient Egyptian past life and my current sister Yasmeen was my twin sister in it. This may at first sound like something else but it too is another symbol for devolving spiritual and energetic processes. I remember a very potent scene in this past life when the three Starbeings introduced the two of us to new and much higher energies one day. We had been led into a large open-air stone building where there were two throne chairs positioned side-by-side at one end of the room. The male throne was on the right and the female throne was positioned about a foot away next to it on the left if you were seated in them.

At the opposite end of this large stone room stood the three Starbeings—the Sirian on the left, the Orion in the middle, and the Pleiadian on the right. They all were facing my twin sister and I seated on the two throne chairs. This positioning was meaningful as was everything these Starbeings did. The three of them were very slowly introducing the two of us to some powerful, higher vibrating energies for very specific reasons. They did not tell us what those reasons were prior, but we slowly discovered over time and through these careful Initiations created by the three of them.

Once the five of us were positioned in this manner, very carefully a man carrying the Flail in both hands, slowly entered the stone room from a door to my far right. I could tell he was nervous carrying this powerful and potent tool. Eventually he reached me seated in the male throne chair and handed me the Flail tool in my right hand. Once I had it securely in my hand, he retreated quickly and disappeared back out the door he had entered through.

Next, another man entered the stone room through a door to my far left. He entered carrying the Crook in both of his hands. He too carefully carried this tool and handed it off to me in my left hand. Again, once I had it safely and securely in my hand and felt comfortable holding it, he quickly retreated and disappeared through the door he had entered from.

This was the most difficult and dangerous phase of the Initiation for me and for all of us evidently. I could tell by the serious looks on each of the three Starbeings faces standing at the opposite end of this long room, that this was rather dangerous business. They did not even know if I, and then my twin sister, would be able to pull it off or not. From my perspective, they seemed to almost be holding their breaths in concern over whether or not I could even accomplish the next step.

Once both the Crook and Flail had been delivered to me from two different men coming from two different sides of this building, I had to hold each of them at arm's length far to my right and left sides, then slowly cross them over my chest and lock and hold them in place. The Crook and Flail could never touch each other. This was extremely important and dangerous for reasons I still do not fully remember but it had to do with energy and polarities. It reminds me of touching two live wires and having them spark with flowing electrical current.

From this position of having my arms extended out to my right and left sides, I then had to cross the two tools or energies across my chest and then anchor and hold them both in that position without letting them touch each other. The Crook and Flail were energy tools, not meaningless symbols or colorful adornments for Pharaohs, which they disintegrated into thousands of years later when everyone had long forgotten the Starbeings and Starseeds. This seemingly simple task of crossing the two tools and energies across my chest and holding them there was no easy task however. It felt like each object was a huge, powerful magnet, and as I tried to cross them they pushed and repelled strongly from each other. The pressure and invisible repelling energies coming from both of them was nearly impossible for me to cross across my chest. It was so strong that my arm muscles shook with fatigue and strain from trying to cross them. The two tools and energies could never touch each other, or evidently, something rather unpleasant would most likely happen. I never let them physically touch each other so I cannot say what would have happened but I had the sense that something could have possibly *exploded.*

Once I got through the difficult phase of crossing the two energies and tools across my heart and locked into place, the magnetic repelling energy coming from them instantly stopped. Now all I had to do was sit and hold them in place with my arms crossed comfortably over my heart. The same potential danger and struggle happened again however, when I had to uncross my arms once this process was finished, and literally unplug the energies. One at a time, each of the men would reenter from their opposite side doors again to retrieve the Flail and Crook once we were done. This was simply unplugging and removing what had previously been plugged-in and connected directly through my physical body. If you have ever had to connect jumper cables to your car battery to charge or jump it, then this entire dramatic and elaborate scene will make more sense to you.

Once I had physically collected the two energy tools and got them crossed over my heart and anchored in place, then the higher current was actually plugged-in and flowing freely. That was my twin male-half of this energy task—picking up the two opposite currents, crossing them through my Heart, and holding them in place through my body and male positive polarity throne chair. My doing that enabled my twin sister seated in the female and negative polarity charged throne chair to pick up the invisible phone so to speak, and call Home, or just about anywhere else. In other words, as the male twin I anchored and plugged-in the energies that then made it possible for my twin sister to directly connect with multidimensional information and Starbeings and exchange information when needed or desired.

So many of the ancient Egyptian objects, even what later became known only as the Pharaoh and Queen's thrones, were actually tools to deal with polarized energies within 3D physicality. They were devices and tools that did other things most people have no memory or knowledge of. They were battery jumper cables, flashlights, tuning forks, interdimensional telephones and telephone lines, handheld and thought-directed laser tools that cut through stone like soft butter, plus numerous other very advanced tools. They were not just rooms, or just male and female throne chairs, or just the Crook and Flail. They were different tools—highly attractive and impressive energy tools—but tools nonetheless.

Once I was able to plug-in the two energies and anchor them through my Heart, my twin sister spoke or relayed higher information from other stellar stations and higher dimensions. Through all this, the three Starbeings were teaching us about polarity in 3D physicality, as it existed on Earth in 12,600 B.C., which was different from what it is in these current lives. Back then, we were even slightly less physically dense than humanity is currently. (Prior to the 1999 Galactic Alignment activation I mean.) We Starseeds were learning about being within a world and dimension that was polarized and terribly dense compared to the higher nonphysical dimensions we were much more familiar with.

My reason for sharing some memories from this particular ancient Egyptian past life is to help explain numerous other things in our current lives, because they are very much connected. As I mentioned before, this past life was at the exact opposite point on the precessional wheel, halfway around the great zodiacal circle at the beginning of the Age of Leo. The numerous plans begun back then are being completed by many of us here now in these current lives in this timeline.

Great spans of physical time mean nothing to us at higher, nonphysical levels of existence. There are plans and there are periods of great creativity that coincide with certain astrological energies and other cosmic cycles, and to our Higher Selves and our higher dimensional stellar selves, those plans are what matter. Not that six of the twelve astrological Ages or 12,500-plus years will need to play out before other layers of other plans can finally activate and do what they were designed to do. It is about creativity and soul growth—not linear physical time, no matter how long it seems to us while within 3D density.

Integrated humans here at the beginning of the Age of Aquarius are currently capable of doing what it took a male and female Starseed twins to accomplish at the beginning of the Age of Leo. So many people reincarnate today are transmuting, anchoring, and completing exceedingly ancient work from multiple past lives in different ancient cultures on Earth—not simply very ancient Egypt. Lemurian and Atlantian souls are thick on the ground today because this current transformational and dimensional shifting work is that ancient. Cosmic, ancient players from all over the multiverse are back again now to ride this lengthy cycle to the exciting finish line, and well beyond it.

There is another past life memory from this ancient Egyptian life and time I want to share before we move past this period. I feel it is very important, so much so I am a bit worried if I will be able to accurately describe it and all that it represents. It is highly visual so you will need to go with me on this exclusive ancient ride and visualize in your mind's eye what I am describing. It was, and still is, a beautiful form of cosmic and energetic symbolism and pantomime. Therefore, as I try my best to paint a living and moving image for you to see in your mind's eye, please trust your Heart and feel what all it really represents.

This past life scene has to do with a dance, or rather a special posing and slow moving gesture—a silent pantomime of the movements and phases of the cosmos, plus energies moving down energetically into slower and denser levels and dimensions. Vast knowledge and expressions of it like this were common and normal in the very ancient days on Earth. Humanity was spiritual beings that remembered far more and maintained their connections to the heavens and other nonphysical, higher dimensional energies and beings that exist elsewhere. Ancient humans were very different from what modern-day professionals believe.

My twin sister and I did this moving cosmic pantomime and channeling alone. The fact that we were twin brother and sister was simply another symbolic representation of this larger complex process. Because we were twins in a male and female body, that represented the further splitting or polarizing and energetic down-stepping involution by integrated beings of higher light, energetically moving downward into denser, slower vibrating dimensions and matching bodies. This has nothing to do with higher being better and lower being worse, but with what happens to us energetically as nonphysical, spiritual beings when we move through the different layers, densities and frequencies of energy. Different bodies are required for different dimensions, and life on physical 3D Earth back then required a complete separation of each individual, even down to the polarization of two sexes. Having us, as twin brother and sister, move through these positions, orbits and angles was another important aspect of this entire cosmic energy symbolism.

My twin sister and I were close to the same height and obviously looked much alike. We always started this symbolic dance channeling or pantomime with me, in the male body standing on the right, and my twin sister standing to my left. We would begin the dance standing shoulder-to-shoulder facing the audience. My left shoulder was pressed against my twin sister's right shoulder. We never spoke throughout this dance pantomime, but just held a pose and radiated or channeled as much energy as we could individually.

My left arm, bent at the elbow, was held with fingertips pointing up and palm facing the audience. My right arm was bent at the elbow with the forearm extending parallel to the floor, with that palm facing up or to the sky overhead. Both of our arm and hand positions never changed throughout the whole dance.

My sister's arm and hand positions were exactly opposite mine. She stood with her right arm bent at the elbow, fingers pointing to the sky and that palm facing the audience. Her left arm was bent at the elbow with that palm facing the sky. Both of us kept our arms in strong 90-degree angles because that meant something.

Fig. 2.3. Egyptian Twins Polarity Arm Pose

This side-by-side twin male/female stance with each of our arms bent and held in these opposite angles and positions was a sixth dimensional Sirian symbolic pattern of higher vibrating beings involuting into the slower and more dense polarized physical dimension and world. It represented a nonphysical, integrated, higher dimensional being energetically down stepping into a polarized physical human body within a physical dimension. It was a cosmic, spiritual dance or pantomime showing how higher energy or spirit moves vibrationally downward into life on physical Earth within a physical dimension and body. However, the whole dance represented multiple processes and not just this one aspect.

Both of our upright or vertical pointed male/left and female/right arms represented polarities within the vertical plane of the winter and summer Solstices on Earth. Our outstretched horizontal male/right and female/left arms represented polarities within the horizontal plane of the spring and autumn Equinoxes.

My twin sister and I stood very straight and ridged with both of our arms, hands, and palms in these deliberate tight and sharp 90-degree angels both vertically and horizontally. None of these symbols—including the two of us—represented only two polarities but four, eight, twelve, and so on. You have to think and view in a multidimensional way to see and fully understand what this dance or moving postures represented on multiple levels and dimensions

Standing in our shoulder-to-shoulder stance facing the audience, we would each hold the energies and position for about a minute. Without ever changing our arms or hands from our individual and opposite positions, we would begin to rotate very slowly. I would rotate clockwise or to my right, and she, counterclockwise or to her left until we were standing tightly back-to-back. In other words, we slowly rotated in opposite directions from both of us facing the audience, to now both of us standing tightly back-to-back in profile to the audience. Being in a male body, I now had my left female side facing the audience, whereas my twin sister had her right male side facing the audience. The two polarities further fractured or doubled within each of us and were represented by this first different and further down stepped back-to-back position.

The two of us in opposite sex twin bodies each carried the opposite sex or polarity energy within ourselves however. Male and female became four, and then eight, and then twelve as we further rotated and shifted positions throughout this orbital and cyclical cosmic dance pantomime.

Fig. 2.4. Dance of the Ages Positions

From this new back-to-back position we slowly, and with our backs always tightly pressed against each other, began to rotate clockwise in a full half circle. We never moved or changed our arm and hand positions, only slowly rotated in tight quarter turns or full half turns. We slowly rotated from the position of male on the right side and female on the left, to halfway around which now placed each of us in the other twins' position. Now I the male was standing on the left side of the invisible orbital circle with my right side facing the audience. My female twin was standing on the right side of the orbital circle with her left side facing the audience. In other words, we had fully swapped polarity sides with each other. However, because our right/left arms did not change their positions, the opposite arms on each of us were now facing the viewing audience and this too is an important symbol. From this new position, we stood silent and ridged for another minute or so as we radiated as much energy as we could individually produce.

The next shift was the two of us slowly rotating on our heels a quarter turn again to both face the viewing audience once more, but now from this opposite polarity position. I the male was still on the left side but facing the audience and my twin sister was still on the right side but also facing the audience. We were standing shoulder-to-shoulder once again, but on the opposite sides to where we had started the dance. We held this position for another minute or so.

After that, we each slowly rotated a quarter turn back on our heels to stand once again with our backs to each other. We held this position for another minute, and then slowly began to rotate clockwise standing with our backs pressed tightly against each other's back. We rotated a full clockwise half circle once again to return to the position of male standing on the right, and female standing on the left side in profile to the audience. After remaining in this position for other minute radiating energies, very slowly we both rotated on our heels one final quarter turn from standing back-to-back, to then standing shoulder-to-shoulder facing the viewing audience once again.

The moving energy pantomime was completed once we had moved through all the levels and stages of higher unified energies hitting and then splitting into further polarities the farther it traveled down the vertical line dimensionally. In addition, this entire dance pantomime was also an astrological representation of orbiting through the twelve great zodiacal Ages. It was a unique illustration of the precession of the equinoxes, with the Ages of Leo and Aquarius highlighted out of the entire 26,000-yearlong cycle. The cosmic dance pantomime displayed both energetic changes to higher frequency energies moving down the invisible vertical axis and eventually manifesting within the lower vibrating, dense physical dimension. It also expressed how that higher frequency energy manifested within the physical horizontal plane as fractured, polarized energies within 3D and linear time. Lastly was how that polarized energy played out over a 26,000-yearlong span of linear time through the twelve zodiacal Ages, with Leo and Aquarius highlighted as the only astrological Ages within what we today call the Photon Band of higher dimensional Light.

This cosmic spiritual dance pantomime also represented how spirit manifests itself and reincarnates repeatedly within both polarities, both sexes, and both physical body-vehicles within polarized physicality on Earth. Spirit desired to experience, create, and learn within both sexed/polarized bodies, both polarities of light and dark, seemingly positive and negative, and seemingly good and bad or pleasant and unpleasant experiences and lives. Because polarity does not exist within higher dimensions, we as nonphysical spiritual beings, desire experiencing this split or fracture that is available within this physical dimension. It is an important spiritual and energetic learning that is not easily gained elsewhere, and this is why spirit greatly desires to experience within the third dimension of separation and polarization. It becomes temporarily less unified with itself and fractures within physicality to experience and even struggle within seeming separation amidst different aspects of itself. The current *ascension process* is this energetic process in reverse, or when we begin resolving all of the fragmentation and polarity we so greatly desired to experience earlier, and instigate the process of becoming increasingly unified individually.

The modern-day version of this ancient Egyptian arm position with 90-degree angles at both the elbows and wrists is an unknown remnant of this very ancient representation of energy flowing downward into increasingly denser dimensions from higher ones. It is much more than just an interesting and sharply angular arm, elbow, wrist and hand dance position.

Like the positive/negative terminals or poles on batteries, the two ancient Egyptian male/female thrones—plus the raised platform and steps they sat upon—symbolized this repeated 90-degree angle or energy stair stepping progression within polarization. They showed how higher energy was tapped into in steps and stages and how they manifested with lower physicality at sharp 90-degree angles. The truly ancient Egyptians represented higher frequency energies as vertical lines. When those higher energies connected with, and manifested in the physical realm, they were represented as horizontal lines. Often the large, circular shapes or images above the head represented the resulting connection to higher dimensions once these energy stair steps had been climbed. Everything the super-ancient Egyptians did represent multiple things, multiple dimensions and had multiple functions. Nothing they created or designed ever did only one thing as that was incomprehensible to them being multidimensionally aware beings.

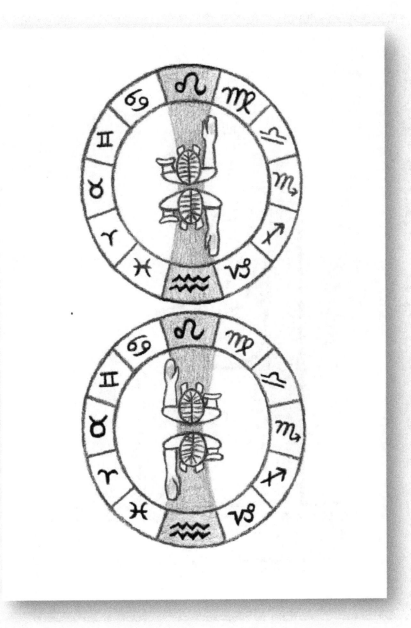

Fig. 2.5. Age of Leo–Aquarius Polarity Integration

Fig. 2.6. Throne Pose or Energy Stair Steps

In this ancient Egyptian past life of 12,600 B.C., I was obviously in a male body. In this current life, halfway around the zodiacal circle of Ages at the beginning of the Age of Aquarius, I am in a female body. This too is directly connected to my ancient Egyptian male past life at the beginning of the Age of Leo. If you look at this energy dance and cyclical time pantomime from both of my incarnations (and many of you reading this), you will understand why I'm in a female body now at the beginning of the Age of Aquarius. That is why I, as a male in this past life, made the first dance positional change in a clockwise direction into what was represented as the Age of Leo. To carry this one more step, my current life's natal chart has the signs of Leo/Aquarius intercepted. Our lives and time now are intimately interconnected with 12,600 years ago at the beginning of the Age of Leo. The larger the view, the more complex and beautifully geometric and interdimensional the overall picture becomes.

One night a year later I heard some newscaster on the TV world news blatantly ridiculing and making fun of something he was reporting on called "Harmonic Convergence". I didn't have a clue what Harmonic Convergence was then or what it meant or represented and that was the very first time I had even heard the term. But despite not consciously knowing what it was, I became instantly infuriated at his infantile and belittling comments about this rare event taking place in Maya Land on August 16–17, 1987.

I still find it intriguing how we can be so deeply and intimately involved with certain aspects of the overall planetary and human ascension, astrological Age change, reentry into the Photonic light and dimensional shifting process and yet not have conscious foreknowledge about certain other aspects of it. This is how the *Harmonic Convergence* in August 1987 was for me. I had no conscious knowledge about it, and yet, I had previously been deep within other Lightworking aspects of the overall planetary shifting and transformational process for many years. Nevertheless, this is often how it works; we do what we are capable of precisely when and where we are supposed to like higher-level, timed-release triggers across the planet. Others do what they are supposed to and are good at in other areas and other events, like *Harmonic Convergence.* Each person, each event, each special and important piece is simply another aspect of a massive transitional energetic puzzle that has been growing and speeding up faster and faster since 1987.

Despite the fact I was clueless about what *Harmonic Convergence* was in 1987, I had already been dealing with other aspects of this massive and ongoing planetary process for many years (and lifetimes) prior as most Lightworkers have. As usual, I was led to a wonderful book, *The Pleiadian Agenda* (1995) by Barbara Hand Clow in February 1995, which was where I finally learned what *Harmonic Convergence* really was. This is often how these other aspects and layers are revealed at exactly the correct time for us individually. It was also when my previous series of lucid dreams with my *crazy twin Mayan brother* and I building an interdimensional bridge suddenly made a lot more sense.

Many of these previous *"new age"* termed planetary activation events are attended from other levels and dimensions than strictly the physical. Numerous Lightworkers do tremendous individual and planetary service work from the dream state because so much more can be accomplished in a much shorter period. In years past, other Lightworkers needed to physically be at the actual locations to receive, activate, and then anchor higher vibrating energies and consciousness into the planet. We each did and do our parts at the appropriate times, locations, and dimensions to assist with the overall planetary and collective ascension process.

After the *Harmonic Convergence* in August 1987, I received a brief break from this early phase of dream state Lightworking and conscious integration of my ancient Egyptian past life, Age of Leo and Photonic energies and memories. It felt to me that what was activated in 1987, suddenly made it a bit easier for me personally for the remainder of the 1980s.

For the longest time I had wanted to get to the coast at night on a Full Moon to see what the ocean waves looked like. It was around late fall and I made plans with my boyfriend at the time to drive to the beach the night of the next Full Moon. The evening finally arrived and off he and I went to the beach to see the surf illuminated by Full Moon light.

We headed for a public beach in SoCal and immediately went straight to the nearby jetty. My boyfriend hopped quickly across the top of the jetty because he wanted to get all the way to the end of it, which he did. I however was having a bit more anxiety getting myself across the huge wet boulders that were the jetty. They looked so much smaller from shore. While he was standing way out at the very end of the jetty communing with the ocean and the beautiful moonlight glowing everywhere, I was halfway behind him, hunkered down, crawling along over the black, wet, slippery jetty boulders carefully in typical *girlie* fashion. I was becoming increasingly concerned over how the surf suddenly seemed to be getting larger and was crashing harder against one side of the jetty. The surf also looked much smaller from shore.

The Full Moon was so bright that it was easy to see everything, but struggling girl-style over massive sharp and wet boulders at night with surf sporadically breaking up over them was getting a bit dangerous. At this point I was on my hands and knees slowly crawling along the jetty boulders thinking this was much safer incase a wave did break over the top of the jetty near where I was. I knew it would be very bad if I accidently were swept into the ocean so close to the huge rocks and rough waves at night. Therefore, crawling on my hands and knees was my solution to this very real and dangerous possibility.

I had reached the halfway point on the jetty when I suddenly saw a creature in the ocean water off to my right. I froze in place and then turned just my head to look at it directly. There in the water, clutching the jetty boulders with his black webbed hands was a water Elemental staring intently at me. I stared back at him and then jerked my head around to quickly locate my boyfriend. He was still out at the end of the jetty communing with the powers of the ocean and moonlight. I jerked my head back quickly to look at my Elemental company and he was still there staring at me.

His skin was smooth gloss-black and looked exactly like the black skin of a black and white Orca or Killer Whale. His skin was precisely the same as dolphin or whale skin. His eyes were black also but reflected the pale moonlight as animals eyes do. He was hairless and had no ears or nose and only a narrow slit for a mouth. He was exposed from the waist up only so I never did see what he looked like below the water's surface. As I hung there clutching the wet boulders with the surf pounding and splashing around the jetty and me, he and I stared at each other in the bright light of the Full Moon.

"You could get in the water with me," he telepathed with a slight mischievous grin.

I immediately telepathed back, *"I would probably die if I did."*

"Would that be so bad?" he questioned.

I jerked my head around to quickly locate my boyfriend again just in case things suddenly became even more precarious than they already were. He was still out at the very end of the jetty standing with his back to me, gazing at the black glistening moonlit Pacific Ocean. There would be no immediate help there if I did need it.

In those few minutes of fact-to-face encounter with the male water Elemental, I completely understood how he had no concept of physical life and death as we humans experience it in the third dimension. My death to him meant that I would merely step out of one body (my physical), into another nonphysical one (my etheric), which meant I could then journey with him more easily in his element. That is all my death meant to him and it was not malicious or evil. The whole while he and I are telepathically communicating back and forth, I was becoming increasingly saturated with the element of water, which was more than easy for me with my Pisces Rising. I'm positive it was my Pisces Ascendant that resonated so closely with the element of water and this Elemental, and that was why I was able to see and feel him so easily. I knew he sensed this in me and was energetically pulling on me even harder to get in the water with him.

In those few moments with him—as is always the case in these types of nonphysical encounters—my awareness expanded to take in more of everything that was happening. I saw and felt him and his perspective of me as a human within physicality, and learned a lot about those old stories or myths about Elemental beings and how they could cause humans to become imbalanced from too much of only one element. It was happening to me just seeing, feeling, and communicating with him in those short three or four minutes. I was becoming increasingly intoxicated and influenced by him and honestly feared I could be swept off the jetty by a wave and my boyfriend would not see or hear any of it. I would just suddenly be permanently gone.

Fig. 2.7. Water Elemental Encounter

The male water Elemental never took his eyes off me but continued clutching two of the huge jetty boulders to keep him in place in front of me. I remember thinking during those moments of how his beautifully smooth reflective black skin looked exactly like the black reflective Ocean waters. He was the water—just a bit more solidified than it was.

As increasing fear began overtaking me, I finally hollered out for my boyfriend but my scream could not be heard over the crashing waves and pounding surf. The black water Elemental just bobbed there in the cold black water hoping I would go swimming with him in his realm. I yelled even louder the second time as I glanced sharply over my shoulder at my boyfriend. Still nothing and his not moving for so long made me wonder and worry a bit. I knew I had to get myself back on terra firma so I slowly and very carefully shifted myself on the wet slippery boulders so my head was now pointing towards land instead of out towards the open ocean. When I looked back after this adjustment, the male water Elemental was gone. I crawled very low and slow along the jetty boulders back towards the beach. In what seemed like a very short time my boyfriend was behind me asking why I was heading back in. The surf was so loud we could not hear each other well so I just shook my head at him, pointed toward the sandy beach, and kept crawling. He followed me back without knowing what had happened to me.

I wanted to see the Pacific Ocean and surf under Full Moon light and I certainly got far more than I had expected. This experience had nothing directly to do with the portal house, but I felt it needed to be shared and viewed also. I learned from the encounter that being in a physical body and dimension means we have all of the other elements within our bodies, and much more. Being in the presence of only one element causes us to become rather imbalanced, intoxicated, lost, confused, disorientated, and downright careless and stupid in some cases, obviously. Encountering one element in its natural and undiluted form is almost too much for us compound 3D humans. It can cause us to think and do dangerous and stupid things if we become ungrounded and overly influenced by whatever element or Elemental being or beings we have encountered. I learned that the old stories and myths about the Elementals and their actions are probably true for the most part.

I spent the last couple of years of the 1980s doing numerous Belly Dance performances, teaching Belly Dance classes, and working as a Belly Dancer at a beautiful Moroccan restaurant in the southern California desert. During these years, I also connected with two older professional male Flamenco dancers, and began taking Flamenco classes from them both. Flamenco Dance had long been another passion of mine and I was extremely happy to have found not one, but two professional Flamenco dancers/teachers to take lessons from. In 1989, one of these Flamenco instructors started a small dance troupe and I was one of the members. It was a happy, hectic, and highly creative time and I immensely enjoyed those last few years of the 1980s to dance and dance and dance some more. Mercifully, I was oblivious to all that was approaching for me personally with the start of the next decade, and just enjoyed performing Middle Eastern and Flamenco dance, designing and sewing all of our costumes.

The decade of the 1980s completed for me in numerous yards of colorful imported Middle Eastern Belly Dance fabrics, pounds of colored glass beaded fringe, earthy, pounding Middle Eastern Belly Dance music, and singing brass finger cymbals (Zills). Also in endless yards of Flamenco ruffles, difficult and intricate Castanet patterns and Flamenco footwork, unique new

Flamenco music patterns, actual Flamenco guitar players, and Flamenco dance classes at midnight because that was the only time we all could get together to have them!

My interdimensional ET family and friends were still always energetically nearby, but now slightly less intense and close. The Harmonic Convergence seemed to free me up a bit energetically, so I concentrated more on dancing and learning Flamenco during the last three years of the Eighties. It did feel as if this was a rest and integration period for me. I could now play and have fun in between these intense and highly focused, higher vibrating, interdimensional contact periods with the some of the Starbeings/ETs and other nonphysical beings.

It had to be this way to give me time to integrate and adapt to all I had been through and remembered. Then, I could rest, play, and pretend I was a *normal* human like everyone else again—for a while. Unknown to me at that time, was the fact that I would soon be entering an extremely intense and compressed learning and transmuting phase during the entire decade of the 1990s. Ignorance *is* bliss, and I was profoundly grateful for those last few very busy and creative years performing Belly Dance and Flamenco, before the profoundly powerful and much deeper level transformational process arrived with the start of the 1990s.

PART THREE

ETs, Multidimensional Construction, Ascension, Polarity Battles, Polarity Resolution
1990–2004

The 1990s began with me still performing Belly dance and Flamenco dance professionally, teaching Belly dance classes, taking ongoing Flamenco classes whenever we could get together for them—which was usually around midnight during the week—designing and sewing all my own Middle Eastern and Flamenco costumes, plus many of the male and female Flamenco troupes costumes as well.

I had done a couple local TV commercials for the Moroccan restaurant I performed at three or four nights a week. I had been interviewed and in the local newspapers many times over the past decade for my psychic abilities, my lecturing and doing psychic readings, performing Belly dance and teaching Belly dance, and also with the entire Flamenco Troup. I had been on local TV a couple other times dancing both Belly dance and Flamenco with our troupe. In general, I had a very public life from the mid-1970s through the decade of the 1980s and into the first few months of 1991. All of that was about to end extremely abruptly however.

Just so this does not all sound too romantic or wonderfully glamorous, know that I also cleaned houses during the day and was an assistant manager for the large apartment complex my son and I lived in. Doing all this not only got my bills paid each month, but it kept me from being trapped inside some horrid building for eight to ten hours a day working for someone else. If I needed to scrub other people's floors, showers, and toilets to remain independent and do what I loved doing, then that is exactly what I did during those years. I simply would not work like a slave inside a building for some patriarchal company I didn't believe in. I tried it a few times, and simply could not endure it for long. Having a passion about dance and performing dance was enough to make doing those other, less than pleasant jobs, well worth it all.

I was also doing occasional public lectures on spiritual, metaphysical and psychic topics and did group psychic readings occasionally. I also handcrafted astrological natal charts for clients and interpreted them as well. (This was well before personal computers and convenient astrological software.) It was a very busy but wonderfully creative time.

By the time 1991 began something was happening to me—something was changing and the incredible pressure to flee was increasing each week and month. Suddenly I could not stand working as a Belly Dancer at the best and only gorgeous and authentic Moroccan restaurant in many counties. I suddenly could not stand waiting up until midnight to be able to take Flamenco and castanets lessons from the only professional Flamenco teacher in many counties. Suddenly I no longer wanted to do what I had passionately loved doing all those prior years, and everyone who knew me then was as confused as I was by my sudden disenchantment and need to move on.

I did some astrological transit investigation and discovered that my Uranus Opposition had begun in early 1991. I knew very little about what the *Uranus Opposition* was at deeper levels at that time, or how dramatically it would affect me over the next four years. All I knew was that I literally wanted to run away from home! I had to quit my jobs and get away from all the people, all the performing, the endless work and all the running around southern California every day and nearly every night. I suddenly did not want to do any of it anymore. More than a few people were rather unhappy with me as I unexpectedly and suddenly quit my Moroccan restaurant dance job in April 1991, quit the Flamenco dance troupe shortly thereafter, finished out my Belly dance classes and informed the dance studio that I would not be starting any new classes. I had to end it all because I felt like I needed to escape, be very alone, and very quiet. I did not fully understand why I felt this way all the sudden, but I did know it was being delivered via my once-in-a-lifetime Uranus Opposition transit.

I had saved enough money previously to keep the apartment and bills up and running for a few more months, but I sure didn't have any other backup plan in place. It was a scary and profoundly strange transitional time for me. As the months passed and I talked with Mom on the phone about what all was happening, we both realized what was most likely coming; my son and I would have to move in with her. *How very strange at age thirty-nine!*

After all I had created for myself on my own, after all the years of hard work and diverse creativity, in the end I had to release it all and go back to being the recluse that I also enjoyed being—but at Mom's house. Poor Mom. Poor me. Poor 19-year-old son. What in the world was happening and why was all I could think of at that point.

The entire unexpected situation was very strange and felt like I was being pressured and squeezed out of one world and lifestyle. If my Uranus opposition transit had not triggered this total life change within me, I would never have quit my previous jobs, lifestyle, sold the majority of my very hard-earned possessions, furniture, even my car, and literally exited from the physical world stage at the age ripe old age of thirty-nine. Yet, that was *The Higher Plan* at that time and so, Mom, my son and I all made major adjustments to our individual living habits when I retired from that phase of my life and moved into her portal house in fall of 1991 with my son and our cat.

Mom had happily gotten used to living alone in her home after my younger sister had moved out many years prior, then suddenly here I come with my then 20-year-old son, our cat, and my wild and crazy *Uranus Opposition* back into her quiet and very private life and home! It was a difficult transition for all of us—except my amazing cat Toki Moto. He seemed to take to the Uranian upheavals better than the rest of us did but that was because he was one extra cool and wise master feline dude!

After selling the majority of my furniture and my car, unpacking, storing, and making slight furniture changes at Mom's house to accommodate my son and me, we all slowly adapted to the strange new living situation. My son was working and had plenty of friends so he was gone the majority of the time doing what a 20-year-old male does and should do. I on the other hand, was having a very strange and difficult time. I was having strange physical pains, my teeth suddenly were falling apart and I spent a couple years in a dentist's chair—one of *the* most unpleasant places in the world in my opinion.

My body and I were suddenly changing, and for the first time in my adult Capricorn life, my physical Saturnian body aged slightly which was rather shocking and unimaginable to me. I was surprised because I had looked one way for so long that I honestly didn't think I would age or change much. Go ahead, have a chuckle, but that was how it affected me at the time. There was transiting Uranus doing exactly what it does at that life changing opposition; completely overriding my Saturn and hammering me endlessly with higher vibrating Uranian energies. I was a wild and wooly mess, not to mention that I had suddenly aged. I was also having amazingly strange archetypal dreams during the entire four years of my Uranus opposition. In their weird ways, those archetypal dreams are what helped me the most to move through all I needed to during that potent life and reality changing transit.

All of 1991, 1992, 1993 and much of 1994 was about me repeatedly releasing so very much, while being torn apart and reconstructed at a slightly higher energetic level via my Uranus opposition transit. The

Uranus opposition transit triggered sudden and repeated kundalini risings throughout the entire four-year transit. I was dying and being reborn as something much different—much better—despite how horrible and crazy it all looked on the outside and felt to me on the inside. (I am certainly not claiming that everyone will have a Uranus Opposition transit as I did.)

Because I was a Capricorn and had not aged or changed much physically prior to this transit, my Uranus opposition and the repeated kundalini risings it caused were extra severe. I relinquished so much via this transit, but it was well worth every difficult and fearful transitional moment. It forced me to shatter and transmute my Saturnian energies into something that could then vibrate much higher and faster. Initiations are rarely attractive or easy things to move through, and my Uranus opposition was a very important but difficult transition for me personally. It was however, the perfect preparation for even more complex Initiations to come in the future.

Those four years of my Uranus opposition Initiation where mainly about a dismantling process for me on numerous levels. As my Capricorn teeth fell apart, I lived much of this astrological transit terrified in my dentist's chair, but I finally learned how to let go and flow with those changes. For me, this alone was huge and symbolic of many other things. My body, focus, my old sense of self and world were being transformed into *the next phase* via my Uranus opposition transit. My dreams were also an important nightly landscape where this intense transformational process played itself out throughout those difficult years, and the majority of them were profoundly archetypal.

A few of my Uranus opposition dreams had to do with my having *"forgotten about Fire"*, which I always found astonishing when I would wake up. I had a cluster of profoundly insightful archetypal dreams during the middle (retrograde) phase of my Uranus opposition that dealt with the archetypes of Chiron, which I had not even heard of at that time. I also had repeated dreams about Prometheus stealing Fire from the Olympian god Zeus to give to suffering humanity. Interestingly, I had never heard or read about Prometheus stealing Fire from the Gods either, and how later, Chiron worked out a much needed deal with Zeus to take Prometheus' place of punishment only so he could finally end his unending physical pain and die. Being an Immortal who was mortally wounded is a real *pain.* I was literally living through the archetypal and initiatory energies of both Chiron and Prometheus, but at the time my Uranus opposition transit was happening, I did not consciously know anything about either of them or their myths. Obviously, it does not matter, because when we are dealing with archetypal energies, we simply carry them and live through them ourselves until the transiting planetary lessons and Initiations are completed.

Not only was I going through my *Uranus Opposition* transit from 1991 through 1994, but also during 1992 and 1993, transiting Uranus and Neptune made their rare powerhouse conjunctions to each other in Capricorn. Therefore, I had both transiting Uranus *and* Neptune conjunct in Capricorn in opposition to my natal Uranus in Cancer. In addition, transiting Chiron was conjuncting my natal Pluto during part of 1992, and then in opposition to my Ascendant during 1993 and 1994. (Natally I have Chiron in Capricorn conjunct my Sun which helps explain those particular archetypal initiatic dreams I had during those years.)

I bring these astrological transit tidbits up only to point out that many of us have been, and/or currently are, living through multiple powerhouse transits exactly like this all clustered together at the same time. Our Higher Selves knows we are on a very tight timeline throughout these incarnations, so it will often have us go through multiple rare and difficult astrological transits all at the same time. If we are going through one major astrological initiatic transformational transit, why not combine it with a few additionally important ones at the same time and plow through multiple layers all at once? This is how it has been and will continue to be in these current incarnations of profound transitions and transformations. Normally, certain lessons like this would take a lifetime—or numerous lifetimes to live through—but in our current lives we are rapidly moving (vibrationally ascending) through monumental energy and consciousness changes in a few exceedingly compressed and tremendously intense years. It really is quite astonishing how much we can energetically survive, transmute, and release, but such are our current lives during this amazingly rare time of individual, collective, and planetary transformations.

(I finally realized in early 1994 that I should have been journaling, or at least scribbling down some notes of my higher dimensional visions and insights, ET meetings and discussions, clairvoyant visions, messages and expanded states of consciousness. I probably would have forgotten much more than I have otherwise. It is difficult retaining higher dimensional information once you have energetically dropped back down into lower vibrating, polarized physical reality and its matching state of consciousness. At least by 1994, I thought to start journaling and because of that, I know the actual dates, years, days and times that these events, dreams, interdimensional ET meetings and higher information download actually took place.)

After my very intense Uranus opposition transit ended in 1994, I entered a new phase as would be expected after so much inner and outer transformational work. It was simply the next level and phase after all those life and body changes and inner archetypal integrations and transformations.

In mid-1994 a very new phenomena suddenly began. One day I heard a loud, clear, and very fast high-pitched electronic sounding Morse Code clicking within my left ear. I did not have a clue as to what it was, so I just listened intently to each rapid-fire clicking trying desperately to discern and interpret what I was hearing. I sensed the clicking was information and *talk,* but talk I was not familiar with at all. This was not crystal-clear linear telepathy from Starbeings/ETs as I had been intimately familiar with most of my life. This was something very new and vastly higher and faster vibrationally than anything I had perceived from any ET group prior. It was a very new learning that took me awhile to decipher correctly using much finer perceptive tools and different aspects of my consciousness.

The first year of hearing this higher and incredibly fast clicking transmission, I didn't do much more than meticulously listen to it and scrutinize it intellectually. It sounded and felt to me like listening to someone speaking very fast; I could occasionally hear sentences and paragraphs but couldn't tell exactly what was being said. This Morse Code-like clicking also sounded exactly like the clicking sounds dolphins and hummingbirds make, which I found very intriguing and telling.

After about a year of listening and trying to discern this incredibly fast clicking, I realized I was going to have to attempt different methods to interpret and understand what I was clairaudiently hearing internally. Now every time the clicking would begin, which it did almost constantly day and night for years, I would become very receptive and *feel* the transmissions instead of listening carefully and intellectually trying to analyze it. This worked of course, and I was able to receive much larger impressions of what was actually being transmitted through these clicking sounds. As I made adjustments and adapted myself to this new and vastly higher form of Light transmission communications—instead of the lower but familiar linear ET telepathy—I was slowly able to perceive complex visuals and knowledge. It really was about me discovering that I needed to shift out of linear consciousness and space-time, into increasing nonlinear, more quantum awareness and being. As soon as I discovered this higher and more diffused method of perception and communication, these Light transmissions became much easier to see, feel, and know. (I am still hearing this Morse Code-like clicking fifteen years later, and my mother started hearing it around 1998.)

Two years later a profoundly helpful connection arrived in February 1996 when I discovered

Barbara Hand Clow's newly released book *The Pleiadian Agenda* (1995) in a local metaphysical bookstore. I had not heard of it prior, but was automatically drawn to it and bought it on the spot. The second paragraph in her Preface she mentions how she began hearing—in her head—transmissions from the Pleiadians in what sounded like "Morse Code in 1984". Gasp! I was ecstatic and greatly relieved to learn that someone else, someone I have come to respect and trust very much, was also experiencing this particular weird inner ear clicking phenomena. Now I could focus in on the ultrafast Morse Code-like clicking sounds I had been hearing, knowing they were Pleiadian in origin, and hopefully that would help me to better interpret them. It did, but slowly from my point of perception. It was very new to me and an incredibly higher way of ET, interdimensional communication than I was used to, and it took me some time to speedup, adapt, expand and learn how to grasp.

My hearing this high-pitched electronic Morse Code clicking continued almost constantly and I slowly made the connection that what I was hearing internally was also being perceived as images, concepts, feelings, thoughts, and much more. Higher dimensional information is nothing like physical linear thinking, speaking, or reading. So far, I have perceived it as consisting of chunks of higher vibrating information or Light in the form of large concepts that have knowledge, emotions, memories, clairvoyant visuals, multidimensional teachings, plus other *probable* multidimensional results all within it. It is the opposite of slow and minuscule linear awareness and expression. It is multidimensional and spherical—the very opposite to what we are familiar with in lower vibrating, physical linear reality and consciousness. Because of this, it takes more letting go and getting out of your own way to perceive and vibrationally cope with larger amounts of information and their corresponding emotions and feelings in this nonlinear, spherical sort of manner.

The internal clicking sounds continued over the years and I was slowly able to grasp larger, higher dimensional Pleiadian concepts and information in this new-to-me form of interdimensional ET communications and stellar energy transmissions.

Another important thing happened in November of 1994 that I should mention. One day Mom and I were driving through another town and noticed a new metaphysical bookstore had recently opened. We quickly decided to stop and check it out and see how it felt energetically.

We had just barely gotten inside the front door of the bookstore when we were simultaneously drawn to one minuscule section of books on the opposite side of the store. Without saying a word, we both gravitated to only one book over there. A whole wall of spiritual, channeled, and new age books, yet we only felt this one book calling to us at that time. We pulled it off the shelf, read the back cover, and knew immediately that that was *the* reason we had discovered that new bookstore that day. We bought the book of course and it was Barbara Marciniak's first book of channeled material from her group of Pleiadian beings called *Bringers Of The Dawn: Teachings from the Pleiadians* (1992).

If you have had any connection at any point with the fifth dimensional Pleiadians, then Barbara Marciniak's books will automatically trigger higher dimensional activations within you, your bodies, and consciousness. When the Pleiadians want to reconnect with you consciously, they do, and in very potent and obvious ways and then the so-called *coincidences* begin to the point of being humorous and downright goofy. Just enjoy the wild 5D Pleiadian ride. Pay attention to all the clues, hints, feelings, emotions, reminders and triggers the Pleiadians literally leave littered everywhere for you. It is merely time for you to wake up a bit more and remember more about yourself—from a multidimensional standpoint.

All my life I have been very good at remembering and interpreting my dreams; conscious astral travels, lucid dreaming or dreamtime, interdimensional journeys, and receiving higher information while asleep and out of my physical body and retaining the memory of most of it. I had a nonphysical astral Guide from around age seven through age twenty-nine whose mission was to re-teach me how to consciously maneuver my etheric or astral body within the astral plane as Denise and within the energies present at that time on Earth. In other words, I was an old pro at conscious dreaming or being lucid while in the dream state and retaining the memory of my journeys by the time I was a young adult thanks to my dark brown, hooded, and always faceless Monks robe-wearing astral Guide.

After years of current life childhood astral training, I could easily discern which dreams where coming from my subconscious mind and which were encounters with other very real but nonphysical beings. I could also tell which were precognitive, which ones were meetings with other living humans and family members on Earth, which were interactions with dead humans, and which were carefully designed and inserted from lower, nonphysical frequency beings. I bring this up only so the next information will make more sense.

April 5, 1995 I had *the* single most potent and important lucid dream message I have ever had in my entire life. It came directly from my Higher Self and I knew this while in the dream. It was a most important message from ME to me about something extraordinarily powerful and life changing that was coming a few years in the future.

It was a simple and uncomplicated dream message really, but while in it, I knew it was monumentally important. The whole dream looked like this except it was white letters and numbers on a vast black background.

D

1

47

That was the only visual in the entire dream. While dreaming this and seeing the letter and numbers, I was simultaneously receiving the meanings of what they each symbolized. The D represented the first letter in my name—Denise—but also represented *"The Death of Denise."* The 1 represented January—the first month of the year, but it also represented that *"I would become One."* The 47 represented the age I would be when this intense transformational process would begin within the physical dimension.

This seemingly straightforward dream message from my Higher Self was informing me that a colossal and complex process would start physically for me at age forty-seven—five years in the future from the day I received this dream information. It would evidently begin January 1, 1999, *nine* days after my forty-seventh birthday! I knew from this Higher Self message, that I would begin some transformational process in which I would most certainly die, and yet would not. I knew from this dream message that Denise would enter a death process on multiple levels—both of my ego self, but also of my body, my intellect, and absolutely everything else beginning at age forty-seven and probably in January 1999. I knew from the dream message that it was something completely new and never before experienced in this incarnation or numerous others. I knew it was a time-coded trigger that meant more than I could comprehend in April 1995. I knew what the dream message meant for me, but not nearly how deep, vast, and excruciatingly literal when the process actually began five years later.

Thanks to this one simple but amazingly loud-and-clear April 5, 1995 dream message from my Higher Self, I knew I had five years before the *"Death of Denise so that she could become One starting at age 47 in the beginning of 1999"*. I knew all that—yet I really knew nothing. I thought I understood the day I had this dream, but years later when this process started physically, I discovered I knew nothing about it at higher, more complex energy levels.

With the start of 1995, an intense and constant new level of physical and nonphysical

Starbeing/ET interactions, meetings, higher dimensional information and energy downloads and interdimensional journeys began for me at the portal house. Whatever higher dimensional information I received from different Starbeings/ETs, I always shared with Mom. Physically verbalizing and sharing my nonphysical experiences always helped me ground and anchor these higher frequency Light energies and information, and better retain the memories of all that I had experienced and learned. Sharing the interdimensional information with Mom allowed it to be fully anchored into physicality better than if I was the only one carrying it inside my head and heart.

I had always had an ongoing level of contact with my nonphysical ET family and friends since childhood as most Wanderers, Lightworkers, or Starseeds do. Nevertheless, 1995 began an intense new level of contact with other higher dimensional Starbeings/ETs in a way I had not previously experienced. Evidently, 1995 was an important activation point within this interdimensional reconnecting process, and I suspect many people besides Mom and I had a huge increase in their personal ET interactions and information exchanges around that time. I did not realize this at the time however, only that my personal ET interactions had made a quantum leap into a higher and more intense level of interaction and information exchange. It was a very fascinating, highly concentrated, and oftentimes rather wild few interdimensional ET years from 1994 through 1999.

1995 began with frequent ET contacts both awake and asleep, lucid dreams, conscious meditations and interdimensional information downloads into my consciousness. I often went into what I call *light meditations,* which were really just me sitting down quietly and focusing on opening and becoming receptive and aware of higher dimensional, nonphysical or etheric ETs whenever I sensed or physically heard them nearby. My meditations were never formal Eastern meditations, simply my opening more psychically to the ET beings and higher vibrating energies whenever I sensed them.

One of these ET meetings was with two dear ancient stellar kin that have been nearby since I incarnated in this life. They both always appeared as young males, and one has light blond hair and the other very black hair. In August 1995, the two of them came through very strongly so I went into my receptive state to see what they had to say. The dark haired one, who I have always felt was direct stellar family, entered into the left side of my physical body as light energy and moved inward until it/he aligned in the center of my body. The blond Pleiadian male stood etherically in front of my physical body in my bedroom where I was sitting while this meeting took place.

Immediately they began a short compressed type of *life review* with me that began with an old memory of seeing them both when I was only three years old. I had remembered this particular three-year-old meeting with them on my own prior, but they wanted to go over it again with me as an adult to fill in some gaps in my understanding. So the three of us watched a clairvoyant movie clip of when I was three and living in my young parent's apartment in Culver City, California in the early 1950s. I saw this clairvoyantly but also felt the emotions I'd had at age three when this meeting originally happened. While the three of us watched, the two of them telepathed that they had always been with both my mother and father their entire lives. They also told me they have been with my son as well.

I watched the three-year-old me telepathically communicate with the two of them after they slowly floated through a living room wall in that Culver City apartment, and then hovered a few feet in the air as they communicated telepathically with me as I stood standing against the living room couch. They informed the three-year-old me that they had always been near me and my other physical family members because we were all part of an energetic stellar family.

The scene changed and moved forward in time to when I was five and living in the new house my parents had bought in Orange County, California. They continued to show me how they were always near me and whispering in my ear, showing me something, teaching me something, and always helping me to remember who I was at higher levels and why I was reincarnate on Earth again at this particular time. I clairvoyantly watched their movie clips of my childhood and teenage years with the two of them and felt very good about what they were reviewing with the now adult me. It was indeed a mini life review, showing me that I had always had higher dimensional stellar beings assisting me and helping keep me on track with why I was reincarnate at this particular time.

During 1995, I began clairvoyantly seeing a grotesquely huge tsunami coming in from the south and destroying pretty much everything on the west coast of the USA. What I was seeing clairvoyantly was so gigantic that I didn't think it was even physically possible! I had never read about or heard how large tsunamis could actually become, so what I was repeatedly seeing clairvoyantly really frightened me. The repeated psychic tsunami visions I saw between 1995 through 2001, were so enormous that it must have meant something catastrophic had happened globally. I had the impression that most of California had started sliding or dropping off into the Pacific Ocean and that was what caused the gargantuan tsunami I was constantly seeing clairvoyantly.

I have clairvoyantly seen numerous horrible things in my lifetime, but seeing this tsunami coming in twice as tall as the surrounding hills in the area where we lived in southern California, was almost too much for me. What I saw was always the same—a huge tsunami coming in from the south-southwest and flooding inland more than a hundred miles. California was literally dropping off into the Pacific. Clairvoyantly seeing this was like having some weird ancient cellular memory of planetary disasters reactivate within myself. It was beyond horrible—it was primal and ancient. It was great Mother Lemuria flooding, it was much later Atlantis sinking, and, it was a strong *probable* near-future reality for us in these current lives. Seeing this hideous image for many years was extremely difficult and I knew it meant it was something that *could* easily manifest physically during my lifetime.

Because the clairvoyant image lasted for so many years, I sensed that it would happen if, *if* we did not soon make some very important changes energetically. What I did not realize the first couple of years clairvoyantly seeing this huge tsunami, was that it was what would happen if we did not do what many of us Lightworkers were already doing at that time. After witnessing this total destruction to the entire west coast of the USA repeatedly, I slowly realized that it was a clairvoyant reminder of what is probably going to happen soon if we Lightworkers did not get things done in time. It was a simple and crystal-clear visual message; make the changes to self and the collective energetically now, or this planetary disaster will most likely happen to clear and clean out all of the old, dark, lower or negative human generated energies globally.

What started out as *the* most ghastly clairvoyant vision I have ever seen—and I have seen numerous profoundly disturbing images—this *probable* tsunami event became nothing more to me than a monthly reminder of unpleasant things to come, *if* we did not create the great shift within ourselves now. In 1995, it was looking like it was a situation of humanity evolving quickly into higher consciousness with plenty of higher Heart, or, massive planetary cleansings with a very long quiet time afterwards.

The next potent ET event happened in August 1995, but was different from what I was used to. I suddenly woke up at 3:06 AM because extremely brilliant blue-white light was pouring in through only one-half of my bedroom window. I woke up suddenly, sat up in bed, and stared at this intense but exceedingly beautiful brilliant blue-white light pouring in the window and wondered why it was coming in through only half of it.

The next second I realized that this same intense brilliant blue-white light was shining in through my partially opened bedroom door also. There I was, wide-awake and sitting upright in my bed staring at all this amazing light filling my bedroom at 3 AM. I am watching the light get brighter and closer because it is literally moving down the hallway towards my bedroom. It is still pouring in through one-half of my bedroom window from outside, but it is also moving towards me down the hall from within the house too.

In those couple of minutes observing the light, I did what I always do when the super weird arrives—I discern as best and as fast as I can! I want to know if it, whatever it is at the time, is something positive or not so positive. Therefore, that is exactly what I did with this brilliant blue-white light; I psychically and energetically felt and read it as best as I was capable of at the time. It felt to me to be extremely high and very positive energy and consciousness, so I sat there in my bed and waited.

In a few seconds, the light coming down the hallway pushed my bedroom door fully open and my whole bedroom lit up entirely with this very brilliant blue-white light. I did not physically or clairvoyantly see any bodies, but I energetically felt two Lightbeings within the radiant blue-white light. That dazzling brilliant light did not hurt my eyes as physical light would have and it felt so pure and extremely advanced. It was such marvelously higher consciousness and energy that I had difficulty not becoming stupid and overly emotional in its presence. I unfortunately have zero-memory of what happened from this moment on. All I remember is that I was sitting up in my bed at 3:06 AM fully conscious, watching and waiting for that light to reach me in my bedroom. Then this light pushed my bedroom door fully open, and as I gazed into it next to my bed, I felt two Lightbeings within it—and then it was the next morning!

I know, I know, I am very disappointed too believe me. I would love to remember what all happened once the two Lightbeings entered my bedroom that night. To this day, I have no conscious memory of anything after seeing the brilliant light and feeling two Lightbeings within it. There must be reasons for this too, so it remains a mystery.

The next Starbeing/ET contact happened in September 1995 in the evening. I smoked cigarettes then and had gone outside on the back deck to have one because the house was a smoke-free zone. As soon as I was out there I could feel an ET presence on the deck with me. I telepathically let them know I was aware of them and was ready if they wanted to talk or manifest in some way.

Instantly to my right I clairvoyantly saw a five-foot tall pillar of slowly moving smoke. I also saw three large black shadows, round and moving slightly side-to-side, and to my left was a large round sphere of sparking electricity. (That is only what I saw and not what they actually were.) I telepathically informed them that I was seeing and feeling them, but that I would like them to wait until I got back into my bedroom and become more prepared to communicate with them.

After I got back into my room and more open psychically, I instantly could see and feel humanoid looking ETs standing there in my bedroom. Etherically there were two males and one female. They clairvoyantly appeared as rather young ETs, more like students actually. I could sense none of them had ever been physical (or human) before and that this was their first time interacting with a Wanderer in a physical human incarnation on Earth. This is *almost* humorous and certainly a bit weird and awkward for us all. It felt to me like this female ET was meeting some far-removed, distant relative she had never met before and was trying her best to create a very professional impression. After all, she too had her mission.

While we are all getting settled and adjusted to each other and the different dimensional energies, I was hearing very physical sounds like bumps and bangs coming from outside. I am also seeing numerous different pinpoints of brilliant light popping, flashing, and flaring all over in my bedroom. Just part of the process of two different dimensional beings and energies doing what was necessary in 1995 to be able to get vibrationally close enough to clearly interact and communicate. I would increase my frequencies a bit so I could perceive and communicate with the higher dimensional ET beings, they would have to slow down a bit for me in physicality, and then we could energetically meet somewhere on *middle ground.* At this point, this was our energetic interdimensional meeting and communications formula.

The female ET in the small group stepped forward a bit more towards me, while the two male ETs stood on her left and right sides and slightly behind her. This triangular stance seemed to be a very common geometric formation many different etheric Starbeings/ETs used when interacting with me in physicality (during the 1990s). The female ETs name was Si-Re-Ah and this is very unusual for me, only because I do not even think of ET beings as having names really. Their amazing personal energy is there primary identity to me. Nonetheless, this particular young female ET introduced herself as Si-Re-Ah. The two males never said anything, but continued to anchor and hold the energetic space open and protected from their vibrationally higher and faster side of the dimensional Veil.

After a few moments, I noticed a typical looking Gray ET had joined us and was now standing to my right, a few feet away from Si-Re-Ah and in front of the two male ET humanoids. I instantly liked him very much and surprisingly knew exactly what it felt like to be inside a Gray ET body looking out through those huge black almond shaped eyes! He made me feel extremely happy, as if I were meeting an ancient dear friend I had not seen in a very long time. It was an extraordinarily strange but deeply wonderful and happily familiar feeling. Was I having an extraterrestrial Gray past life memory also? The Gray and I telepathically and empathically embraced like this for a few seconds and Si-Re-Ah waited patiently for us to finish our intimate emotional greeting and exchange. I knew in those moments that I have been an ET with a body that looked much like this Gray ETs body. It was so intimately familiar and in exactly the same way that certain other beings and animal's bodies have always been to me.

Next, Si-Re-Ah began explaining a lot of very detailed, complicated, and highly technical information about how they have been and still are doing higher dimensional construction work all around our physical house and property. Again, remember that many ETs do not usually talk in a linear fashion as we do, but transmit multidimensional information in the form of telepathed words plus much higher perspectives and knowing, multiple clairvoyant images, and emotions simultaneously in one immense chunk of complete data. That is communicating with someone in 3D to them, and you have to be on your toes to grasp it all in just a few seconds.

At one point during all this Si-Re-Ah became a bit impatient with me for not being able to grasp all she was explaining and showing me. Because I had been dealing with mega body aches and pains, another abscessed tooth and assorted other physical body pains and such, I wasn't in the mood for any *attitude* from anyone—Extraterrestrial or otherwise! I telepathically told her we could trade places and she could be down here in polarized physicality feeling like utter shit the majority of the time, dealing with all I was struggling with, and then we could see how well she might grasp and retain everything a nonphysical, higher dimensional being was transmitting to her in a matter of minutes.

"Social Worker ETs! I tell you—they just don't understand how brutal and heavy it is down here in polarized physicality. No respect from the younger ET generations," I hotly thought to myself.

After I hit her with *my attitude,* she backed-off immediately. She honestly had no idea of what life was like here in 3D physicality and I knew it. I could easily feel the Gray fighting to remain silent and not say something prickly and humorous at that slightly awkward interdimensional moment. It really was just too cosmically amusing.

Si-Re-Ah continued, very patiently and much slower now, describing and clairvoyantly showing me how they had been building (etheric) vertical and horizontal interconnecting geometric energy patterns around our house and property for the past few years. It was, and is, amazing information, not to mention visually stunning in its interdimensional perfection and complexity. She proudly and patiently showed me different etheric layers of shapes and rotating and counter rotating rings and other things I did not recognize, that put together, slightly resembled some type of colossal counter rotating etheric gyroscope. It was not a "gyroscope" at all really, but that was the only thing it slightly resembled physically that I recognized at that time. Many years later, I discovered it looked much like what is called a *"Merkaba"*, or two counter rotating energy fields.

According to Si-Re-Ah, this large etheric device is a, "...*very simple Portal, Star Gate, and Grid Point.*" It is where they and we can interdimensionally connect at this time in 1995. I clairvoyantly saw that interdimensional devices such as this weird etheric gyroscope-looking device above our house was somehow connected to transparent tubes, like invisible energy roads where higher dimensional energies came through and imprinted upon the physical dimension. They were *interdimensional bridges* across which more complex planetary grid points and grid system were energetically overlaid atop Earth's old, much less intricate and expiring grid system.

Clairvoyantly I saw the lower frequency planetary grid system appearing as simple squares touching each other at their points. This new and vastly more intricate planetary grid system was obviously able to carry infinitely higher frequency energies due to its more complex geometric shapes. Visually, it looked to me like we were in the process of quickly evolving from a simple 3D planetary grid system of squares, to a much more complex and higher vibrating grid system capable of holding vastly higher dimensional energies around planet Earth. It was a profoundly beautiful and impressive sight and the two wildly different geometric grid patterns said it all; we were in the process of evolving, both as a species, and as a planet.

It was easy to tell by how much more complex this new higher frequency grid system was that humanity and life on Earth was *finally* going to become a great deal more interesting and pleasant. Evidently, Earth was in the process of being completely rewired or upgraded to be able to house tremendously higher vibrating cosmic light and energies. Naturally, that also indicated that humanity had to be going through some major inner changes as well; otherwise, what was the point? I knew in those few first seconds of clairvoyantly seeing this new and vastly more geometrically complex planetary grid system, that whatever humans were going to be living on this new higher frequency Earth, would absolutely and completely have to be an energetic match to it. If not, then they would simply have to exist somewhere else that was a vibrational match to them.

Different nonphysical Starbeings/ETs had also been building these interdimensional devices near many reincarnated Lightworkers, Wanderers and Starpeople's 3D physical homes across the planet for a few years at that point in the mid-1990s. What Si-Re-Ah had shown and told me was about more of them and us Lightworkers/Wanderers working from both sides of the dimensional Veil to energetically replace Earth's expiring old lower vibrating grid system with a higher vibrating and much more complex (5D) one. This was about higher frequency planetary grids and grid points, interdimensional portals, etheric bridges and sky tubes that connect physical Earth with higher vibrating dimensions and energies for current interdimensional construction purposes. The many reasons for all this would continue to unfold over the months and years because this is an ongoing alchemical process for Earth and humanity.

In years and decades past, we Lightworkers/ Wanderers have been working the Veil or dimensional boarders from this 3D physical side, while many of our higher dimensional family and friends (and other aspects of ourselves) remained on their side to assist us here, but also build, work and help from their side as well. Interdimensional ET construction work crews existing within multiple dimensions to each do what they can, where they are at that time, for multiple reasons for everyone everywhere.

In October 1995, I had another intense ET contact and exchange of information. As usual back then, anytime a higher dimensional, nonphysical ET being would come close to me energetically, my physical body would hurt in some way only due to the vast difference and pressures of energies. It was like trying to run 220 electricity through a much smaller and simpler 110 electrical line. I would often become nauseous, dizzy and very heady feeling, and physically strained and weakened a bit when they were nearby energetically. That was often my clue—during the 1990s—that I had unseen ET company. That was how my physical body registered those particular higher dimensional energies and positive ET beings at that time. It was a stretch for both sides to make up the vibrational range between us, enough for undistorted clairvoyant and telepathic communications to happen. If my physical body hurt a bit because of this at that time, then so be it. It was a small price to pay and I knew it would not last forever. Eventually, I would catch up and there would be a much easier and more comfortable vibrational match between my physical body and these higher dimensional beings and energies.

This time in October, Mom and I had been outside on the back deck talking. Suddenly I got nauseous and dizzy and Mom said her head suddenly felt three times larger than normal. That was our clue that ETs were nearby and wanted to interact with us. I looked out at the open sky and saw a brilliant silver-white flash of light exactly where my eyes were looking. That was another typical ET signature (at that time). I was so nauseous however that I didn't know if I would be able to get through this interdimensional ET meeting without vomiting all over the back deck!

Mom and I talk about how we are both feeling due to some ET group wanting to communicate, so she decided to go in the house and let me do my thing with the incoming ET transmissions. As soon as she got in the house, I telepathically and clairvoyantly saw a Gray in my mind's eye. He was the one who flashed the silver-white light in the sky for me to see. He is out there, low in the southern sky, but there are also other energies out there behind and beside him as well. Far to my left in the eastern sky was an Orion ET that I have known and loved for many Ages. (This is all happening from a nonphysical, clairvoyant and etheric level and not a physical UFO sighting type situation.)

The Gray starts telepathically communicating first and he tells me many things, far too many of which I unfortunately forgot. It was oftentimes very hard to retain everything I saw and was taught by these different ET beings. It is so easy and natural at the time of the meeting and exchange of information, but often rather difficult to bring all of the information back to lower 3D consciousness and physical reality and not lose portions of it.

He is explaining how people like me and other members of my current physical family—Wanderers, Lightworkers, Starseeds—are much like lightning rods for them and the higher dimensional energies. We literally ground higher dimensional energies in polarized 3D physicality through our expanding consciousness and physical bodies. It is one of our many jobs on Earth at this time. It is also why we often feel so nauseous, dizzy, ungrounded, large headed, spaced-out, and in physical and emotional pain. We are channeling higher dimensional light energies right through our lower frequency and still much denser physical bodies and that typically causes some level of physical pain and pressure.

He continues to tell me that by doing this through our very physical bodies we are helping humanity by making higher energies and Light available on Earth. We are here on Earth like spies in a foreign land, holding and anchoring much higher frequency Light, information, energies, and consciousness through our dense physical bodies. This is how it had to happen on Earth—unseen and unknown by anyone else. Those who had been running and controlling the planet for eons certainly would not appreciate what certain Lightworker and Wanderer people were doing with positive nonphysical ET beings and higher dimensional energies. Therefore, we were here in disguise, unseen and unknown, and did what we were here now to do for self, humanity, the planet and more. We were Lightworkers who had been functioning in stealth mode for the majority of our lives.

This Gray continued clairvoyantly showing me how people like me (Lightworkers/Wanderers/Starseeds) had done this many times in other incarnations and times around the planet. However, we have needed to remain well under the radar of the lower vibrating world while we did the higher energy work we are so good at doing. We were indeed much like spies in a foreign land, quietly and steadily smuggling higher Light energies and greater information down into this dark, controlled, and isolated planet. We were energetically bridge building in numerous different ways.

At this point I telepathed to the Gray that I did not feel like I was actually doing as much as he was suggesting. My concept of "*doing*" was more along the lines of hard physical work, which is ridiculous of course with energetic work like this, yet my ego and intellect occasionally did stupid things like this to both them and me! He instantly reminded me about my other dimensional inner-planes bridge building work with my *Crazy Twin Brother* ten years prior. I smiled and he nodded patiently. OK, I got it, yet again.

He continued reminding me that the physical work I had been doing over the past year and a half redecorating, painting, and wallpapering the inside of Mom's house was another aspect of this same higher energy work with them. He said it was another way in which we were vibrationally increasing our physical reality to match with the incoming higher energies. He reassured me that everything I had, and would be doing physically to the inside and outside of the house and yard, were directly connected to interdimensional building and upgrading. I already knew this but still needed reminding a few times by some of the different ET work crews from their side of the Veil. They knew the reasons for my repeated self-doubting, and I suspect many other Wanderer Lightworkers have experienced this too. It is so easy to become beat-down by the density and darkness of this place and simply need repeated reminders from Home and higher vibrating kinfolk about what we Lightworkers actually are accomplishing within 3D. Therefore, they often give us pep talks as reminders and ways for us and our work to be validated by them as often as we need it during the difficult early phase of planetary work and service.

Suddenly my Heart chakra fluttered open again and I became emotional. I immediately felt stupid and telepathed to the Gray to please not leave or break our interdimensional connection just because I was getting emotional and tearing up. I told him it was oftentimes so much more difficult and painful doing what I had been,

176

that I was exhausted and in physical pain most of the time and so on. He patiently allowed me time to complain about how hard it was here in physicality, cry, and momentarily feel sorry for myself. He certainly was not the first nonphysical ET or higher dimensional being to give me emotional and psychological whine-time like this and I was always grateful for it. I have never had any ET or higher dimensional being scold me for whining or complaining about some miserable, painful and difficult phase I was experiencing doing my Lightwork from within polarized physicality. Many of them know exactly how difficult and painful it is being within polarized 3D in a physical body while carrying higher frequency energies. The occasional whining, crying, discomforts, bitching and complaining is heard and recognized interdimensionally—and that made me feel better about it all actually.

I asked him when The Shift (consciousness, energy, dimensional) was going to happen because I was profoundly exhausted and it was becoming increasingly difficult and painful down here. He replied by clairvoyantly showing me a clock face that read twenty minutes to eleven. Later he showed me a second clock face and this one read 1:30. Unfortunately, I did not understand and did not bother asking him to explain because I was becoming fatigued from our lengthy but wonderful higher contact.

The next month, November 1995, I went into one of my light meditative or psychically receptive states to deliberately access higher frequency information. I wanted to go back to my past life in Egypt of 12,600 B.C. and investigate the Great Pyramid to see what I could remember or rediscover. Once I was there beside the Great Pyramid, I leaned against the west outer wall and instantly projected inside of it.

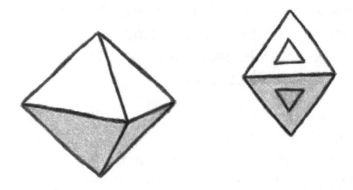

Fig. 3.1. Great Pyramid Octahedron

Next, I see the Great Pyramid shaped like an Octahedron. It had a mirror image of itself below ground, connected at the base to the pyramid that sat above ground. Both Pyramids had different rooms and tunnels within them, but the Lower Pyramid was used for very different things than the above ground or Upper Pyramid was. I am not saying this Lower Pyramid was, or is physical, only that it existed and still exists today on the Inner Planes. Many of the buildings, temples, pyramids, Sphinx, and other structures in very ancient Egypt were designed and created to be accessible using ones nonphysical bodies, as well as the physical one. The very ancient Egyptians were multidimensionally aware people and their buildings and structures naturally reflected that.

Farther within this clairvoyant journey, I started seeing a phosphorescent green glow inside the Lower Pyramid. Because I had seen this same phosphorescent green colored light before as a child and as an adult in this incarnation, I became mildly concerned. My experiences with this particular phosphorescent green light had always frightened me because it usually was connected to some dark or negative type energy or being. Because of this, I automatically reacted to seeing this same colored light deep inside the Lower Pyramid near the capstone. I internally asked why this particular colored glow frightened me so, and as usual in altered states like this, I get an immediate answer.

The answer that came was complex, deep, and profoundly important to me personally. The insights revealed were that some 12,600 years ago I had gone through an etheric level Initiation within the Lower

Pyramid. During it, a further splitting or separation of an aspect of me happened. The newly fragmented aspect of me that separated during that Lower Pyramid Initiation became a separate entity, and it increasingly became very frightening to this aspect of me. This further separated and polarized aspect of me only became highlighted and more potent over the millennia—as they naturally do—until we fully reintegrate them, usually many lifetimes later.

Once I had this information, my inner heart remembered what the Lower Pyramid represented to the ancient Egyptian peoples. It was another powerful symbol of how we—as spiritual energetic beings—split or polarize once we have entered physicality in physical bodies. The Upper Pyramid represented the conscious self, living in the bright daylight of the Sun. The Lower Pyramid represented the less conscious self, unseen and living in the dark that eventually manifests in all of us at some point within a physical incarnation on polarized 3D Earth. It is simply another aspect of life within the dense 3D realm where levels of polarization and further separation from our Higher Self and Source naturally happen. This is not something *bad, evil, or wrong;* it is something we as nonphysical beings greatly desire to experience, learn, and further create within.

The additional fragmentation that occurred within the Lower Pyramid became something that, to this aspect of me, seemed evil, dark, negative, profoundly frightening and terribly powerful. It was simply a projected, separated aspect of me, but from my perspective, it was *Evil* and had nothing to do with *me.* I did not understand that it was an aspect of me so naturally it had to be someone or something else that existed outside of me. This is how classic projections and polarizations often happen within the physical realm, and that it usually takes so very long to even realize, let alone start to work on and eventually reintegrate and resolve.

At seeing and understanding this great descending and fracturing process we each go though due to having vibrationally dove into the dense physical realm, I instantly was no longer afraid of the phosphorescent green glowing light. I understood that this separated or projected aspect of me was that very same thing, that frightening monster, that crazy male being that wanted to kill this aspect of me—or so I had always feared. He, It, did not want to kill me really but only to come back Home and be reintegrated with this aspect of me. *He/She/It wants desperately to return Home and be loved and whole once again with this aspect of me.*

Once I understood what had happened and why, I immediately grabbed the phosphorescent green glowing light energy and rolled with It, hugged It, loved It, reabsorbed It, and drew It back into this current aspect of me. This one seemingly insignificant and simple process was one of *the* most important for me of this incarnation. I was greatly pleased with myself for finally figuring out this ancient situation and taking the first huge step in reintegrating It back into this current me in this life and time. It took me forty-three years of this current life—not to mention the last 12,600 years—to reach this special point of readiness and fearlessness. In other words, half a precessional cycle around the great astrological wheel, from the Age of Leo, to the beginning of the Age of Aquarius. It was a great day indeed and I swear I felt the heavens smile the moment I understood and reintegrated that ancient and intimidating aspect of myself. It is that huge and that simple.

Many of us have gone through this same energetic involuting or devolving process where we have aspects of ourselves separated from other aspects of us. Separated and projected aspects of us fracture off only to play polarized roles for us at other levels and dimensions, especially while we are learning and creating within extremely polarized physical reality. Once we reach a certain level of development we must reintegrate all our many separated parts, projections, fragmented aspects, unloved monsters, demons, murderous and maniac selves; those dark, dangerous, and seemingly insane aspects that we have become separated from over the millennia for the very purpose of learning what polarity is and how it feels and functions here in 3D.

The more depressed, the more fearful, disempowered, misunderstood and frustrated you may currently feel, it is most likely you being terribly tired of having separated aspects of you strewn all over the planet for a very long time now. It is time now for all of us to pick up these fragmented pieces of ourselves and love every one of them no matter how horrible, repulsive, or frightening they may seem to these not yet fully integrated aspects of us doing this spiritual work. They are nothing more than dejected, pissed-off, frustrated, and wounded aspects of you and I that are equally exhausted from playing the dark Bad Guy role so that you and I could learn about polarity and further separation from Self and Source. I have learned, repeatedly, to just get over the high polarity drama and deal with it because then it is honestly over and you are completely free of it, whatever *it* is for you personally.

Parts of the Lower Pyramid dealt exclusively with these types of spiritual energetic separating and polarization processes and leanings, hence why it was unseen and belowground. For me, the moral to this ancient and difficult learning was that it takes so much more energy to keep running away than it does to stop, turn around, and finally embrace the monsters chasing you. They are merely other aspects of YOU and they too greatly desire to return Home now.

A couple weeks later in November 1995, I took note of the fact that the years of 1996 and 1997 would trigger even greater changes in many more people across the planet. Brainwave patterns would begin to evolve and change, ESP abilities would begin appearing in people who had not been psychic at all in any way prior, some people would start noticing that linear time and physical reality was becoming increasingly strange, nonlinear, and morphing in peculiar ways not yet understood by many people. In other words, I was sensing some more of what was approaching, not only for me personally, but for increasing numbers of people across the planet during the next two years.

From 1994 through 1999, higher dimensional information and different ETs were constantly available and present (nonphysically) for me. It had always been extremely easy for me to make the energetic adjustments needed to speed up enough to perceive certain beings and energies within higher dimensions. I quickly learned however exactly how difficult it was to retain all of what I had perceived once it ended and I was energetically back in a lower dimension and state of consciousness again. I would speed up a bit vibrationally to where the ETs and other higher level information was, but when I released and dropped down again, almost immediately aspects of the profound insights, knowledge, visions and discoveries would start to evaporate. It took some serious determination and tenacious focus doing repeated interdimensional consciousness traveling before I learned how to grab hold of the higher information and retain it fully once I was back in the lower, slower, and denser 3D world and consciousness again.

This process is not much different from learning how to adjust rabbit ears antenna on the top of an old television set to improve reception and pull-in certain channels you want to see. It is much the same with learning how to pickup and fine-tune our consciousness to be able to literally tune into higher dimensions and some of the beings that naturally reside within them. This is the direction humanity is currently evolving towards and it will be deeply satisfying for all involved.

Another weird anomaly that started during 1995 was physical banging or knocking sounds on the outside walls of Mom's house. From the sound of these knocking noises, it seemed to us that they were only a foot or two below the roofline of the house. That meant the banging, pounding, tapping, and knocking sounds we both heard repeatedly for over a year were happening around eleven feet above ground level and primarily on the front north wall of Mom's house outside.

Nonphysical ET beings will do all sorts of strange and almost comical things to get your attention and let you know they are nearby and want to communicate. Knocking, pounding, tapping sounds, sudden scents of burning pipe tobacco, burning incense, mixed flowers, roses, cinnamon, eucalyptus or combinations of those scents have been common ways they let me (and Mom) know they are energetically near and wanting to chat. Also small portals or vortexes suddenly manifesting inside your house, usually near the ceiling where the vertical wall or walls connects to it (just like the poundings or knockings), are common locations for positive ETs to come through into lower frequency physicality. At least this was the case during the 1990s that Mom and I experienced numerous times.

December 1995 brought two clairvoyant ET contacts. Earlier this particular day they had been banging and knocking on the outside north wall of Mom's house for a couple of hours (this became another common anomaly during 1994 and 1995), and we had both looked outside repeatedly to see if anyone or some physical object could have been the cause of the very physical banging sounds. We never found anything physical, plus Mom's entire property had a 6-foot tall fence around it and the front gate was always locked. The only way onto the property would have been for a human to jump the fence, run up and pound on the exterior walls at ten or eleven feet high, and then run back and jump over the fence to get off the property.

We heard these wall knockings and pounding sounds while we both were standing outside looking directly at the exterior north wall and there was nothing physical causing these particular sounds.

After a few hours of random wall knockings and thumps and bumps, I felt them very strongly within my bedroom, which was also a common occurrence. I immediately went into my light meditative state to meet clairvoyantly with them. Instantly the one much-loved, ancient male ET being I had remembered since childhood was there ethereally and slid into my physical body as he often did from my left side. I should add that I do not know if he actually did etherically enter my physical body as I have described; I know that is how I clairvoyantly perceived his actions. In addition, he and all the Starbeings/ETs clearly knew how I felt about allowing other beings, entities or anything into my body. I was psychic enough to not need or desire any being or entity to enter my body to either channel or as a medium, and I had made this personal desire and rule very clear as a child in this life. I was intent upon this because I have always sensed I am supposed to do these things myself in this lifetime. It is the next stage of development for me.

Because of my *no channeling any beings other than my own Higher Self rule,* I sensed that this one and only ET being simply superimposed his energy body over my physical body and never did really enter it. In other words, he aligned himself vibrationally with me to more easily communicate while I was fully conscious.

Once he was energetically in place, I said to him, *"You are the one I have always loved the most. You are me aren't you?"*

He replied, *"You could not love me the way you do if I were not an aspect of you."*

At one point while he and I were telepathically talking, a beautiful female ET I had never seen before suddenly appeared clairvoyantly right in front of me. She glided up to my body quickly and in one graceful move, bent forward slightly from her waist and inserted some very long, thin etheric something into my left eye all the way into my mid-brain. At first it looked—from my perspective—as if it was her extra long and thin pointed index finger. It may have been, or it was an etheric tool she was holding. Whichever it was, I thankfully felt nothing physically and sat there in my chair without moving, as I didn't want to disturb this strange new process. After all, some etheric, stunningly beautiful female ET had swiftly inserted something about a foot long through my left eye deep into the middle area of my brain! I was not about to panic, jump up, or run away screaming. I could easily discern that both these ET beings were very positive and highly evolved nonphysical, other dimensional beings. I sensed whatever they were doing was to help me, not harm or control me.

After she was finished, she stood back upright again, took a few steps backwards so I could see her better and smiled gently at me. I smiled back and telepathed, *"Thank you."* At that, she vanished.

Fig. 3.2. ET Pineal and Pituitary Adjustments

I telepathically told my inner beloved male ET being that she just adjusted some brain gland inside my physical brain. He smiled and said I was correct. He informed me that the energies, my different energy bodies, and all of the changes currently happening were progressing so well and so fast that they had to help some of us in physical bodies (Wanderers, Starseeds, and Lightworkers) with certain energetic adjustments or upgrades to continue doing all that we had been doing in physicality. His explanation made perfect sense to me. I intuitively knew what he was saying was true, and in typical Denise fashion, did not intellectualize much about any of it because I could sense and discern at higher levels the necessity for these etheric body adjustments.

To make this next insight a bit easier, let me backtrack briefly. I had long been a lover of semi-precious gemstones and had collected them for many years. Nothing expensive, just simple gemstones and many only in tumbled nugget form in long necklaces. I had hung these many different gemstone necklaces on a wall in my bedroom, mainly because I enjoyed looking at the vibrant colors and feeling their different energies. My eyes enjoyed absorbing the colors and energies of each of the different gemstone necklaces displayed like this. They were visual therapy as well as being objects I wore around my neck and wrists.

Next, an etheric ET used my numerous gemstone necklaces hanging on the wall as an example of a complex concept he wanted me to understand better. He told me that, like my different gemstones, there were different Rays or Energy Groups and that we all belonged to one of these different colored Ray Groups. Groups such as the lapis lazuli color Ray, the amethyst color Ray, the emerald, or the gold Ray, the aquamarine colored Ray, the citrine, the carnelian colored Ray and so on.

He next showed me about how we, from our individual colored ray groups, separate or further individuate even more. Instead of there being just one huge single blue energy Ray and Ray group, there become millions of us individuated blue ray beings, or green ray beings, gold ray, purple ray, yellow ray beings or souls and so on. There are many individual and different colored gemstone pieces or souls within each ray color. I really enjoyed this clairvoyant visual lesson because I could easily see and understand the vast concept due to my different colored, different energetic gemstone necklaces.

He and I continued telepathically talking about these different things, but the bottom line kept cycling back up repeatedly; it was the *"you create your own reality"* reminder. In regards to this, he asked me what I want to have happen to Earth and myself. He was trying to get me to know in my being and not just intellectually, that I was the one (as are you) who was to create the reality I (and you) honestly and deeply want on Earth now and in the very near future. I am the one to do this in my body, my heart, my mind, my very being. It is yet another aspect of why we are reincarnate on Earth at this very important time.

After the meeting and lesson, my beloved blue ET friend gently disintegrated into the background of my awareness. I had the sense he stayed longer than usual this time only to make sure I was doing fine with the etheric brain gland (pituitary and pineal) adjustments made earlier by the female extraterrestrial. I was indeed just fine.

After he left, I continued my altered state and inner travels by myself now that both ETs had departed. The rest of this insight had to do with my blood family on my Mother's side. I saw how certain ET energies are carried into physical Earth life by certain family members and often on both sides of the blood family. I knew which of my relatives on both my Mother and Father's sides carried the ET or higher dimensional, stellar energies just as I had been shown via the different gemstones and different colored ray groups. It was fascinating. There were also some minor insights about Jupiter and Saturn and how within 3D physicality, they too carry energies that are much like certain Stars, such as Sirius (Jupiter) and Orion (Saturn). Our natal charts reveal some of these higher dimensional stellar Ray Group energies if we can sense and discern beyond traditional astrological knowledge.

A week later, I was in a store shopping when I was—once again—hit with intense higher energies that usually made me nauseous, dizzy, in physical pain and deeply exhausted. It became so bad that day (in December 1995) that I actually laid down on the floor right in the store like little children often do. It was that or risk vomiting in public. I'll take the dirty public floor thank you very much!

So there I am, doing the unthinkable for me at the time, which was being vulnerable in a public place and all I can think of is to put up an invisible energy shield around me to keep other people away because they wouldn't understand what was wrong and might call an ambulance. While I'm laying on the floor in this store trying to remain invisible and not vomit, I clearly realized that the cosmic, solar, and astrological energies were only going to continue increasing each month and year, for many years to come, and that I had better learn how to cope with it all right now. That, or never leave my higher vibrating house again.

I could physically feel all my upper chakras vibrating from my Heart up through my Crown. It was wonderful and slightly intimidating all at the same time, which is rather common with these intense higher energies being exposed to lower vibrating physical bodies and energies. Eventually my nausea eased up and Mom and I quickly headed for the seclusion and energies that our higher vibrating home provided.

In February 1996, I had a very interesting interdimensional journey. I sat down and went into my receptive, expanded state with the intention of returning to where I had come from prior to this incarnation. As usual, I easily and quickly got results. Instantly I saw a beautiful open-air temple made of lapis lazuli hovering out in deep space with stars sparkling brightly above and below it. It was a beautiful vision and a deeply familiar and much loved nonphysical location.

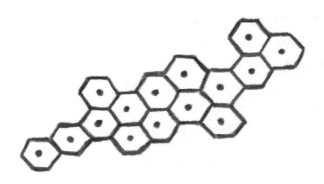

Fig. 3.3. Sixth Dimensional Geometric Blueprints

Next, I began seeing many hundreds of hexagonal shapes against a vast black background. There were many hundreds of perfect six-sided geometric shapes all connected to each other like huge honeycombs hanging silently above me. They represented numerous things— one of them being hexagonal crystals within our physical blood and cells. While I was watching these hundreds of connected hexagonal shapes hanging there above me, I realized they were geometric blueprints or patterns for actual objects within physicality. In other words, these many hundreds of perfect six-sided shapes I was seeing were higher dimensional patterns of different things as they exist within that particular dimension of geometric shapes. They were 6D geometric blueprints and patterns, as they exist within that dimension for other things that exist in lower frequency dimensions below it. What struck me viewing many of the 6D geometric shapes were how stunningly perfect they were. It reminded me of exactly what the ancient (6D) Sirian ET taught us Star Seeds in 12,600 B.C. Egypt about geometric, morphic patterns.

I next saw, off to the right side of my lapis lazuli gemstone temple, a large round table that perfectly mirrored the blackness and glittering stars overhead. The symbolic table so perfectly mirrored the galactic space above, that is was difficult to tell where one ended and the other started. There were a group of especially unusual looking beings seated at this round table so I went over and joined them as I knew I belonged there too. I easily found my chair at the round table and sat down.

I let my eyes scan slowly around this table at the marvelously unique, nonphysical beings seated there and felt more safe and at home than I ever had throughout my entire life on Earth. My eyes landed upon a couple of ET beings seated at the table that had a flesh colored cloud where a head would typically have been. Other of these ancient and exalted galactic beings looked like swirling colored lights contained within an invisible humanoid silhouette. A couple other of these greatly evolved beings at the table had bodies or vehicles that were only living geometric shapes. They were absolute perfection to me and profoundly beautiful and emotionally moving.

After I had visually gone around the table and viewed each of these wondrous stellar ET beings seated within the floorless, deep space temple, I realized that this was just a modest corner of what I could remember of the 8D so-called "Galactic Federation". I must admit I am not terribly fond of that name or title only because it has been so horribly distorted and Hollywoodized. These magnificent eighth dimensional beings and location was only a miniscule section that I called *my temple*. It was another important higher dimensional Home station for me at that time.

My deep space temple was 8D Orion and lapis lazuli or Orion Blue colored with the gold sparkling stars all throughout. It was the Orion ETs energy from my past life in Egypt at the beginning of the Age of Leo. It was also the higher dimensional meeting place where certain great beings oversaw numerous things—grand, massive, cosmic things. They discussed immensely long plans and multiple plans within other multiple plans, and carefully considered all of the possible outcomes from each and every single potential. They were great celestial designers and overseers of entire systems and the countless worlds within them. They were not *gods*; they were amazingly evolved, nonphysical beings who exist within that particular dimension and frequency at that time, and that is why the name *Galactic Federation.* Like great-unseen parents, they direct and supervise the entire Milky Way galaxy from this breathtaking dimension throughout incredibly vast cycles and orbits.

My interdimensional journey switched again at this point and I was now seeing the male I had been in my ancient Egyptian past life. These same 8D Orion energies where there then and I realized I was just seeing more of the interdimensional connections running throughout my many Earth incarnations. I was viewing the male I had been in that ancient Egyptian past life, and he was seated in an altered state himself, either in a room within the Great Pyramid or in a room beneath it. There was a human male assistant with him and it was his job to physically and psychically watch over and guard the other man's physical body while he was out of it and traveling interdimensionally.

Once everything was prepared, I as this male past life self intentionally directed my etheric body up and out of one particular airshaft in the Pyramid. I was going back Home for a brief visit to Orion and then Sirius. My etheric body intentionally shot up that so-called airshaft like a bullet fired from a long riffle barrel. While this was happening, my physical body quickly began disintegrating and eventually disappeared completely. The other man guarding my physical body during this first phase was there only to make sure nothing interrupted my complete dimensional shifting process. As soon as my past life male body had fully disappeared, his job was finished and he left the room.

I had this past life vision only because I had wondered how this male past life self died in my life in Egypt with the three Starbeings. I remembered that this was the customary way we exited our physical bodies back then; either temporarily to go back home for different reasons and return a few hours later, or, when we desired to permanently exit that life and body on Earth and return home for a much longer visit. We often used the airshafts and certain other chambers within the Great Pyramid as interdimensional transit tubes for our nonphysical bodies. It was unthinkable to die and leave one's physical body behind for someone else to have to deal with, so we would fully dematerialize it when we were permanently exiting that life and body. These very ancient Egyptians never buried or entombed dead physical bodies. The majority of people could intentionally dematerialize their physical body once they were permanently finished with it in that physical Earth incarnation. They would simply speed up their vibratory rates fast enough to literally disappear physically.

It is astonishing how severely distorted so many very ancient ways of being, living, perceiving and even death and dying become over the millennia. To these ancient and highly multidimensionally aware people, it would have been unimaginable to bury someone who had permanently vacated their physical vehicle. It would have been perceived as dirty, irresponsible, thoughtless and disrespectful to Earth and everyone else to do so. Millennia later, long after the Egyptians had forgotten how consciousness had originally been there, who had been there and how multidimensional they actually were, this whole process digressed into the elaborate rituals of embalming and entombing and so on. It was— as is usually the case—the exact opposite of what actually happened many thousands of years earlier.

I was still feeling very exhausted and usually in a lot of physical pain as well during this time. The more intense physical pain and being sick started in

1995 and continued through the 1990s and beyond. At this point I didn't know what was causing me to feel so ill much of the time, but eventually I discovered that much of it was solar related. Whenever the Sun was producing any solar flares or extra activity at all, it instantly registered in my physical body as stabbing ice pick-like pains in certain bones, body aches, low-grade fevers, chills, intense exhaustion, and what felt like the flu yet was not the typical flu. I simply felt terrible most of the time and sensed that much of it was caused by higher solar and cosmic energies triggering changes within my physical body, DNA, nervous system, brain, heart, and my other nonphysical bodies as well.

In March of 1996, I had another interesting higher awareness despite being so ill and in constant physical pain. I was extremely exhausted that day and had been listening to my inner ear Morse Code clicking that ran continuously. It was so fast and clicked away constantly day and night and I desperately wanted to understand it better than I was. That evening I went into an expanded state to attempt to decipher the high-pitched electronic sounding Morse Code clicking from what sounded like inside my left ear.

As soon as I close my eyes, I could see humanoid shadow shapes and figures of other dimensional beings moving right in front of me only a few inched away. I am stunned to realize that nonphysical, positive, higher vibrating beings exist in another level and frequency mere inches away from us here in physicality. Physical distance means nothing in the way we usually think of it, and many other life forms and beings exist all around us, only inches away. Because they exist within a different vibrational range than we do in 3D, we usually cannot perceive them despite them being in our space, and us in theirs. I knew in that moment that this phenomenon is no different than multiple radio and/or TV waves all existing within the same space, yet we can only perceive one of them at a time because we are in physicality, and those are the rules here. Only one station is perceived at a time unless you are psychic that is or rapidly evolving.

In the next instant, I saw a bright flash of light and suddenly there is the Sphinx. The Sphinx is the pineal gland—the pineal is the Sphinx! What? I am suddenly aware that the Nile is the human spine, the Delta the Crown chakra, the Great Pyramid, the Sphinx, the lesser pyramids are the many endocrine glands within the human brain. What? I have the feeling that if I could overlay a transparent map of Upper and Lower Egypt over the human body, and more specifically the human skull and brain, we would see an astonishing alignment. What? Really? Yes, I do believe so. All of ancient Egypt mirrored or reflected certain cosmic and stellar locations, but it also mirrored the interior landscapes of our bodies.

Because the very ancient Egyptians (and others) were multidimensionally aware and functioning beings, they built things and structures that were multidimensional codes, libraries, models, maps, star maps of and for Earth, and human bodies. An object or building was never just an object or a building. The ancients simply did not perceive reality in a disconnected and linear way, and because of that, their structures and buildings did far more than what modern-day "professionals" can even comprehend. (This is finally changing however.)

Some of what the Sphinx does, the human pineal gland does. Some of what the Great Pyramid does, the human pituitary gland does. There was so much more of this type of higher dimensional information, but unfortunately, I started to lose my focus and connection. It is terribly frustrating knowing that so much extra exists but that I could not grasp more of it and bring it back to share.

Earlier I had mentioned how Mom and I stopped into a metaphysical bookstore in November 1994 and were immediately drawn to only one book that day. It was channeled Pleiadian material from Barbara Marciniak. From that day on, I would read all other of her books aloud to Mom so we could discuss the material. It seemed that by my reading all of Marciniak's books aloud in the living room every evening (and a couple other authors books as well), we made it that much easier for certain higher dimensional ET beings to make interdimensional contact with both of us. On the other hand, this all could have been cleverly designed by some Pleiadian ETs to get Mom and me into a jointly receptive state so they could more easily come through the dining room portal and communicate with us more directly. The Pleiadians especially seem to excel at creating these types of seeming synchronicities for us in physical 3D.

This became so common that we never knew what wild phenomena or anomalies to expect each time we sat down together to read aloud one of these Pleiadian books. It became an interdimensional ET circus in Mom's living room whenever we would do this. Literally, within minutes of our sitting down in the living room chairs to read aloud for a couple of hours, a clearly visible portal would manifest near the ceiling and wall by the dining table next to where we were.

Our cat would go nuts every time I would start reading aloud too. He could instantly feel and see the higher dimensional ET energies connecting to the house, Mom and I, and he would meow loudly right over my reading. He would walk back and forth over both our laps while I was reading aloud, trying to stay focused on the book material and ignore him. (The dining room portal would physically manifest during this time.) All the while, the cat is meowing, purring, singing, rubbing and carrying on as if he was high on catnip. Once the portal appeared, he would jump up on the dining table, stand up on his back legs crying and try to get up and into the portal itself. Our cat wanted to go back home in a very serious way. I could certainly relate.

This ritual with the cat usually happened every time we would start the book reading, and after that, the higher dimensional ETs would come through. It often took a lot to get the cat calmed down and quiet because he absolutely loved these particular higher ET energies and wanted to physically get up to that portal. Thankfully, it was very near the ceiling because I have no doubt that the cat would have physically disappeared into it if he could have reached it.

It was a wonderful, wild, amazing time for all of us—cat included—and we did much more than just read aloud believe me. We had nearly constant ET contacts in the house because of our reading that particular material at that time which obviously triggered even more expanded states of consciousness within Mom and me. After awhile it was obvious that the reading aloud had morphed into interdimensional ET contact that was an extension of the information and Pleiadian energies in those books. At different points during the years of this process, the book reading became secondary to what we both were experiencing directly in the house via the interdimensional ETs and higher energies coming through and teaching us directly. It was definitely a very nice dual learning between direct etheric ET contacts and reading those wonderful channeled Pleiadian Marciniak books.

I don't remember the exact month and year that this next business started, but it was either 1995 or 1996. Each morning I would go outside and sit on the back deck, smoke a cigarette, and survey my little corner of the world. I would look at the yard and the many birds feeding at the bird feeder and bathing in the large shallow concrete pond I had made for them. I would view the sky and the sunlight, the surrounding land and hills outside our fence line, and easily feel the higher energies present. It was my morning reconnection practice with the physical world.

I will never forget the very first morning that this happened however. I stepped out the back door, lit a cigarette, and looked out to the south of our yard and it looked just a little bit different to me that day. The sky too was just a bit different, the yard looked just a bit different, the rolling hills and open fields to the south and east of us all looked slightly different. I smoked and pondered over the possible reasons for why physical reality had changed slightly from the day before.

From that morning on, I would make sure to view the yard and everything in it and the sky and sunlight to see if I noticed any further changes. I could easily see and feel that *reality* had indeed changed slightly. This perception was more felt than keenly physically seen, and yet, these slight changes to physical reality were clearly and visibly there. The world was literally changing energetically a little bit each day and week and it was increasingly easy to see and feel this fact. It was a fascinating process repeatedly watching physical reality morph and shape-shift into something slightly different each week and month. It was nothing huge that you could easily point out and then go investigate. It was more subtle and energetic, and over the months, it became undeniable.

Another anomaly that began during this same time and continued for many years after, was going outside and physically seeing what looked to me to be some type of white mist or fog in certain areas. It was not physical mist or fog, but energy, and it seemed to swirl slowly and move about much like fog does. Again, this was just how I personally was seeing certain higher energies manifesting within lower vibrating reality at that particular time. I would see this same white mist or fog-like energy not only in our yard, but also while driving and while in certain shopping stores.

Inside certain shopping stores, this white fog would be so thick that I could hardly see or read the large signs inside the stores. I would blink, squint, and struggle to see clearly, but I usually could not see through this dense fog-like energy. As soon as I stepped outside of the store however, the fog or mist anomaly would be gone. This told me that the manmade energies inside those particular stores were much lower frequencies than just being outside.

I also started seeing new colors while I was outside in the sunlight during. I was seeing many of these new colors in what were normal shadows while outdoors. Instead of the shadows looking the way they always had, they suddenly were strange colors I had never seen before. Because I was seeing new colors, it is very difficult to describe them. The best I can do is to compare them to other colors, and even that is not completely accurate.

One of these new colors I was seeing at that time looked like burnt orange where shadows were. I also would see new colors just floating in areas in the back yard about four feet above ground and they would remain hanging there in space. I found it difficult to walk through them because they felt so solid to me even though I could see through them. Same with the shadows—I was not so sure I wanted to walk on burnt orange colored shadows for some silly reason.

I was also seeing new colors up in the open sky. Again, they were patches of much higher iridescent colors that are extremely difficult to describe only because there is nothing physical to compare them with. They were beautiful and radiated light and were not flat, matt, or dull. I believe I was simply seeing some higher frequency colors that exist beyond the normal range most humans in 3D can currently perceive. If I could see, hear, and access other higher beings and information, it makes sense that with reality changing as obviously as it was in 1995 and beyond, that other people and I would begin seeing higher vibrating colors (and numerous other things) too.

Another thing that changed at this time was how flowing or moving water looked to me. Water always looked like regular water up until one day in 1996. From that point on, water looks denser and thicker to me, more the consistency of honey or syrup. Much of the time water appears to me to look and feel like nearly set jello. It is quite beautiful actually and has more energy and *soul* in it than old lower vibrating water did. I suspect we will perceive far more changes like these over the next few years.

Another common anomaly I saw starting in the mid-1990s was what looked to me to be heat mirages. I would see them in the house, in certain shopping stores, while driving, and while outside. They too were beautiful glimmering silver-white energies that shimmered in the air like floating portals. They looked like heat mirages but were not the typical, physical heat mirages. They were higher vibrating energies intermingling with lower vibrating physical energies. From my perspective at that time, they appeared year-round like floating, shimmering, beautiful heat mirages in the strangest of places.

Another exceedingly interesting but confusing anomaly I began seeing around 1996, was what looked like heavy, same-sized white raindrops all falling at exactly the same angle and speed. I would usually see this phenomenon when I was inside the house looking out a window. It was always the same; heavy white colored *energies* that looked to me like large raindrops falling. The drops were larger than normal and all perfectly equal in size and shape. Because we had mini blinds on all our windows, I first assumed it was some weird optical illusion I was seeing and nothing more. However, I saw it so often that I began physically experimenting with raising the mini blinds to see if that caused the phenomena to stop. It didn't, so it was not the mini blinds causing some type of optical distortion. For some reason I believe looking through the mini blinds made it easier for me to clairvoyantly see this energy phenomenon at first. Later I could see it with or without looking through mini blinds as it was there constantly wherever I looked out a window anywhere.

This anomaly continued for many years and I still occasionally see this heavy white rain-like material falling today, some thirteen years later. After doing all the intellectual, analyzing, pondering, questioning, physical experimenting and other mental gymnastic to try and figure out what I was seeing, I finally went into an altered state to perceive it and/or ask for higher insights if needed. Almost as soon as I relaxed and got out of *intellectual and physical detective mode,* I perceived that what I had been seeing were actually photon light particles constantly *raining down* on and through Earth, and literally everyone and everything on the planet. This instantly made so much sense and answered all my previous questions.

Over the years, I have watched these photon particles continuously raining down and uniformly hitting Earth at a particular angle. Ever so slowly over the years that angle has inched its way up to where it currently is today. It now rains down in a straight vertical line. I have seen this falling white rain or photon particles slowly inch along from a slight angle, to directly overhead over the past thirteen years. Question is which has really moved or changed? Earth or these photon particles? I sense the Earth has changed its position within this photonic light or raining down of photonic light particles and that is why it now clairvoyantly appears to me to be falling or raining down from directly overhead. I sense this means Earth is now (fall 2009) fully and completely orbiting well inside this Photon

Band of Light, and will remain within it for a very long time.

I have since discovered that some people called this the *"Galactic Precipitation"* or the *raining down* of higher energies and Light upon Earth and humanity. From how it always clairvoyantly looked to me, it was indeed raining cosmic Photon Light or *Galactic Precipitation*.

September 1996 fall equinox brought in a massive surge of energies for me. On each of the equinoxes and solstices, I always went into a light meditational state, which again just means I sat down somewhere quiet and became much more passive and open, yet highly focused at the same time. I would become very relaxed and receptive, but at the same time, highly focused and ready for whatever might happen, manifest, or be remembered or realized.

Because the fall equinox and season are very energetically potent to me personally, I suspect that is why this particular clairvoyant journey was extra special. I eventually realized that I was actually traveling to higher dimensions and perceiving, what I was capable of perceiving at the time, of what exists within them. As the Sun entered Libra, I went more fully into the sixth dimension than I ever had before. I am particularly fond of 6D and the few Sirian beings I know, and always greatly enjoy viewing some of the incredibly perfect geometric shapes and living energy patterns that exist there.

Once I was in an altered state this day, I instantly clairvoyantly saw a scene from my Egyptian past life with the Starbeings. I saw myself as the male I had been then working with those much-loved three Starbeings—the 8D Orion, 6D Sirian, and the 5D Pleiadian. We were preparing a celebration ceremony in that life and time—and I Denise—was simply viewing that ancient past life event from my current life and timeline.

Once these three Starbeings had the energies opened and set just the way they needed to allow some other extremely ancient Elder Starbeings to come through, the real party began. It was a grand memory for me (Denise) to once again be seeing and reliving what I had experienced in that male past life in 12,600 B.C. It was exactly like having a family reunion with relatives you have never personally met before. You have heard about them, you have listened to other family members share their personal stories about them, yet, you have never met them yourself. Then one day at some big family reunion, there they all are and you get to actually met them and finally have your own personal stories about them. This clairvoyant past life vision memory was just like that—one big multidimensional ET family reunion.

With the energies prepared by the Orion, Sirian, and Pleiadian Starbeings from this side, these other ancient Elder Starbeings from their respective higher dimensional stellar systems, came through and into ancient Egypt that day. It was a rare treat for all of us (in my past life), because these great ancient beings from Home did not come to Earth physicality much, even back then. They suddenly *came through* and simply stepped down from up in the air a few feet and manifested into our dimension. They were stunning and magnificent higher dimensional ET beings. They were the great and extremely ancient Elder Lion beings from Sirius, the great and ancient Bird beings, and the third group was beautiful and radiant humanoid beings from eighth dimension Orion.

As they all *stepped through and landed* gently within ancient physical Egypt, the three Starbeing teachers greeted them first while the rest of us Star Seeds excitedly waited our turns to meet each of them. It was almost too much to endure for the teenaged male past life me who lived then. These great Elder beings from their respective dimensions radiated such different energies than we did, that it was intoxicating just being physically near all of them. It was like having ancient angelic beings suddenly manifest within physicality at your family reunion simply because they too are your distant relatives.

The great Sirian Lion beings made the male past life me (and current Denise) swoon just from seeing, smelling, hearing and feeling their energies. They were spectacular creatures that stood anywhere between seven to ten foot tall. They had humanoid, bipedal bodies like ours with the main difference being they had beautiful lion heads and paws and were covered in short, soft, golden-tan, light tan, to pure white lion fur. The male Sirian Lion beings were regal and magnificent and they radiated such ancient knowing and profound love it was hard to comprehend and highly intoxicating to be near.

The female Lion beings were only slightly shorter than their male counterparts were, and were very beautiful, gentle, and deeply loving beings as well. They wore tiny glittering trinkets and objects tied in their glorious long manes. To the male past life me, they felt as if they were very ancient grand artists and creators. The energies they radiated are nearly impossible for me to describe for the simple reason that we have nothing on Earth today that is remotely comparable to them and their energies. They were our higher dimensional great, great, great, stellar grandparents and they loved those of us here on Earth very deeply.

Fig. 3.4. Ancient ET Lion Beings

The next small higher dimensional group that joined us was the equally ancient and impressive Bird beings. These grand beings also had humanoid bodies, but with stunning falcon bird heads. They were only slightly shorter than the Lion beings and were much more muscular, strong, and dense or solid feeling. They were grand and incredibly ancient beings as well, but their energies were extremely different from the Lion beings. The Bird beings were more focused, serious, and reserved than the affectionate and kindhearted Lion beings.

Their energies were equally intoxicating but in a very different way. They seized your attention in a different way from how the Lion beings did. The Lion beings felt like proud, protective elderly grandparents who deeply loved us. These particular ancient Bird beings were slightly less emotionally warm and charitable and felt considerably more mentally focused and highly alert to absolutely everything. They were not dangerous feeling at all, just resolute and focused in a very different way than the Lion beings. They gave the impression that they were on a very large and important mission and absolutely nothing would distract them from it, not even a group of excited young Star Seeds in ancient Egypt.

Fig. 3.5. Ancient ET Bird Beings

As I (Denise) clairvoyantly watched this past life cosmic family reunion in Egypt of 12,600 B.C., I smelled that blessed and much-loved scent that has been with me all of this life—the enthralling smell of birds and bird feathers. I just about come unglued when I smell that distinctive bird smell and I instantly want to bury my face in their feathers and breathe the beloved scent deep into my lungs. As I watched this past life scene play out like a clairvoyant movie, and I again saw these magnificent Bird beings, I easily knew why I had always loved the smell of birds and bird feathers in this current life. That scent reminded me of this particular ancient stellar group and some of its extremely magnificent bird headed kin.

The small Orion party was stunningly beautiful, human looking Starbeings with intense faces and eyes. Their height was around 6 foot and some had blue-black hair while others had silver-white hair. Some had deep sapphire-blue eyes and the others had light silver colored eyes, but they all had flawless milk-white skin. Many of them had a pale blue tint of color beneath this milk-white skin that simply made them even more beautiful and extraordinary looking. Both the males and females dressed in rich deep purples, indigos, royal blue, teal, and dark gold colors. It seemed they all preferred wearing pure dark colors, which was a stunning contrast next to their milk-white and pale blue undertone skin and intense otherworldly eyes.

This Orion group was very much like the one male Orion being in this Egyptian past life. I (Denise) knew there were other body forms or vehicles that the Orions could have use if they wished, but that day at the cosmic family reunion, they decided it would be best for us Starseeds to see them in this radiant humanoid form and not their lightbodies or something more vibrationally exotic and comfortable for them. They resembled a small assemblage of colorful and radiant Starbeing royalty that bordered on the angelic.

At one point during this clairvoyant past life vision, I (Denise) knew that all these (past life) other dimensional stellar beings saw and felt me here in this incarnation and timeline clairvoyantly viewing them and my male past life self in ancient Egypt. This is very typical from what I have repeatedly experienced throughout this life. We here in linear 3D physicality have a radically different perspective than these higher dimensional, nonphysical, Starbeings/ETs. To them, and increasingly to more of us, everything is happening simultaneously and they only need to focus in on different stations or points to perceive us in our different incarnations and timelines. This was very interesting for me (Denise) to perceive this ancient/current event from all of these different perspectives. I am certain each of these ancient Starbeings/ETs deliberately did this to help Denise in her life and timeline to experience this expanded view and past/current life memories.

This clairvoyant vision and multiple timeline meeting did however make me, Denise, very nauseous for a good while after it ended. It was a great conscious, multidimensional reach for me then and I maintained it for a good while too. Becoming dizzy and nauseous afterwards were simply some side effects of my having consciously held open larger chunks of my own multidimensional consciousness in 1996.

November 1996 I had another interesting higher dimensional journey that I truly enjoyed because it was in 6D again. Within a few minutes into this inner/outer interdimensional journeying, I remembered having been taught about sixth dimensional sacred geometry in my male ancient Egyptian past life from the Sirian Starbeing. As I have that thought about different geometrical shapes, I also mentally said to me, *"They are conscious living beings!"* That realization and memory was the trigger for all that instantly followed.

Immediately in front of me, I was clairvoyantly seeing amazing and beautifully perfect geometric 6D shapes. Each of them was living entities, but also living patterns or blueprints for numerous other objects in physicality. Here are a few illustrations of what I clairvoyantly saw on this particular 6D journey. There were more than what I have drawn here but unfortunately, I forgot many of them once my consciousness dropped back down to 3D again.

Each of these sixth dimensional geometrical shapes was living things. The round wheel shaped image was a higher dimensional ET being, but it was also an energetic blueprint for other objects and things in lower vibrating dimensions including the third dimension.

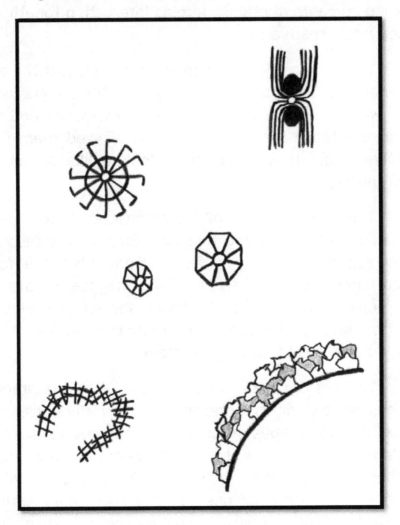

Fig. 3.6. 6D Blueprints or Morphogenetic Fields

The large black spider-shaped image seemed to be what certain energies look like when they first manifest at this level, and then when they are caught in other energy flows and pulled along to create additional things. It was not a spider at all, but energies and moving currents of other energies interacting together in a beautiful creative dance.

The two smaller octagon shapes were just the tops of enormous things I was seeing. I didn't know what they were, only that I liked the way they looked and felt. I had the sense that if I could have viewed them from another angle they would have looked like something else entirely.

The crooked band of interconnected hatch marks was like cells connecting to each other to manifest and grow something vastly different from what the four-sided hatch marks looked like. This image also gave me the sense that if I could have shifted my viewing position enough to see it from another angle, it too would have looked entirely different.

The bottom semi-circular image with the stacked shapes on top of it represented the *Nothingness* that those craggy shapes attached themselves to so they could develop, grow, and expand. Eventually those other shapes would develop up to the point where the whole thing would morph or gestate into something entirely different. These energy shapes were alive and developing into what would become very different looking objects.

I had another interesting lucid dream in November 1996. Over the decades, I have had numerous lucid dreams very much like this one, which just means I was functioning within another of my bodies (etheric) in another of the many different dimensions and layers within the dimensions. We all do this, but I have been able to remember more of these interdimensional journeys, meetings and teachings than most people have in the third dimension.

Because I can discern which level I am functioning on while in a dream, I know when I am actually with another living human, or a higher dimensional Starbeing/ET, a nonphysical being, a negative entity, and so on. This lucid dream was an etheric and *real* meeting with an ET that I have interacted with many times in the past but never saw face-to-face. He always stood just behind my right shoulder in these etheric dream meetings so I never saw him. I also never sensed any negative or devious motives or energies from him either.

In this particular lucid dream, I suddenly found myself in a massive underground structure beneath a large and well-known shopping Mall here in southern California. I was walking along this massive underground building with my unseen ET friend floating behind my right shoulder and telepathing back and forth with him about what is happening, where, and why. As he and I are walking through this enormous underground structure, I became aware of some human male soldiers in uniforms walking with some different ET beings in the opposite direction. Some of these human soldiers were in camouflage Army clothing and some other human men were in formal military uniforms. They were walking and talking with Gray ETs, some other large insectoid ET beings, very tall thin ones I had not seen before, plus some very attractive humanoid looking ETs. At this point, I seriously wanted to see the male ET being who is behind me! As soon as I have this thought, I telepathically hear and feel the ET behind me chuckle and emanate pleasure. You can't get away with much with the ET beings!

What was so strange to me seeing all this was how absolutely normal looking and feeling the whole scene appeared. This scene was no different than if we all had been aboveground, inside the shopping Mall, hunting for a pair of purple shoes or something. It was *business as usual* in other words and I found that rather interesting.

I thought to myself in this lucid dream, *"Is this physical 3D or are these underground structures in 4D, 5D, or what?"* The unseen ET behind me instantly replied, because there really is no private thinking to yourself in these type situations.

"Both. In some buildings, it is underground 3D. In other physical buildings, it is superimposed etherically over physicality from higher dimensional levels. You know—like at Wal Mart." At this, the unseen ET smiles and I know it and he knows I know it. As crazy as all that may sound, it is perfectly normal when interacting with nonphysical, other dimensional ETs.

The Wal Mart reference he made was due to some physical events Mom and I had experienced in an actual Wal Mart shopping store months earlier, which I will share later.

The unseen ET voice continued telepathically informing me that *"We"* build these higher dimensional etheric structures where 3D physical structures have been built. According to him, the reasoning for this was because it was much easier for them—groups of different positive ET beings—to ethereally build right on top of certain physical buildings, usually large shopping stores, grocery stores, and large Malls to energetically affect and occasionally interact with multitudes of people. He said it was a very fast and easy way to introduce the human masses to higher frequency energies with no drama or trauma and most of them never see, feel, or sense anything. In other words, in 1996 it was another way to introduce humanity to higher vibrating energies with no trauma or fear.

Those of you reading this who have had the recurring dreams over the years of being in some large shopping Mall, a Library, University, Collage campus, Auditorium, Theater, or Hospital and running into different ET beings there, I hope you are recognizing the interdimensional connections within all of this. Those of us who are Wanderers/ Starseeds/Lightworkers, typically have these types of etheric dream encounters and ET meetings most of our lives. In many cases these dreams are the easiest and fastest way the Wanderer—in a human body and physical incarnation—is reintroduced to why she/he is back in 3D Earth physicality now. If the Wanderer/ Starseed/Lightworker is more psychically open and can safely cope with conscious, interdimensional meetings and retain the memory of them, then that too happens with these types of lucid out-of-body dream meetings. These are both individual and group Lightworker/ Wanderer dreams or out-of-body gatherings we have with some of our ET helpers, guides, interdimensional family and friends.

(Another aspect of this that many of you may relate to as well is the etheric dream meetings Lightworkers/Wanderers/Starseeds have within other people's houses across the country. We do not physically know each other and yet, many of us have remained in higher-level contact with each other through these etheric dream meetings with other Lightworkers/ Wanderers/Starseeds and sometimes with ETs present as well. During the 1980s and 1990s especially, we needed to meet like this to exchange information and remain up-to-date with our unfolding Lightworker missions and planetary service work. It doesn't matter that we may never physically know or met each other; we have been in contact with numerous other Lightworkers living within the same country we do for decades. Stealth mode has been used by us for a long time to remain in contact etherically and exchange ascension related information with each other when needed.)

Years ago, I read about some people suddenly seeing strange beings or ETs appear and disappear in different shopping Malls in the USA. Earth has had so many Starbeings/ETs working from their nonphysical side of the Veil or border while numerous Wanderers/ Lightworkers/Starseeds worked from *inside* this physical dimension and lower system here. Occasionally people would see these nonphysical ET beings pop in and out of different physical locations because they were portal areas. In some dreams, many humans would also use these same interdimensional portals to step through into a higher dimension and visit their ET friends and guides briefly while asleep and out of their physical bodies.

Over the last few months of 1996, I became increasingly obsessive about being outside and working in Mom's yard every day. I suddenly wanted to remove all of the old evergreen plants she had planted years earlier, and replace them with flowering plants and vines. What? Why? What is this all about? It's not as if I have extra money or endless physical strength and energy—quite the opposite actually! Yet, this is how abruptly my phase of completely re-landscaping every inch of Mom's quarter acre began. Doing this difficult outside labor suddenly became my new intense focus for reasons unknown to me at that time.

I felt somewhat better after I had worked myself half-to-death outside in the sunlight, the air, dug in the soil, listened to and watched the many birds and hawks all around me. Many of these birds, including big beautiful red-tailed hawks, hummingbirds, mockingbirds and others I'm not familiar with, would fly right up to me and land only four or five feet away. It was magical having them come so close to me while I was digging, watering, planting, pruning or raking outside.

Bottom-line question was—is my mental and psychic focus being deliberately shifted now? Is it being unplugged and scrambled for some reason I am unaware of at this point? Am I now supposed to be outdoors for the majority of time each day, working hard physically out in the elements and sunlight? Am I supposed to be doing this now because I suddenly cannot mentally focus as I have effortlessly been able to my whole life? Why am I, for the first time in forty-six years, suddenly *off my higher contacts?* Why can't I effortlessly and immediately connect with my interdimensional ET friends and family and all the other higher dimensional beings as I've always been able to? What in the world has suddenly happened now and why?

In mid-November 1996, I had another lucid dream teaching from another dimension. I had been asking my Higher Self and guides to be more involved with me on a daily and nightly basis, and to help me have this be even more conscious. I repeatedly asked to be more consciously aware of what all I did while functioning in other dimensions. Evidently, it was working because it was becoming easier for me to retain more information from my interdimensional travels while awake and asleep.

In this particular lucid dream, I found myself hovering out in some starless black vastness. I could hear and feel unseen beings pointing out highly unusual looking shapes that would suddenly appear within this vast blackness in front of me. They would discuss these unique shapes with me as my consciousness hung there viewing each of them. As strange as it all seemed, this higher dimensional classroom felt deeply familiar and very comforting to me. I had done this many times before, but was only now starting to consciously remember these particular interdimensional refresher courses certain guides and assistants where giving me.

I saw something that looked, from my current perspective, to be enormous and was a long narrow square pipe sort of object with tiny grooves and patterns along only two of its sides. From my perspective, this object looked like it was almost as long as one could see. I have no idea what size it really was and any or all of them could have actually been microscopic in size.

The next cosmic image that appeared was a three-sided pyramid and for some reason this was highly important. This structure, plus numerous others that I had already been shown in this same manner, were geometric shapes of things inside our physical bodies plus other external objects. Many of these 6D morphic objects or patterns were the very structures inside our cells, our blood, our endocrine glands, our nerves, our brains, and our tissues.

The unseen being carefully highlighted the three points on this pyramid making up one face or plane of the triangle. Just these three points where amazingly important and meant something on their own. Each aspect, each section, each point, and each plane of the entire three-sided triangle meant something, but when combined it meant something else entirely. It was so beautiful, so complex, and so utterly perfect at each individual level that it almost made me melancholy. The sheer perfection and purity of these geometric shapes made me so happy and almost sad or lonely at the same time.

These unseen beings told me so much about so many different geometric shapes and other objects I had never seen before, but I was struggling a bit with the more technical side of the information. These unseen beings struggled a bit with why I could not understand some of this information. It was basic sixth dimensional information that I was already very familiar with. They were terribly confused over my having forgotten so much that was so basic. They were not angry at all, just highly confused over why the Denise aspect was having such trouble understanding what all these shapes and forms really were at other dimensional levels. Many higher dimensional beings have to deal with us Wanderers and Lightworkers reincarnated in 3D again, who then forget so much of what we already know at nonphysical levels of being. It is usually a lot of work for both parties to get the needed higher dimensional information to the Lightworker reincarnated back in slower, denser physicality, typically with varying degrees of amnesia.

The geometric shapes and forms continued for a while longer with me struggling while the unseen teachers were confused over my struggling. I heard one of these unseen beings comment about why I could not remember all of the shapes when I was intimately familiar with all of them and much more, *"In both physical and nonphysical craft."* I thought in response how frustrating this was for all concerned, and then suddenly woke up. I looked at my clock and saw I had only been asleep for about an hour.

Later in this same evening, I had another lucid dream around 4 AM. Again, I was far out in deep space looking down on the most stunningly beautiful, sparkling, glittering gemstone-like multicolored nuggets. There were multiple millions of them everywhere, glittering like perfectly faceted diamonds, emeralds, sapphires, rubies, citrines and so on. I hung there in space, staring in astonishment at how incomprehensibly beautiful every one of them was. A few moments later the unseen being asked me what I thought these glittering objects were. All I could respond with was, *"They are beautiful..."*

The unseen being replied, *"They are all of the souls incarnate on Earth now."*

December 1996 I had another lucid dream where I saw a single perfect geometric shape. Again, I was out in a place of blackness with nothing else in it that I could see or sense. Suddenly I saw a huge object come flying in from one side. From my perspective, it looked gigantic but I had nothing else to compare it to, so again, I do not really know what size it was or if that even mattered.

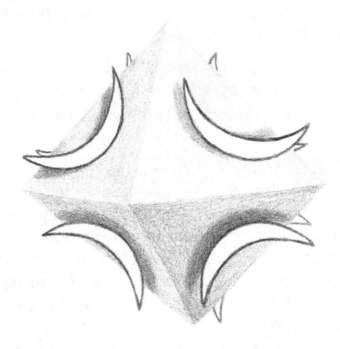

Fig. 3.7. Merkaba Craft and Being

It was two, four-sided pyramids or an octahedron. On each of its four faces—top and bottom—were sharp crescent moons facing outward like weird antenna. It certainly was not aerodynamically correct, yet the second I saw it, I knew it was sheer perfection. As I stared at it, I thought it was *the* most beautiful and perfect object I had ever seen in my life. I have no idea why it affected me so deeply but it did. I even said in the dream that I thought it was *"perfect".* I also knew from looking at it as it flew past me in the vast blackness, that it was a living, conscious, higher dimensional being. I also knew it was a type of ship, craft, or vehicle as well.

Only four days later I read—for the first time—that some nonphysical 6D Sirian ships or UFO vehicles are two, four-sided pyramids called *"Merkaba ships".*

■ Suddenly in January 1997, I am having one hell of a miserable time nearly all the time. I am abruptly falling apart physically and mentally and I don't know why. I had already been feeling sick and in pain for the past few years, but now my normally razor-sharp mental focus had melted into a puddle of unrecognizable and embarrassing mush. What was going on now? I have always been able to instantly, effortlessly mentally and psychically zero-in and focus on anything whenever I wanted. If I wanted or needed to step into an altered state of consciousness to access higher-level information, I could within a couple minutes. If I wanted to zone-out or space-out and become unfocused to better perceive other levels of reality, I could effortlessly do that at will also. This was normal for me and something I was intimately familiar with being a psychic sensitive my whole life. It was simply how my mind worked and I knew how my mental and psychic processes functioned like the back of my hand. They were well-honed muscles and I knew exactly how to get them to access other dimensions when I desired or needed to.

So, what in the world was happening now that I had just turned forty-six? Why was I suddenly not able to mentally focus on much of anything? I simply could not remain mentally focused for longer than a few seconds when other bizarre images of people, objects, energies and strange things I have never seen before would invade my mind's eye and completely flood my inner clairvoyant field of vision. These objects, these strange things I am suddenly seeing in my mind's eye are foreign to me. In addition, the worst of all this is that I have suddenly lost my lifelong ability to mentally and psychically focus on whatever I want, whenever I want, which was a fate seemingly worse than death to me at that point.

I was profoundly frustrated with whatever it was that had happened overnight to my highly developed abilities to mentally and psychically focus and be aware of things around me within about a half-mile in all directions. Every time I attempted my old tried-and-true methods of focusing and expanding my awareness to another level of perception, I ran into this crazy chaos and seeming static. Within my mind's eye, I saw these new foreign images and scenes that I could not recognize or interpret as anything. I suddenly could not remain mentally focused and clairvoyantly on-point no matter how hard I tried and it was deeply frustrating and confusing.

Am I supposed to just go with this insane, weird, and very new flow and not fight it at all? Why when it is so terrible, chaotic, and seemingly meaningless? Am I being blocked or rerouted for reasons I cannot discern yet? All I knew at this point was that I was miserable and extremely frustrated by it all.

January 22, 1997 was yet another of the new and seemingly endless abnormally horrible days. Suddenly and very rapidly, these *horrible days* were becoming normal for me. I felt sick and in constant physical pain at this point, had almost continuous mental blur and interference not to mention increasingly emotional sensitivities and sudden outbursts of crying. I was also usually dizzy and in pain and would have sudden mild to moderate nausea like morning sickness when you are pregnant. I would suddenly burst into tears over anything, even exceedingly stupid TV commercials! I was highly unimpressed and frustrated with all of it, whatever it was. To add to the overall unraveling and generally repulsive picture, I was also suddenly and uncontrollable gaining weight for the first time in my life (with the exception of when I was pregnant with my son). Oh dear god, anything but *weight gain!* Take the mind, take the highly developed mental and psychic focus and control, but do not let me gain weight please!

"Sorry, gotta happen. You'll understand much more about why later," replied the ever-present and always helpful voice inside my head.

It is not enough that my mind is suddenly gone, that I cannot think or focus or connect with the greatest-of-ease with higher dimensional ETs as I am so used to. Now I am going to get fat too? You have got to be freaking kidding me! Yet, I knew that the inner voice of mine was always right so I slowly learned to accept even this miserable body change along with all the others.

I was very glad to see the Sun disappear that day so I could try to rest and maybe even access a higher level of awareness again, and amazingly, it worked. However, I started to slowly realize that much of what was happening to me and making my body hurt so badly, was connected to the Sun and sunlight. More about that later because I did not fully understand what the Sun was doing in 1997, only that I could far too easily feel every little bit of it right inside my aching body and bones.

That night after the Sun had gone away for a blessed few hours, I was able to access a higher level of consciousness once again and some nonphysical ETs and Lightbeings were immediately present. It appeared they wanted to communicate with me as deeply as I wanted to connect with them again. The message they delivered was vast, multidimensional, and highly complex and I did my best to keep up with this particular information they gave me on January 22, 1997.

This particular journey began on what sounded to me to be a rather dark note. They telepathed, *"the large Dark Ones"* were currently in the process of returning and would be here soon. Really? Weight gain, mentally fried, constantly in pain, teeth falling apart, *plus* Big Bad Dudes with attitude from deep space too?

"Isn't this going to be fun?" I thought loudly. They did not appreciate my sarcasm and continued telepathing more information right over my modest crap-attitude.

"Humanity will be informed by the media that it is comet Hale Bopp but it is the ancient Dark Ones returning now," one of the higher dimensional beings telepathed.

"They are not really happy about this either and they know the Great Cycle is almost over. They are aware that it is simply time for them to change, grow, and evolve now also," the higher being finished telepathing.

Because this type of higher telepathy is not strictly a linear communication like it looks and sounds in those typed, quoted lines above, I receive much more information, knowing and visuals at the same time the sentences were telepathed. I simultaneously understood that those mysterious and frightening sounding "Dark Ones" were nothing more than ancient aspects of us that were powerful and rather nasty guys—from our current and restricted perspectives that is. The interesting part was that we needed to integrate all of them back into us now and they needed to integrate us. This was a two-way street and we all had plenty of upcoming inner polarity work to do according to this particular message.

These higher beings used the term *"Great Cycle"* to indicate the entire period from when the few decided to create all this and insert themselves into it eventually becoming the many, to the end of the Mayan calendar.

I was also informed that I should simply, *"Forget the world."* This meant to keep my eye and heart on my mission and simply ignore what the rest of the world is, and will continue to be going through. It is that or risk *falling* vibrationally back into the old lower frequency world repeatedly and then having to energetically climb my way back out again.

I also understood that the intensive yard work and landscaping I suddenly had a burning desire to do every day was another aspect of all this. I was at the point where Jade One was being fully integrated into Denise in my incarnation here now. Jade One was/is a male past life self of mine who ascended during his incarnation with Master Hotei, the Laughing Buddha. (See *The Temple of Master Hotei: A Unique Past Life Memory*.) I in this timeline was utilizing Jade One's expertise in landscaping and garden maintenance because Mom's entire property needed to be reworked with higher vibrating plants, trees, flowers and energies. Jade One was an expert in higher energy gardening and creating, so I tapped into and utilized his/my past life abilities for use within this life and timeline for similar reasons.

I also clairvoyantly saw a three-sided triangle fit nicely right inside my Third Eye (Brow Chakra). As I viewed it shining there perfectly, I realized I was only seeing one plane or face of a much larger and more complex Icosahedron within my Third Eye. It was a strikingly beautiful sight and I thought rather amazing that it was etherically inside my head.

There was much more I was told during this particular altered state but unfortunately, I was not able to retain all of the higher information and visions. A couple hours later while in bed and half asleep, I was jolted awake by the loud sounds of five fast metallic taps in the ceiling right above me. These five metallic sounding taps came in groups of five. This happened five times while I was laying there listening and counting the tapping sounds. A few hours later it happened again, waking me up a second time hearing a group of five fast metal-on-metal sounding taps in the side of the house near my head this time. There was nothing psychic or clairaudient about these sounds as they sounded fully physical.

What this told me was that even asleep, even if I don't always consciously remember my interactions with my group of higher dimensional Starbeings and teachers, they are always nearby talking, teaching, reminding me and helping keep me on track and on time here in 3D physicality.

February 1997 I entered a higher state of awareness and accessed more information that was rather interesting. This primarily had to do with all of the interior decorating I had been doing during the previous two years. I had started wallpapering and painting my bathroom first, then my bedroom, and it just kept spreading on out into every other room throughout the house. The only room I did not paint and wallpaper was the kitchen, but everything else got a much-needed upgrade. Despite all the hard work, it certainly made the house look and feel much lighter and improved physically and energetically. What I was to learn in this evenings higher dimensional journey, was that even my desire to redecorate the inside of Mom's house, plus paint the outside of it, was connected to everything that was going on interdimensionally. It was quite amazing really, as I had never thought my sudden desire to alter the colors and look inside Mom's house was connected to what the etheric ETs were building vibrationally around and above our house.

I remember Mom and me commenting one day about how we had chosen very specific geometric wallpaper for every room in the house. Each room was different wallpaper with different colors, but each wallpaper design was geometric patterns. Once we consciously realized this, things started to make more sense as to why I had been triggered to do this extensive amount of interior decorating in the form of wallpapering and painting in the first place.

This evening's interdimensional journey began with my clairvoyantly seeing our twelve zodiac signs superimposed over other larger constellations in space. These other constellations were larger cosmic archetypal energies than what Jupiter, Mars, Venus and so on are to us on Earth. Depending upon where one is physically or non-physically located and focused, there are archetypal energies that coincide with those different layers and levels up to a point. This particular night I was simply viewing a slightly larger group of these energies and archetypes than usual.

Next, I returned to my favorite lapis lazuli temple floating silently out in what appeared to be deep space within the eighth dimension. My three beloved ancient Starbeing family and friends from my ancient Egyptian past life were there waiting for me. The Orion, Sirian, and the Pleiadian wanted to inform me about my current intense interior decorating phase. What they had to say however let me know it was not strange at all. In fact, things were finally starting to make much more sense.

The three of them informed me that the geometric patterns on all the different wallpapers Mom and I had chosen were reflections of the higher dimensional, nonphysical work and building they were doing. So too were the garden lattice panels I had recently bought. These garden lattice panels are 4x8 foot wooden panels used for outdoor decorations, privacy dividers, or for garden vines and plants to attach to and grow upright. These lattice panels have open diamond shaped spaces in between the long crisscrossing wood or plastic strips.

I had added some of these wooden lattice panels to the carport (open garage) area for privacy and to block the relentless SoCal sunlight from baking the car much of the year. I could then plant flowering vines on the other side of the lattice panels to block even more sunlight from hitting the car. I had also added more of these 4x8 foot lattice panels to other areas around the front and backyard for flowering vines to attach to and create a solid wall of plants between us and the nasty west side neighbors and energies.

What I had not even noticed was that these diamond or octahedron shaped open spaces in the garden lattice panels were very much like some of the geometric patterns on the wallpapers we had chosen. There were diamond shapes, triangles, wavy lines, circles, squares and dots. Not a flowery or fruity wallpaper anywhere!

The Orion being informed me that the garden lattice panels I attached in the carport area now matched my entry point there at my lapis lazuli temple in 8D. I stared utterly dumbstruck at him trying desperately to grasp and visualize what he was telling me. The three of them cannot believe I have not already figured all this out or instantly understood what I had just been told. They cannot believe I have been doing all the hard physical work inside the house for the past two years—and now re-landscaping the entire outside property—and I still do not consciously understand how it is all a matching vibrational extension within physicality, of what is being constructed in the higher nonphysical realms! How can I be this smart and this dumb at the same time? Quite easily it appears.

The Pleiadian said, "*We were directing the colors and textures.*"

The Sirian said, "*We were directing the geometric wallpaper patterns inside, and now the outside lattice panels.*"

The Orion said, *"We were and are still directing you to build in specific locations, directions, and heights both inside and outside of your physical house."*

At this point all three of them are clairvoyantly showing and teaching me about how interdimensional energies work. They tried to help me grasp these concepts by showing my how water exists in one state as a liquid, and how it can exist as ice in another state, and vapor in yet another state and so on. I understood that symbolism easily and was then able to translate it into what else they were showing and teaching me.

I finally understood that many different higher dimensional Starbeings had been—from their side of the dimensional Veil—constructing different nonphysical moving structures energetically over specific physical locations and that they all were grid related. From my perspective, these nonphysical devices or structures were geometrical shapes that rotated and spun like multiple counter-rotating tops. I also understood that at their different dimensional levels, these geometric shapes and structures did specific things, but here in 3D physicality, they would look and do different things much like their example of water, ice, and vapor or steam.

My hard physical work redecorating the inside of Mom's portal house, and then outdoors re-landscaping the entire quarter acre, was energetically connected to what they were building. I realized that all of the physical work I had been doing to the house and yard was simply to increase its denser, slower frequencies to vibrationally catch-up with and match what they were building at higher dimensional levels. Our house and property had to be rewired and upgraded energetically on the physical plane to match and accommodate the higher frequency energies coming in through this new and vastly more complex grid point over Mom's property and the surrounding area.

My multidimensional ET friends and co-workers knew nearly everything about this mission, whereas I didn't completely but worked very hard nonetheless. I knew it was profoundly important and at that point, it didn't matter too terribly that I could not remember absolutely every detail about my personal interdimensional Lightworker mission. I knew I would eventually if needed.

This interdimensional construction project had been going on for a couple of years now and I was finally able to string my weird dreams, interdimensional journeys, and the ET contacts together to finally perceive a much larger portion of The Plan from a higher perspective. It was quite an impressive vision. An interdimensional and vastly higher vibrating geometric planetary grid system with one intersecting point right at and around Mom's property! Ah—I see now. They, we, are building a new and much higher and more geometrically complex energy-carrying planetary grid system. In addition, one of those numerous physical land areas where multiple etheric gridlines connect is right on top of Mom's physical property. That is why that land and area is so important. That is why Mom's property and the surrounding land are so highly polarized. That is why Mom and I live here and are anchoring in 3D what is being constructed at higher dimensional levels for humanity and Earth. This information certainly helped answer a couple dozen questions I'd had for years.

One evening in February 1997 close to 10 PM, it was raining heavily and unexpectedly the front doorbell rang. Mom and I just about jumped out of our skin because the entire property was fenced and each evening I locked the front driveway gate from the inside. The only way onto the property would have been to jump the six-foot fence or gate. Secondly, the front doorbell was one of those old types that only rang when you pressed it. It was an old manual doorbell, not one of the newer remote sensor types. Therefore, to have the front doorbell ring would have required an actual person to jump the fence, run up silently on to the wooden front porch, press the doorbell and then promptly disappear.

As soon as we heard the front doorbell ring, I quickly turned on the porch light and ripped the door open. There was no one standing there on the porch and

I didn't hear any footsteps or see anything. I immediately went outside to look for anyone anywhere on our property. There was no one there. I then went into *psychic sensing mode* to feel and perceive if there had indeed been someone physically inside our fence line. There were no human impressions, but there were ET energies up in the air above the house. So now, besides knocking on the exterior walls of the house, some of these ETs are also ringing the front doorbell to get our attention!

It was during the spring of 1997 that I began seeing something new and unusual in the sky during the day. They looked exactly like large transparent tubes coming down from very high in the sky and actually into the surface of the Earth. I could clearly see them, but being transparent, I could also see the normal landscape behind them. I used to sit on the back deck to smoke a cigarette and stare keenly at them. I only saw them during the daylight hours and they were usually only visible for a few minutes before they would disappear. I also saw them out in the large crop fields on both sides of the road as I drove to or from town. I only saw these transparent sky tubes of light in large open fields and never in any other location. After viewing them many times over a week or so, I finally shifted into psychically sensing and reading them energetically as opposed to simply viewing and intellectually analyzing them.

I had the immediate impression these large transparent tubes came from higher dimensions down to 3D Earth, and not up from Earth up into the sky or space. I had the strong sense they were interdimensional freeways for interdimensional energies. They felt like some type of vertical portal used as energetic freeways to get certain things from one vastly higher interdimensional point, down into 3D Earth physicality. I never physically or clairvoyantly saw any beings, ETs, or anything else inside any of these sky tubes however. They reminded me of those small transparent tubes you find at certain banks or drug stores that transport money or prescriptions inside a small plastic container that a vacuum then quickly pulls from point A to point B within the clear plastic tube system.

I also had the sense they represented the fact that new higher frequency energies were finally reaching Earth because enough lower dense energies had been sufficiently broken up and cleared at this point. They were like giant tubes or transparent hollow straws that allowed massive amounts of higher vibrating light energies to be transmitted and transported down into the third dimension, Earth, humanity, and all life here. To me they represented just how much planetary darkness, lower consciousness and lower frequency energies had already been broken up and transmuted by 1997. I loved seeing them manifest out in the open fields and countryside month after month and knowing that all the miserable, painful, sickening and often repulsive inner polarity resolution work I had been doing for so many years was actually showing positive results in the external, physical world around me. Seeing higher frequency anomalies like these massive transparent sky tubes made it a bit easier to continue living through all that I had been.

(In December 2004, I bought Barbara Hand Clow's book *Alchemy Of Nine Dimensions: Decoding the Vertical Axis, Crop Circles, and the Mayan Calendar* (2004). In it, she talked about how large tubes of light come down from high in the sky and then through them, the crop circles are transmitted energetically and imprinted into Earth, crop fields, and humanities consciousness. Until I read her book in 2004, I had never heard about this interdimensional sky tube transmission phenomenon. I absolutely believe her claims about them, because I have repeatedly seen these tubes of light in the field next-door to our portal house and in other local fields here in SoCal since early 1997. If you are familiar with how higher dimensional Light is down-stepped and transmitted, say from 8D down into 7D sound and light, then down into 6D geometrical shapes and patterns and so on, then these interdimensional sky tube delivery systems make perfect sense.

Fig. 3.8. Interdimensional Sky Tubes

I feel the reason why the sky tubes I saw numerous times during the late 1990s never produced any physical crop circles, was that enough people would not have seen them. I did sense they manifested next-door to our portal house and other nearby fields because a tremendous amount of higher dimensional light was being energetically drilled right into Earth, and of course humanity, in those physical locations. It was yet another higher dimensional activation tool helping humanity transmute and carry higher energies within our bodies and consciousness through the ongoing alchemical ascension and dimensional shifting process.)

March 21, 1997 I had a strange dream that I did not totally understand at the time. A few years later I did. In this dream, I was outside with many other people because we all sensed something strange was coming. We all were scanning the skies when it suddenly started raining and then hailing wildly. Within a couple seconds, there were mild earthquakes under our feet and we kept looking around and at each other wondering what was happening.

After the rain, hail, and earthquakes stopped, we all watched as these strange geometrical shaped objects started flying past us overhead. There were hundreds of thousands of them and they were alive, transparent geometrical shapes moving or flying in a massive geometrical pattern in the sky above us. Other flying shapes twisted, snapped, curled, and danced their way across the sky overhead along with the main larger objects. These particular shapes were not flying in formation as the geometrical shapes had been. The whole scene was actually quite beautiful yet also a bit frightening so I woke myself up at this point.

I understood this dream symbolism was indicating that physical reality itself was energetically changing, which of course also indicates that much of humanity is as well. Because I could more easily perceive higher 6D morphic shapes and patterns of certain things, I believe that was why I saw the energies in that particular geometric form. The rain, hail, and earthquakes suggested to me that more physical Earth changes would mean Earth was also going through major aches, pains, sicknesses and transformations just as I was. However, I would rather take rain, hail, and earthquakes any day over the mega-sized tsunami I had been clairvoyantly seeing for years. Some extra heat, Earth shaking and quaking was vastly better than the entire western states of the USA dropping off into the Pacific. Despite being a bit frightening, I knew this dream symbolism was really a very positive sign.

May 27, 1997 I finally got another insight into what is currently happening to me personally, and no doubt numerous other Lightworkers/Wanderers around the planet at this same time. This was actually a reconnection back to a dream I'd had twelve years earlier in 1985. It was evidently time for me to connect more of the invisible dots to get a better understanding about what was currently happening to me and many other Lightworkers globally.

In my original 1985 dream, a small group of people from around the world and me were waiting in front of the Great Pyramid in Egypt in current time. We did not consciously know or recognize each other as

"Lightworkers" as we all stood there waiting, but we all understood we were there to participate in something very rare and significant. Previously, we had each been invited to be at the foot of the Great Pyramid in Egypt on the eve of 1999, and so, there we all were waiting for whatever was going to happen.

The next scene in this 1985 dream was of some local Egyptian men in their native, long white galabeya's suddenly appearing from around a corner of the Great Pyramid. They carefully and slowly maneuvered multiple huge metal scaffoldings out into an area in front of the Great Pyramid for all of us to view. We took a couple steps back and watched them push a group of these giant elevated scaffoldings into place in front of the Great Pyramid.

On top of each of these scaffoldings were what looked to us to be massive statues of all the ancient Egyptian, Greek, and Roman gods and goddesses. They were all lying immobilized on their sides like frozen gray giants as the local Egyptian men respectfully wheeled them out before us and then quickly disappeared once again.

We stood watching, waiting, wondering what in the world was going on. After a few minutes, there was a loud cracking sound overhead and lightening dramatically flashed perfectly across the sky as if on cue. Next, we could see that very slowly and carefully all the giant statues of the ancient gods and goddesses were waking up, moving, and coming to life way up on top of their scaffolds. (Sounds like a strange take-off of the old Frankenstein movie doesn't it?) We on the ground all squealed with excitement at the rare and unique event we were personally witnessing. Slowly, every one of these ancient archetypes came to life and stepped down off their scaffold to walk the Earth once again.

This May 1997 meditational insight was entirely about my older 1985 dream. In it, I finally and fully understood that we physical human Lightworkers watching those ancient gods and goddess come to life and crawl down from their lofty scaffolds, were symbolic of what was happening to us. We were witnessing other ancient aspects of ourselves waking up and coming to life once again so that the great gap between them and these current aspects of us in human form today would be no more. It was a grand symbolic integration process and was directly connected to the ending of 1999 and transitioning into the twenty-first-century. More of my old questions were answered this day, but with further mysteries to unravel as well. After this May 1997 insight, I seriously wondered about what would energetically be arriving with the year 1999 to activate this incredible level of individual integration.

On June 26, 1997 at 4 AM, Mom suddenly woke up for some unknown reason. She can see from her bedroom that there is a light on in the living or dining room, so she got up and went out to see if anything might be going on. Once she got out there she discovered it was the dining room ceiling light over the table that was on. She turned it off and went right back to bed.

Every night before I would get into bed, my ritual was to go through the house and make sure I had locked the front and back doors and that all the lights in the house were turned off. This was, and still is, my nightly ritual. I know without any doubt that all the lights were off when I went to bed after Mom had. If any light had accidently been left on, I would have easily seen it as soon as I had turned my bedroom lights out.

This light turning on anomaly was something I had experienced a few times when I was in elementary school, junior high, and high school. I would wake up in the middle of the night because a light was on in my bedroom—one that no one in the family had turned on. I would be scared stupid because of it of course, but I would get up nonetheless and go to the bathroom and on my way back to bed, I could easily see if Mom, Dad, or my little sister were up. They never were when my bedroom light would be turned on in the middle of the night. I always had nonphysical, other dimensional ETs, guides and helpers around me since age three, so this was just one more anomaly to learn to not totally freak-out over in the middle of the night.

The next day when Mom and I were up, she told me about the dining room light being on around 4 AM. I thought it was interesting only because I had slept abnormally well the night before and could not remember anything. No dreams, no waking up multiple times because I needed to go to the bathroom, no tossing and turning, no nothing. It was superb! I slept and did not wake up repeatedly all night as I usually did. To me this typically indicated that I was etherically gone most of the night and probably with my ET co-workers, friends and family.

The rest of June 1997 automatically focused on old family frustrations, wounds, angers, and total misunderstandings between Mom and me. We had mountains of old issues, emotions, wounds, and anger to work through and we both had avoided it for as long as possible. Nevertheless, to continue growing, evolving, and doing all that we were individually and as a twosome, we simply had to work through our past unpleasant emotional issues. It would not be pretty, and it would not magically happen overnight and instantly solve this entire life, plus our past life emotional issues, but it absolutely had to begin now. There was no more time left for avoidance of anything.

As is usually the case in situations like this, because all parties have avoided honestly and directly confronting long-buried wounds and frustrations for so long, no one is practiced in the fine art of honestly dealing with their crap and old emotional issues. Certainly not with the person in the same room with them that is. Therefore, when something finally emotionally boils over, there is usually a lot of ancient and highly misplaced backpressure that erupts all over the place, is ugly, messy, intense, and typically out of place. However, this is usually how we have to dive into our emotional family septic tank and try to clean the dank, stinky place up. June 1997 was the big start of this process for Mom and I and it would take repeated tries before we each excavated all that we needed to. It is a process—an ongoing process that usually requires repeated excavations to reach all the numerous layers of toxic stuck emotional crap and deal with it honestly, then release it, and move on. Mom and I would go through this long and often-difficult process repeatedly over the months and years before we both got to where we each needed to be energetically. We both desperately needed to transmute and release certain current life, and past life issues so we could continue working together and evolving individually in our lives now.

July 11, 1997 I was driving home and noticed that the sunlight and everything else looked very different. It looked extra brilliant and sharp and there was a silver-white colored light everywhere. It was so physically obvious and blatantly there for all to see, I wondered why I had not heard anyone else mention that the light the Sun radiated had changed so drastically.

As I drove I kept glancing up at the open sky, the trees, the leaves on the trees, the freshly plowed fields, and could so clearly see that a profoundly brilliant silver-white light was literally everywhere. It was stunningly beautiful and instantly reminded me of my past life in ancient Egypt 12,600 years earlier because that particular past life had the same brilliant silver-white light everywhere. I had remembered this silver-white light when I was a young child in this life and wondered why the Sun and sunlight was only a soft warm golden-yellow color. Even as a child in this life, I sensed that the Sun and sunlight was only warm and nurturing, gentle and loving solar energy. My ancient Egyptian past life memory was of a much higher stellar silver-white light that was extremely bright and intense, yet did not harm one's eyes or skin. As a child in this life, I always wondered about why the Sunlight was not this stellar silver-white light I remembered from my ancient life in Egypt. The seasons and gravity—not to mention human cruelty—were also huge confusions to me as a child in this life however.

As I drove home viewing this brilliant and very different sunlight illuminating everything, I remembered this particular silver-white light was how everything looked and felt when the Sun and Earth were within the Photon band of higher dimensional light at the beginning of the astrological Age of Leo. I suddenly became ecstatic. Here we were again, 12,500-plus long and very dark and difficult years later, exactly halfway around the great wheel of Ages entering the Photon band of higher light again at the beginning of the Age of Aquarius. All I could think was, *"It's about time! Now the much higher changes to humanity and Earth will happen extremely fast."*

Later in the evening, I watched some ridiculous and typically incorrect program on TV about *Ancient Pharaohs* and realized this was another one of those higher dimensional *"synchronicities"*. A time-coded event perfectly designed and directed by my Higher Self to get me aligned with multiple incoming realizations. I watched the TV show, cursing under my breath the whole time about how outrageously incorrect the majority of these type programs really are. At the same time however, I was expanding my awareness at another level because I could feel higher information and unseen energies lining up like a long string of jumbo jets waiting for takeoff.

By 9 PM, everything was finally ready to get airborne. At this point, I suddenly realized that I had been leaning to my right while seated in my chair, telepathically talking with an ancient Egyptian man I knew in my past life in Egypt of 12,600 B.C. I was watching TV, but at the same time leaning to my right having a telepathic conversation with this very familiar ancient man from my past life! As I became fully conscious of the fact that this telepathic conversation had been going for the past half-hour or so, I remembered that this ancient past life man had been trying to communicate with me for the past two months. Suddenly realizing this, I instantly muted the TV, closed my eyes and settled back to get much more directly involved with whatever needed to come through to me right then.

I asked him who he is. The answer came flooding in as if it had been held back behind some invisible barrier for eons of time. He was/is my personal Guide, my personal nonphysical assistant. It had been imperative that I never clairvoyantly saw him before but all that needed to change right now.

Evidently, if I had seen him before face-to-face, eye-to-eye, it would have changed how I felt about him and made it exceedingly more difficult for he and I to even communicate with each other. He has been, forever, my *Shadow Guide.* He has been nearby but hidden in the shadows during my incarnation in ancient

Egypt and so many others as well, including this one. He watched me intentionally and consciously exit my male life in Egypt and travel out those unseen interdimensional tubes (airshafts) out of the Great Pyramid and back to Sirius, then Orion, and then through the massive Orion portal.

In this current life, he was the frightening, faceless male who nightly stood behind my bedroom curtains waiting for Mom and Dad to tuck me into bed. He would wait patiently for me to exit my physical body so I could then astral travel with him. It was he who wore the heavy brown hooded Monk's robe with no face beneath its hood, who taught me how to direct my astral body and go wherever I wanted or needed at night. He had been with me in this particular Monk's robe form from early childhood until my late twenties.

He proceeded to clairvoyantly show me the zodiac wheel with brightly illuminated points around it within the different astrological Ages where I had physically incarnated on Earth throughout the past Great Year (26,000-yearlong cycle). Once I had viewed each of the points of light that were my multiple and simultaneous incarnations on physical Earth, he pointed out the great circle again. Instantly, beautiful different colored lines of light appeared that connected every one of the illuminated points or incarnations around the zodiac of Ages. These colored lines of light connected with every single incarnation across physical linear time on Earth creating different geometric light patterns exactly like *aspect lines* in a person's astrological natal chart. It was the same exact concept as natal astrology, but at a higher and much larger and more complex soul level. He was showing me something that could be called a *Soul Chart* as opposed to a single incarnation's astrological *Natal Chart*. It was beautiful beyond words, and I was very proud of and comfortable with my unique Soul Chart in much the same way that I have been fond of my current life's astrological natal chart.

My Soul Chart, with its multiple angled lines of different colored light connecting every incarnation I have had during this great cycle, represented ME (not Denise) at a higher level. It was not representative of my entire selves because it only represented my *physical incarnations on Earth within the past Great Year*. I, or rather my soul, had other charts like this that dealt strictly with other lives or incarnations if you will, within *nonphysical* dimensions and realities as well. One could then view both of their physical and nonphysical Soul Charts and more lines of light would connect between them which revealed further interdimensional connections between the many different aspects of one's current life self, multiple 3D past life selves, and interdimensional nonphysical selves. It was a grand, expanded sight and realization, and despite it sounding multidimensionally complex or confusing, it was so perfect and made complete sense to me the moment I saw my overlaid, transparent and multiple Soul Charts.

The next thing my Shadow Guide discussed with me was how important it was for me to be consciously aware of the numerous energetic connections between my male past life in Egypt with the three ETs at the beginning of the Age of Leo, and this female life now at the beginning of the Age of Aquarius. There is a tremendous energy bridge between these two astrological Ages and all of our past/current incarnations within them. The reason he was emphasizing these two astrological Ages and my incarnations within them both, was that I and many other Lightworkers are and will continue to be transmuting tremendous amounts of lower energies/issues within ourselves, the planetary collective, and within the Earth from the beginning of the Age of Leo through to our current lives and time. That is half of the Great Year or about 12,500 years. All previous lower vibrating energies within all aspects of myself, and also within the planetary collective in the form of fears, traumas, hates, murders, wars, rapes, tortures, violence, disempowerments, slavery and so on, needed to be transmuted by myself and the other Lightworkers first. Many First Wave Lightworkers would be doing this difficult, unpleasant, dark planetary and collective energetic mop-up process before the next phase could obviously begin.

I instantly understood that it was us First Wave Lightworkers doing the planetary collective astral or fourth dimensional (4D) transmutation mop-up that would create a higher roadway out of the lower polarized physical dimension, consciousness, and energies. My Shadow Guide also informed me that he is the one who was often with me in certain lucid dreams but has always remained unseen and often behind my right shoulder. Yet tonight, he has made himself far more know to me than ever before, so this must be a good sign of my ongoing polarity resolution work and integration process.

The thing about this particular experience that was the most interesting to me was that it was not a meditation. It was not my normal expanded state where I go through a few steps to focus and reach an altered state to access higher vibrational information either. This situation was so easy, so natural, and so effortlessly right there beside me. There were no alterations, energy steps or layers to climb to reach this expanded state as it was just right there beside me, and in me, and I truly enjoyed it. It felt so much more natural to me than what I had always experienced as a psychic prior. There was finally so much less vibrational distance for me to negotiate to access higher knowledge and higher energies. What a joy and how wonderfully familiar it all felt.

July 1997 and I am outside doing yard work when slowly and relentlessly some of my past-perceived negative actions kept bubbling up from my dank, dark, basement gut. I kept trying to ignore them but they were not having any of it today. Nope, they were coming up and out because it was time and they absolutely had to. They could no longer remain suppressed and ignored down in my deep guts anymore and they were literally being squeezed and pressured up and out now no matter what I tried doing to ignore this slow-motion birthing process.

I continued to try overriding this important and normal healing process that particular day for some stupid reason and kept trying to draw my thoughts away from these past guilt-ridden sexual actions. I may be making this sound as if I did something truly horrible but I didn't. It was some of my past emotional sexual energies all tied up in sticky, ugly guilt, and long packed away in a dark corner of my inner basement. Nevertheless, housing this level of stuff any longer was not an option with all of the higher frequency light energies and inner transformational work I had been doing. These past emotions and energies were birthing their way up and out despite my ridiculous efforts to ignore them for a bit longer.

It was like giving birth—this thing is simply coming out now so just stop fighting the process, take advantage of the contractions and push it out! Over a half-hour of my trying to override this positive purging process, it simple overpowered me and thankfully came out anyway. Because I had kept this particular sexual guilt suppressed for so long, I started to have the dry-heaves outdoors while I was doing yard work! I instantly became sweaty and suddenly my back was hurting so badly I thought I was going to pass out. I literally regurgitated some previous sexual guilt emotions that day while outside working in the yard.

I quickly headed indoors to lie down just in case I did pass out. I was crying, retching, sweating, and shaking as more layers of my past sexual guilt energy came loose and were purged up and out of my dark inner basement chakras. It was perfectly, repulsively, and horrifically wonderful actually. I knew without any doubt that this—and everything else like it—must be transmuted now. None of it and I can co-exist as we have for so many years. Lower and higher frequency energies cannot exist comfortably or for very long within the same space, so all of my lower vibrating emotional energies in the form of fears, guilt, anger, wounds, hate, and projections simply must be purged, transmuted, and fully released. This is the ongoing and multiple layered energetic purging and transmuting process. It is literally living the alchemical process right inside my (and your) physical body and different energy bodies. It usually is not an attractive process and causes plenty of physical and emotional pains, especially if you are trying to prevent some aspect of it, but it is so very worth it to be completely free.

Next, I went through another series of unpleasant dreams that all dealt with my past relationships with both the ex-husband and most of the boyfriend relationships I'd had after my divorce. It rarely is enough to go through these inner energy exorcisms just once because we have multiple layers of them within our different energy bodies to work through, and that takes time, years in fact. At least I certainly did with a few of my past guilt-ridden sexual relationships. All my lower chakras—what I have referred to as my Basement—must have been one big sticky, dank mess that required repeated cleansings on both the physical and astral levels. In addition, I learned that it was not because of any actual deeds or actions I had done physically, but much more about the emotional energies in the form of fear, guilt, and anger primarily, that I had covered those physical actions in.

I had multiple clusters of these types of unpleasant dreams for a couple months where I had to repeatedly do further inner clearing work with old sexual relationship wounds, anger, disappointments, projections and everything else. In other words, a lot more inner purging work while both awake and asleep were required before I was completely free of these old lower issues and stuck emotional energies. As usual, it was very intense and laborious but an absolutely necessary and unavoidable inner house cleaning. If we want to honestly be free, we simply must do this type of intimate inner personal transformational energy work, and typically repeatedly and on multiple levels. Hang tough and just dive in because real freedom and empowerment are the results of your labors.

August 1997 I had a nightmare about an old boyfriend who, in this dream, was not really that boyfriend but an entity using his image as a vehicle to trick and manipulate me. Because I have always been able to wake myself up when the going gets excessively dangerous or scary out there in Astral Land, I did just that and woke myself up. Once awake I did what I always do which is to glance at the clock to see what time it is. It was 3 AM.

I lay there a couple minutes thinking about the nightmare and how something nonhuman and unpleasant had used the image of a loved one to manipulate me. This certainly was not the first time I had experienced this particular low astral tactic and phenomena. I had become very good at being able to energetically sense if someone (human or nonhuman) within the astral was not who they appeared to me to be. This nightmare was another of these cases. It was an entity using the image of a person I knew to cause specific emotions in me—primarily fear and anger. Because I recognized all this, I knew I should not let myself fall back to sleep right away. In many cases the negative astral scenario simply picks up again and continues if you do fall back to sleep. You have to create a meticulous energetic break between you and the astral entity/entities, and in some cases that means you do not go back to sleep for at least a half-hour or longer. That is what I was going to do; lay there and not fall back to sleep until it was 3:30 or 3:45 AM.

I rolled over on my side and suddenly felt the top mattress push up under my hips from below my bed. This was not a psychic impression but a very physical and physically real moving of my mattress under my rump and hips. The top mattress did this physical push up move, then drop back down to normal move, then push back up move again a few times as I lay there on my side trying to not fall back to sleep. At the same time this happened I heard Mom moving around in her bedroom and was actually glad she was awake. I wanted to get up, turn my bedroom light on, and thoroughly break this negative astral connection.

I not only heard Mom moving, but also heard sounds like objects on her dresser and chest-of-drawers being shuffled around too. The sounds were all very clear and easy to hear physically. Because I believed she was awake, I got up too and turned my light and TV on, went to the bathroom and then headed for her bedroom to see why she was up at 3 AM. As I got to her bedroom door, I could clearly see her lights were off and hear that she was sound asleep. So then—what had made those noises in her room? I suspected it was the same astral entity from my nightmare and who had physically pushed my mattress up underneath me repeatedly. The dimensional Veil is not only exceedingly thin now in 1997, it is completely nonexistent in many places.

This was another negative aspect of being a Lightworker, a Seer, and an interdimensional traveler and it was something I have had to deal with throughout my entire life. As much as I hated it, it was another lifelong aspect of my being a sensitive and clairvoyant Lightworker within a lower frequency polarized world and dimension and it would continue until I literally evolved beyond it. Because I knew I would have a difficult few hours, which is a polite way of saying I would experience some level of psychic attack if I fell back to sleep without doing anything to energetically protect myself, I called in some positive higher energies to help protect me the rest of that night.

Along with all the other layers and levels of repeated inner clearing and energy transmuting work, a couple of important past life memories suddenly arrived too. They needed to be remembered so I could transmute any residual issues they caused that were affecting me in this current life, body, and personality. The evening of August 10, 1997, I had just crawled into bed when an ancient past life dying memory abruptly exploded in my conscious mind. I had no sense that this memory had been laying-in-wait for me that night, but it certainly highlighted physical problems I have had all my adult life in this incarnation. In that regard, this was a highly positive past life death memory for me.

Lying in my bed I was clairvoyantly seeing and physically and emotionally feeling this one scene from an ancient past life on Earth. I was a tall, thin, refined and elegant male dressed in colorful clothes in this past life, and in this one and only scene, it was close to noon because the bright sun was directly overhead. It looked and felt like mid-spring and was very beautiful with abundant lush plant life growing everywhere. I was alone walking along in some vast pristine wilderness in an open meadow with low hills wrapping around perfectly in the distance. It was a stunningly beautiful place and what I was doing out there all alone I did not remember completely. That aspect of this past life was not what was important—how I died in it was.

As I am walking through this pristine meadow by myself, I suddenly heard and saw some horrid scruffy, dirty, stinking, knuckle-dragging type human male rushing out of nowhere from slightly behind me on my left side. Without making much noise, he rushed up from behind and hit me in the left side of my head with a heavy tree limb. I went down on the spot and never got up. He was so terrified of me that he just ran up, bludgeoned me, and immediately ran away. I don't know if he even understood that he had killed me.

This particular past life memory consisted of remembering this one important scene of being bludgeoned and dying shortly thereafter from those wounds. As I lay on the ground broken and dying, I knew with that one blow that he had broken my jaw and many teeth, fractured my skull above my left ear, that my left eardrum was ruptured, and that my neck was broken and that I was paralyzed from the neck down.

In that split-second, the impact and trauma of those fatal past life injuries affected me to such a degree that I still carry the etheric imprint of some of them in this current life's body. These past life physical wounds and emotional trauma were what needed to be consciously remembered, integrated, transmuted, and then fully released within me in this life and time. These devastating physical head and neck injuries—not to mention a general level of overall distrust of the locals— all had to go finally within this current me.

What was interesting to me is that in this current life I was born with mild scoliosis and have had TMJ (jaw joint) my entire adult life. The misaligned vertebra and pinched nerves in my neck have been a source of constant pain and have caused other bodily problems as most spinal issues do. I hoped that this was going to be my big release thanks to remembering this particular past life's injuries and death. I certainly was able to better understand many of my current body problems and release this past damage and trauma. The rest of that past life did not matter at that time—only that I finally emotionally dealt with those past life injuries. My death in that past life was not the issue, but those lingering physical body wounds certainly were.

Sometime in August 1997, I had a very interesting and fully conscious interdimensional ET meeting. I had just gone to bed, turned the lights out, and was still very much wide-awake. Because it usually takes me some time to relax and slow down physically and mentally, I typically lay in bed in the dark for a good hour or so before I actually fall asleep.

As I lay there in the dark doing exactly this, an immense and ancient nonphysical ET being decided it was time to reveal himself to me clairvoyantly. Unexpectedly I had an extreme close-up clairvoyant image of an ancient Reptilian being staring at me through an invisible, interdimensional window about five inches away from my physical face. Even though he was intentionally revealing himself and his race to me by doing this, he kept this first conscious meeting at close-up eye level only. He was deliberately revealing only his right eye and right side of his face to me during our first initial encounter.

As I stared at this amazing and highly impressive clairvoyant image, I did what I always do in situations such as this; I psychically scanned him to get a sense and feel about this being and what was happening and why. The only problem was that he had intentionally shielded himself from my doing this. He had a type of psychic shield or barricade in place that prevented me from doing what I usually can do quickly and easily. As soon as I discovered that he had blocked me from reading or sensing him in this way, I telepathically told him that it did not matter because I could still sense other things about him nonetheless. Rather brazen for my first Reptilian face-to-face! He telepathically said nothing in response to my bold statement but continued to hold this interdimensional viewing window open for me to see this small section of his face in extreme close-up.

Despite his only revealing this small section of his face and one eye to me, and despite his blocking me from psychically scanning him for information, I still was able to perceive a few interesting tidbits from this first Reptilian meeting. One of those things was that I knew instantly he was a *he*—a male being. I also sensed that he was very, very, ancient like the Lion and Bird beings I knew in 12,600 B.C. Egypt who were profoundly ancient even back then. I also knew he existed within another dimension and was not physical.

I easily sensed he had intentionally created this meeting between us because he wanted me to know that he and his race of ancient Reptilian beings were indeed real. He also wanted me to understand that, as is the case with certain other ET races, there were *good guy* Reptilians, and there were *bad guy* Reptilians. (You know—exactly as we have within the third dimensional human race with good guy and bad guy humans.) Without telepathically saying anything to me, he easily let me know that he was one of the positive Reptilians. He most likely would not have revealed himself to me if he were one of the negatively charged or negatively focused Reptilian beings. Most all negative beings prefer to remain unknown and invisible to those of us in 3D that they are using and affecting in some way. Positively charged or positively focused nonphysical beings are not like this at all and they know exactly when it is time to connect with us in physicality.

About two weeks after this first Reptilian meeting I was watching the world news on TV and clairvoyantly saw a few of the *bad guys* or negatively focused Reptilian beings superimposed ethereally over certain American and foreign politicians and world leaders. This time I saw those Reptilian beings full-sized and could somewhat judge their size, shape, and height because they were transparently superimposed over those human males. Assuming that the average height of those human politicians and world leaders was around six-foot, then these Reptilian beings I was clairvoyantly seeing were approximately eight or nine feet tall.

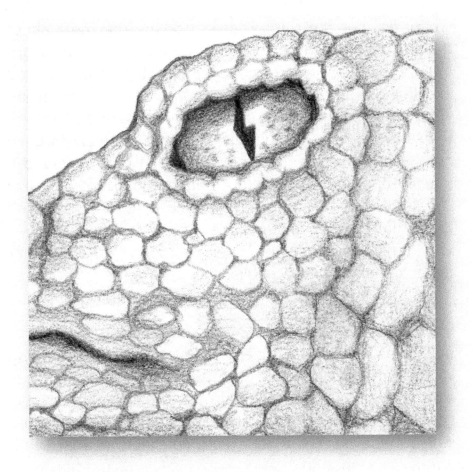

Fig. 3.9. A Reptilian Encounter

The other thing I found interesting about these Reptilian beings was how extraordinarily strong and muscular they were considering they were not physical. They reminded me of human heavyweight professional body builders in that they were thick, dense, massive, and heavily muscled from their necks down to their feet much as they are. They were impressive bipedal creatures, but the thing that struck me the most about them was their incredible intelligence and razor-sharp mental focus. They are amazingly intelligent beings and exceedingly quick and keen mentally. Many of them are very light to nonexistent on the feeling and Heart side of things however, which is typical with negatively focused nonphysical beings, entities, and ETs. But, if you can imagine an eight or nine-foot tall bipedal lizard built like the largest sized human body builder, but with a mind that would leave you and me dazed in the dust, then you have a sense of what some of these other dimensional, ancient Reptilian beings are like.

After seeing a few of these negatively focused Reptilians superimposed over some of those human politicians, I realized that my first eye-to-eye meeting weeks earlier was indeed with a positive Reptilian. I was slowly discovering a few more of the interdimensional cosmic players—both positive and negatively charged—which made perfect sense to me considering what I was going through and how I was evolving consciously. I knew because of the first positive Reptilian meeting that it was merely time for me to become more consciously aware of additional ancient interdimensional players, creators, ETs, stellar kinfolk, and that includes some of the plain old scary looking and feeling types too. It also includes our having to know more about how vast and amazingly creative this Plan has been, and occasionally meet some of the big scary looking and feeling nonphysical beings that have existed all along. It is simply time for us awakening humans to consciously remember and know much more about what we are involved in—past and present. No fear or guilt, disempowerment or judgments, only consciously knowing more about what has always been anyway.

August 20, 1997 after settling into bed, I intended a physical body healing for myself. Because of all the ongoing inner energy work I had been doing, I was still very ill and in constant pain the majority of the time. This particular night I intended to create a healing for myself to help with my nearly constant physical sicknesses and body pains.

This is one of those moments we hear about when we should, "*be careful of what you ask for.*" I received a healing all right, but I had to go way down into The Pit as I call it to receive it. Does it matter that I had to once again dive into the dark, dank, Underworld to confront some very ancient, monstrous aspect of myself? Not at all. Doing so is another aspect of *The Process* and I am getting damned good at it at this point!

Almost immediately after intending a healing for my physical body, I clairvoyantly see that my physical bed I was laying in has suddenly also become a 24-karat gold sarcophagus inside the Kings Chamber in the Great Pyramid. I absorbed the energies emanating from the 24-karat gold-lined sarcophagus in the Kings Chamber in that ancient timeline, but also in my actual physical bed in this timeline as well. As I am doing this, I clairvoyantly see the beautiful lotus flower drawings that were so common in ancient Egypt, and suddenly recognized that they look very much like the Pleiadian star glyph simply turned upside-down. I also see the head of Horus superimposed over my face and they feel unified energetically.

All of a sudden, there is a seven-foot tall, solid black male energy standing right next to the sarcophagus/my bed and he rumbled darkly and with great revulsion, *"Your nakedness disgusts me. You will not succeed."*

His unexpected appearance and negative comment really startled me for a couple seconds. Then I, in my bed, and the other female past life me in the sarcophagus within the Kings Chamber in the Great Pyramid, remembers and realizes that this is part of an Initiation she/me/we are living/reliving. She and I simultaneously and very intently yell at him, *"I will succeed, I already have succeeded, and I will always succeed!"*

Having proclaimed that, she and I both wrapped our arms around the giant fearsome black male stranger. I (Denise) suddenly remembered that the Pleiadian gave me a large gold key to keep in my heart years earlier, so I honestly loved this big intimidating, threatening, black monster male image and directly sent as much love into him as I was capable. He instantly evaporated into the dark shadows of my bedroom/the Kings Chamber, and she and I instantly both understood we each just passed this particular Initiation.

My physical body and spine abruptly filled with so much inner heat so quickly I could not believe it. I laid there in my bed with grateful tears rolling down my face as this inner fire and my wide opened Heart felt as if I might not physically survive that amount of higher energy pouring through it. However, that is a typical ego-based thought and fear over these types of higher energies and transformations. The burst of inner fire and higher Heart energy was the healing I had intended for myself minutes earlier. Energy that has been blocked or cut-off for long periods always feels to the ego self as if it will destroy you/it when it comes flooding back in once again. That too is another aspect of the alchemical transformation process. Fear not and just let the energies do the transformational work on your ego self and consciousness.

The next morning I told Mom about my vision and follow-up Initiation experience. She informed me that she too had a dream experience last night where she was provided with a test and needed to make important decisions. It seemed both Mom and I had individual Initiations across space-time the night before.

(I had a second past life in ancient Egypt as a female approximately 3,500 years *after* my first male life in Egypt 12,600 B.C. with the three ETs. The above initiatory memory was one of hers/mine from within both of our individual but simultaneous timelines. Always remember that just because we call them *"past lives"* does not mean they exist in the distant linear past. Our past lives and selves exist simultaneously and we can connect with any or all of them and they with us at any point.)

October 13, 1997 I had a lucid dream experience that introduced me to what *holographic* meant. In this lucid dream teaching I saw, knew, and completely understood that separation is indeed an illusion—a very important and deliberate illusion however. I had read about Earth life being an illusion years earlier and intellectualized over the concept as we all do. However, this night I *experienced it*, remembered it as an unfolding process, and saw it symbolically. This type of direct higher experience is drastically different from a strictly ego-based, left brained intellectual opinion. The two things are drastically different and must be personally experienced to know how true it really is.

I saw and remembered that we can access and manifest anything and everything for the simple reason that we literally are an aspect of, and connected to, everything. I saw a huge piece of glass or mirror floating out in deep space and it symbolized *Source* or *the All That Is.* Next, this huge mirror broke into trillions of tiny pieces that flew out in all directions within the vast blackness. These tiny pieces of broken mirror represented each of our Higher Selves. This one image explained the complex concept of holographics to me in a very easy and simplistic way. We are indeed all One, but even more importantly, we are also unique individuated aspects experiencing within our own individual journeys, and that is why the mirror chose to fractured Itself in the first place.

This important complex concept and symbolism was so childlike in its simplicity that it was almost amusing. However, this is often how higher complex and multidimensional spiritual concepts have been revealed to me—in almost childish cartoon form. The experiences and interactions within illusion and separation are equally as important as is the state of greater unity. One is not more grand or better than the other is. Spirit, not being polarized, simply does not perceive in that way.

December 21, 1997 and I used the dynamic winter solstice energies to interdimensionally journey and access higher light information. During this journey I perceived that, *"the goat must change from 3D Lead into higher Crystalline Diamond now".* I perceived that all of the dense, physical Capricorn/Saturn 3D energies were in a process of transmuting into a higher vibrating, more crystalline-like transparent structure. It was an important visual symbol of what I had already been living through the past few years, but was obviously now needing to increase dramatically. This information was letting me know that much more alchemical work was still ahead for this Capricorn goat and for all of 3D physicality as well.

The last week of January, and again on February 1, 1998, Mom and I both had more clairaudient experiences of hearing large, nonphysical bird wings flying above and around our heads.

We had both previously had experiences of smelling birds or bird feathers—a scent I adore actually. There is something deeply loving, protective, nurturing and familiar about this particular scent for me. For some people its smelling roses when none are there physically. I however go weak in my Capricornian knees over the enchanting smell of bird feathers. I know this is due to my first Egyptian past life memory of the very ancient falcon-headed ET Bird beings, plus another past life many thousands of years later as a Native American Shoshone woman.

When this particular phenomenon happened to both of us, I was not terribly surprised actually. Mom and I were out shopping when suddenly we both simultaneously hear abnormally large bird wings moving air very close over our heads. We both looked at each other wide-eyed, and then grinned like excited little kids. For these sounds to be what we both heard, the bird wings would have needed to be huge, and for some reason that made us both very happy and excited.

The next time this same bird wing-flying phenomenon happened a week later, Mom and I were again in some store shopping. This time I was the only one who clairaudiently heard the huge bird wings flying over my head. After a few minutes of listening to this and smelling my beloved bird feather scent, I clearly felt something touch the top of my head. Because I am not a big fan of spiders, my first (ridiculous) thought and fear was that a spider had gotten into my hair. Stupid yes, but that's what my mind immediately did despite my having heard the bird wings overhead.

I went running over to Mom like a frightened child, swiping wildly at my hair, starting to panic in public. I hollered at her to check my hair for bugs, bird poop, or anything, which she did immediately. Nothing was in my hair of course. Hearing that I was bug-free and safe I broke into tears right in the middle of the store, which was 1,000% out of character for me. I have always preferred being in stealth mode when I am in public, so running around flailing and crying was certainly not my normal behavior at all. We stood there for a moment longer and then realized it was obviously time for us to return home.

The night before the 1998 summer solstice, I had a cluster of potent insights and later in the evening, dreams. While sitting alone that night I suddenly knew that the hot flashes of menopause are so much more than what most doctors believe or know. I suddenly knew they were a very potent way that middle-aged women were able to transmute enormous amounts of previously accumulated lower emotional energies within themselves. Hot flashes are kundalini fire that helps repeatedly burn away and transmute a lot of the earlier residual *girlfriend, lover, wife, and mommy* energies that need to be transmuted at that stage so the woman can continue growing and evolving beyond her earlier identities, abilities, and consciousness. Hot flashes are profoundly important in the process of inner energy clearings and transmutations of the many previous stages in a female's life. The sacred inner kundalini fires of hot flashes repeatedly burn away all previous lower beliefs, habits, emotional addictions, and residual or stuck energies and are obviously a necessary part of our evolving into the next stage of our lives during our late forties and fifties especially.

Secondly, I clairvoyantly saw two Tibetan Monks turning on or activating energies to help all of humanity with this ongoing and increasingly intense and compressed evolutionary (ascension) process. I did not know exactly what they were doing and felt it was more of a symbolic gesture than something physical they were actually turning on.

Thirdly, I had another etheric contact with a young boy who looked to be about nine years old. Despite him appearing to be just a mire child, he had higher knowledge and soul maturity as if he were a very ancient master. I learned over time that he too was another aspect of me, almost like a guide, and he and I had many wonderful telepathic conversations about different important things over a period of a couple years. At the end of those two years, he too left me because our work with each other had completed. Evidently, I needed to know he existed and was another aspect of me and consciously interact with him and vice versa. This particular night we discussed how holographic things worked and why, also about 6D geometric energies and how they are vibrational blueprints for all other things within the third dimension. We also discussed how these current aspects of ourselves, our so-called past life selves, our multidimensional selves and our Higher Selves are all fragmented pieces of the All That Is or Source, which is extraordinarily holographic. Whenever this young boy showed up etherically like this, it was always an exceedingly fascinating and enjoyable conversation and

I became acutely fond of him and our short couple of years together.

The next day—the day of the summer solstice—Mom and I sat outside on the back deck and talked for many hours. It was during these last few years of the 1990s that I realized I was increasingly channeling or tapping into my own Higher Self. I had no interest or desire in channeling any other being or small group of higher dimensional beings, but I certainly did want to have increased conscious connections with my own Higher Self. After a year of Mom and I having hours-long talks like this I realized that about thirty to forty minutes into my talking strictly from a Denise perspective, I would vibrationally speedup, enter a higher state of consciousness, and had tapped into my Higher Self. I was increasingly channeling bits and pieces of wisdom directly from my own Higher Self in a fully conscious state. Denise did not go elsewhere or step aside as many channels do. My sense of self only expanded a bit more and I was suddenly saying things as deep knowing and understandings from this higher perspective. What a phenomenal treasure-trove of endless wisdom exists for each of us when we are able to commune directly with our Higher Selves.

It was no longer about being psychic, but about a much more direct conscious connection to my own Source—my Higher Self. Over time, this connection has only become more clear, easy, and normal to me. It is vastly less dramatic, colorful, and theatrical than psychic, clairvoyant, or clairsentience (ESP) abilities. Wisdoms from your own Higher Self are unemotional higher *knowing* with no linear intellectual *thinking* involved. It is awareness and knowing—not egoic thinking, intellectualizing, or lower ego-based emotions. You simply *know* higher, larger, and much more complex things without any ESP abilities or colorful high drama. One is like being in your early twenties and learning about life and reality; the other is like being an Elder Master who calmly and easily knows so much more but without all the emotional ego drama and intensity. I'll take direct Higher Self knowledge in a heartbeat over being psychic any day! That is how wonderful it is, and we are rapidly evolving now towards fully conscious Higher Self connections.

The day of the summer solstice was first spent talking for about an hour with Mom. My talking as Denise would vibrationally increase and expand after awhile into channeling portions of higher information directly from my Higher Self. I talked for hours that day and had a higher perspective of so many things in my life, my family's lives, past lives, and past astrological Ages, and how they are all intimately interconnected with this current life and time of compressed evolution. Our Higher Selves see the Big Picture from such a different perspective than we do that it is rather shocking. It was a very good summer solstice indeed.

Months later in December 1998, I had a dream and suddenly felt compelled to wake up and turn over on my side for some reason. I woke myself up, turned on my side, and then flipped my pillow over because it had gotten flat. While I was doing all this I saw something from my bed floating at my eye level about two feet away from my face. It was a perfectly flat, two-dimensional image of a milk-white skinned ET head. No body, no limbs, no neck even, just a flat two-dimensional ET face floating there in the darkness next to my bed in the middle of the night. In that moment I knew it was the ET who had told me to wake up and turn over. Evidently, he wanted me to see him very clearly and to be wide-awake when I did.

Because I had not been sleeping well anyway, I did not appreciate being woke up to see him or anything else for that matter. The ETs could come and chat all they wanted while I was awake and not disturb what precious-little sleep I am able to get occasionally now. I told him in this less than appreciative state in the middle of the night to not bother me with any, "*…negative shit and to go away!*" What in the hell was I doing! I certainly hope he knew how terribly sleep deprived I was at that point and did not have anything too interesting to tell me about. I will always regret my rude behavior and attitude with him that night.

Fig. 3.10. Flat ET Face

January 1999 and I'm sitting on the toilet when a profound insight enveloped me. Hey, we've all had it happen! You're sitting there not thinking and suddenly you align a little bit better with the Multiverse for a few seconds and experience an expanded state of awareness. You know more than you did a slit-second ago, and that knowing permanently alters you for the better.

What I knew in that brief moment was that everything within the third dimension—including my entire life—was an illusion. I knew that 3D was like a dream, real, yet not real from another point of view. Of course, the big question then might be *what is real?* It is all real, it is also an illusion, and it is perfect for what we, as spiritual beings, intended to use all of it for. *Real* and *illusion* are limited ego-based terms we feel we need when attempting to describe cosmic plans we don't yet fully remember or understand from our narrow 3D state of awareness.

During my toilet-seated moment of profound cosmic insight, I had the sense that I had been existing deep underwater during this entire life but was now quickly rising toward the surface of the water finally. I knew that when I reached the water's surface I would break through into an entirely different level of awareness and being. I also knew my doing this would automatically transform me into a different species that would energetically match its new higher frequency environment. I knew I was currently within the ongoing process of vibrationally evolving up and out of the deep, dark, Waters of Illusion that polarized 3D ego-based consciousness is. I could see the bright light above and feel the surface of the water only a couple feet above my head now, which showed me how far I had already risen within the dark and unaware depths.

The surface of the water was so close now but I was not completely ready yet to make that huge shift into existence on the other side of the Waters of Illusion. This is what we have been working towards for so long. I wondered if when the Sun enters the Photon band of higher frequency light around December 21, 1998, if that will be what helps draw so many others and me across the surface cusp of the Piscean Age waters finally.

January 12, 1999 I had another of those extra important experiences and insights. They all were terribly important and very interesting pieces of the greater overall picture, but this one was a bit more unusual than what I was used to. It held tremendous quantum information and understanding that changed my viewpoint on so many things that day.

I had been waiting to meet with my son to have a long-overdue converstation with him about drug addiction problems he had been battling. While I was waiting for him to get home from work and call so we could get together, I started feeling horrible physically. I automatically assumed this was due to my having tons of past mommy anxieties and guilt over these old drug issues with my only child. My issues with my son were simply one more emotional and energetic situation I needed to fully deal with within myself, and also with him, to help us both. No stone will be left unturned remember?

While I waited for him to call, my body was reacting to previous years of frustrations, wounds, anger, maternal guilt, divorced single parent guilt, and all of the emotional junk we so expertly stuff down and out of sight for numerous personal reasons. Of course it all just sits down there rotting and fermenting, becoming even more potent and toxic and hasn't really gone anywhere. The emotional energies inside us don't magically go away just because we have learned how to carry on over the top of them. In this particular case, many of my old toxic emotional issues and blocked energies concerning my son were trying to get up and out now too, right along with all the other family member stuff, past boyfriend issues, and absolutely everything and everyone else. What a dark, hot, lower-level volcanic mess!

So while I'm sitting there becoming physically sick from my own suppressed emotional energies with my only child, my much-loved Pleiadian male friend from my past life in 12,600 B.C. Egypt dropped in. I knew this meant he had something important and timely to share, so I instantly went into a receptive and expanded state to more directly interact with him.

I clairvoyantly saw the Pleiadian in a brilliant white robe standing outdoors in the silver-white light of the Photon light. Everything is glowing white light everywere and looks so clean and pure, so honest and perfect. The Pleiadian's white robe, his long straight blond hair, his perfect sunkissed skin, and the very air itself are all shining brilliant sliver-white light everywhere. There are absolutely no shadows in this higher dimensional Photonic light. No lies, no distortions, no illusions, no manipulations, no shadows, no hiding, no lower vibrating anything—only higher dimensional Photon Light and the higher Heart consciousness it automatically produces.

Standing to the Pleiadian's right side is a majestic full-grown male lion. Hovering in the air above his left shoulder is a large white sphere. The Pleiadian doesn't talk or telepath to me as he usually would, but instead goes into a pose and turns slowly, giving me plenty of time to carefully view him and feel the energies he is deliberatly emanating and displaying. He has something imporant to say, and today, this was the technique he was using. He was posing and radiating energies for me to both see, feel, and then interpret on my own.

I will admit it was an impressive sight and reminded me of what it might be like viewing a brand new archetypal Tarot card for the very first time. Everything was brilliant white within greater brilliant silver-white radiating Photonic light. I had plenty of time to view and feel the Pleiadian, the large regal lion at his side, and the silent hovering white sphere floating above his left shoulder. I had the impression all three objects represented one overall similar energy and that I needed to connect it to something else I didn't understand as yet.

In the next moment the white sphere turned into a cluster of small multi-colored geometric objects and the Pleiadian's brilliant white clothes turned into his more familiar ancient Egyptian multi-colored gemstone encrusted robe. He maintained his pose during this transition from brilliant silver-white Photonic light, back to more normal physical energies and colors, and then back to brilliant silver-white light again. Was he showing me about cycles or transformations within cycles? Was he showing me how certain energies appear within normal physicality, and also within higher Photon light? I felt he was trying to show me all this and much more.

I suddenly sensed that just out of view to the Pleiadian's left, stood the male I had been in my past life in Egypt with he and the Orion and Sirian Starbeings. I could feel him standing there waiting for the Pleiadian to finish whatever it was he was doing. He did not sense or see me (Denise) here in my life and time watching the Pleiadian posing, but I knew the Pleiadian was up to something very new and important with both of us.

The Pleiadian was gently and slowly introducing the male past life me to this current life me here in my timeline exactly opposite them way back in 12,600 B.C. He was going slowly with this because he knew the male past life me would have a bit of a shock seeing me—Denise—here in this reality. In my own way I was holding a pose too, waiting to see what the Pleiadian was going to do next with this past life male me. I could clairvoyantly see him talking to the male past life me who was now also visible to me, and I to him. The Pleiadian was explaining about why it was necessary for the *anchor person* in this (my) timeline to be in a female body.

As I listened to the Pleiadian talking to the male past life me in his life and time in 12,600 B.C. Egypt, I knew that so many of us reincarnated now at the beginning of the Age of Aquarius are in female bodies because we had ascended or had intentional and fully conscious deaths early in the Age of Leo while in male bodies. It had to do with the necessity of having the majority of reincarnated Lightworkers be in female bodies now to reintroduce and anchor the long-banished Goddess energies and consciousness. We are to help override the current dark and perverted patriarchal energies and consciousness in our current lives, and being in female bodies energetically assists with this process.

When Goddess consciousness was alive and well back during this ancient Egyptian past life, the majority of us were in male bodies. Now, in these current lives at the end of the long partriarchal planetary rule, we are reincarnate in female bodies for the obvious polarity reasons; to integrate and resolve any and all of this longstanding polarity, both within ourselves individually, but also the collective and the planet. You see, WE are our *soul mates.*

The Pleaidian wanted me to view and hear the conversation he was having with the male past life me about Denise in her life and timeline. It was a extremely special experience for both he and I and one I will never forget. As I listened to his (my male past life self) fears and confusions as to why this me—the *anchor person*— had to be in a female body, and small sickly one at that, I understood more than just what was being said by the Pleiadian.

I realized I had to be in a female body in this life and time period, and that I had to physically look very nonthreatening and inconsequential. I had to not standout in the current planetary patriarchal world, so being a small insignificant female was—amongst other things—camouflage. We Lightworkers reincarnated today in female bodies wouldn't be seen as a threat to the patriarchy, and therefore would have an easier time flying under the planetary psychic radar because of it. This was extremely important because we needed to get a tremendous amount of energy work accomplished within the planetary Darkness decades before the higher cosmic Light could arrive.

As the Pleiadian was explaining all this to the male past life me, who kept glancing at me (Denise) while I was watching and listening to both of them, he kept shaking his head in disbelief. He thought it a terrible thing to be so seemingly handicapped in a female body and be so sick and in such constant pain, not to mention having so much toxic energies to transmute when my mission was so important in completing this massive, ancient business. He thought it a real hardship for this version of me (Denise) in this horribly toxic and incomprehensibly dark and vastly lower time on Earth. The Pleiadian repeatedly reassured him that this had all been carefully planned long before either aspects of us had incarnated, and that contrary to how things may appear, everything was going along quite well actually. Eventually the male past life me accepted that I (Denise) was the perfect woman for the job, but he too found the whole thing pretty amazing.

I have experienced meeting a couple of my already remembered past life selves in this same manner and always with a Master Teacher there as the higher third party between the two of us in our two different lives and times. (See *The Temple of Master Hotei: A Unique Past Life Memory)*. I realized that this too was another aspect of becoming more interdimensionally and quantumly aware on a conscious level. We are quickly evolving to be able to carry more awareness of not only multiple dimensions, but also of our simultaneous lives and selves existing across Earth (and elsewhere) in different times—our so-called *past lives*. I hope you can more easily see now that there is nothing *past* or linear about any of them.

Experiencing this was basically my becoming a bit more consciously aware of more aspects of ME and connecting with them as opposed to being consciously disconnected or isolated from each other. It is an ongoing and expanding process of conscious reintroduction to multiple aspects of self, with increasing conscious connection to Higher Self as all of our creator parent. Higher Self's creator parent is Source or the All That Is, and on and on it goes. This simultaneous, multiple selves awareness was another (ascension) aspect of me slowly learning to *consciously* adapt to functioning within a larger quantum state and not only within a singular, linear, ego-based consciousness and space-time awareness. I feel this is rapidly going to become humanities new and normal Aquarian Age consciousness; awarness of multiple, simultaneously existing selves and lives, plus much closer alignment and conscious connections with our individual Higher Selves. In other words, we are evolving back into increasing states of quantum interdimensional identity and consciousness both on and off of Earth. Increasing awareness and communications with different Starbeings, ETs, and other dimensional beings is another aspect of our current consciousness evolution.

January 1999 I had one of the most horrific, negative, lucid dream experience I had ever had to date. I was much more used to clairvoyantly seeing and empathically feeling these types of actual physical events that happen to other people while I was awake. I'd had other psychic dream-state experiences like this before, but this one was so brutal, so evil, so dark that it affected acutely me for many days. Little did I know at the time this first dream experience happened, that this too was merely another aspect of my being a Lightworker. I put two-and-two together shortly after this appallingly negative experience however.

From the dream-state I suddenly popped into an already begun event somewhere in current England. It was an actual physical event that happened to other very real living people there. A young boy about age ten was walking home when he had gotten cornered at the end of some ally or small side-street by a group of five young adult males. They looked to me to be in their twenties. These twenty-year-olds were closing in around the young boy, taunting and insulting him, threatening and demeaning him. The poor child was terrified and he knew he was in very serious danger with this group of human monsters.

I was an invisible psychic observer, there to witness and emotionally and physically feel all that the boy and each of the young males felt during this entire torture, gang rape, and eventual murder. Once I had done that it was up to me to energetically transmute all of the dark energies and emotions generated by those horrible actions, and also from the boy's tremendous fears and pain in response to those actions. This is Lightworking the Dark at its most potent and intense. Having to witness and feel all of the players within some lower, horrific negative event, plus all the different energies they produced because of what each person did was unbelievably bizarre to me. It is like decending into Hell to clean up and transmute another repulsive corner down there; doing so affects you deeply and permanently. These are things, events, actions and feelings I have never experienced in my life and never would have on my own. However, this is what many Lightworkers have to do to transmute and permanently remove the massive amounts of human generated dark, negative, lower frequency energies on Earth across time.

Within a few moments my consciousness was placed inside the young boy's body so I could see and feel—firsthand—all that he was. My awareness was still very much mine, but I was within the young boy's body witnessing and feeling all that he was from his perspective. He was absolutely terrified and I felt every bit of everything he went through in that atrocious event. I do not think I have ever loved someone as much as I did him while I was with him in this intimate way.

Next, my consciousness jumped into each of the adult males doing these horrendous things to the boy. I got to physically and emotionally feel what each of them felt. It was a lowly feeding frenzy, a mindless bloodlust, a savage group possession, an ancient negative male sexual perversion that was obviously exceedingly dark. It was a sinister hoodlum ritual without any conscious ritual on their part. They were hungry, so they fed, and someone died because of it which is usually the case in lower physical 3D.

These adult males physically tortured the boy, repeatedly gang raped him, tortured him some more, then murdered him with knives and then disappeared back into the city. The violent, dark, energetic storm and damage they and their actions left in that tiny physical location in England was immense. Keep in mind that this was only one physical event in current time in one physical location on Earth. There are hundreds of millions of such actions and events that have taken place all around the planet for the last 12,500 years. This and more is what many Lightworkers have personally lived through, felt, transmuted, cleaned, cleared and released over recent years. It is the darkest and most negative energy work one can imagine. It is also an important remembering for the Lightworker because it allows us to experience this intense level of darkness, negativity, fear, hate, and all the rest of it within physical bodies, with polarized minds, within a physical polarized dimension and world. These are feelings and energies that most Lightworkers have long forgotten because they evolved beyond the lower levels of this type of 3D consciousness and corresponding energies. They need to remember and re-feel some of it personally to be very aware of what they are doing now and why with their planetary Lightworking for humanity.

January 29, 1999 I and my poor sleeping cat experienced something massive come energetically blasting in from the southeast. I had been laying on my bed resting while the cat was asleep in my bathroom with his back against the south facing wall. I clairaudiently heard something coming from the south through the air from many miles away, heading directly towards our house. I couldn't tell what this was, only that it felt huge, powerful, and traveling amazingly fast about 30 feet above the ground. At least that is how I perceived this approaching thing or energy.

Because I could hear it traveling extremely fast towards our house, I quickly sat up on my bed and psychically sensed for all I was worth. It did not feel postitive. In the next second something actually impacted our house like a massive energy crashing into the wall and blasted right on through it and out the north side of the house. I and the sleeping cat heard and felt the energetic boom and repercussion of it etherically hitting the house. The poor cat woke up and flew out of the bathroom, into my bedroom, and straight into the closet to hide. He remained in there crying and howling and was truly terrified. I could certainly relate.

Whatever this thing or energy was, it was very potent and traveling extremely fast. I felt and heard it coming, then hit our house like a sonic boom and travel right through it and out the north side. I didn't sense it had kept going in a straight line on the north side of our house however, but more like it had reached its destination—our house—were it just blasted through and vanished. I still don't know absolutely what it was and why it happened but the cat wasn't the same for weeks.

Four years earlier in 1996, I felt my beloved and always nearby Starbeing threesome begin to withdraw energetically from me. The 8D Orion, 6D Sirian, and 5D Pleiadian male ETs I had known and remembered from my past life in 12,600 B.C. Egypt, were also my current life interdimensional partners and teachers as well. The three of them, and a few others, were instantly available to me ethereally, clairvoyantly, and telepathically in this life. All I had to do was emotionally desire and intend to communicate with them, and within a minute or so, they were there. They energetically dropped down a bit, I energetically sped up a bit, and we met vibrationally in the middle where we could easily communicate with each other. It had been this way for the majority of my life and I had obviously become very used to them always being available whenever I needed certain information from them. However, things were rapidly changing at this point.

I was evolving, and because of it, the three of them had gradually been retreating energetically. I could feel it happening, yet none of us had said anything about it to each other for the four years it had been slowly building. By January 1999, I knew I finally had to confront them and ask why they were leaving me. One day I went into my usual state of slightly higher consciousness by increasing my energy or spin or frequency to get to that familiar middle ground to talk with them. Within seconds, all three of them were there and I knew they had been waiting for me to finally ask them this very important question.

After I asked the big question they informed me that it was simply time for them to leave me— permanently. The Orion told me what was coming for me was for me alone to live through and that he, nor the other two or anyone else for that matter, would hold my hand through any of it. I did not even care about what this coming thing was because it simply didn't matter to me at that moment. I knew what Orion was saying and what he meant by it and that was what was important to me at that exact moment. I would worry about the approaching *thing* that I alone had to go through later!

He also telepathically informed me that what was coming for me was something I had to go through on my own and no higher being would harm me by helping me through it. He said it was a universal law that they— and all other positive higher dimensional beings—could not, and would not, ever for any reason interfere with whatever it was that was coming that I had to go through. He explained that positive higher frequency beings would never break this universal law and interfere with another soul's mission and important growth process. (Negatively focused beings certainly would however.) It was utterly unthinkable for positive higher beings to interfere, even to seemingly help or assist during certain profoundly important and difficult phases of soul work within an incarnation. They would not risk harming the soul/person by seemingly helping, nor would they risk the energetic consequences of interfering when they knew they should not.

Even though this was the first time any of them had ever discussed this with me, I already knew it well in my deepest gut and my heart-of-Hearts. It was the only way to go, and because of that, it was much easier for me to release the three of them emotionally. It was time to let them go Home, and time for me to get into some serious sounding new level of personal energy work. They had babysat and guided me for many long years during this incarnation, as well as long ago in my past life at the beginning of the Age of Leo. In that moment I knew I had reached the threshold where it was now time for me to begin transmuting in some new and greater way so I would evolve into what they had long been for me—and even more.

I told the three of them that I absolutely understood why they had to leave me. I also had sensed this coming ever since my Egypt past life in 12,600 B.C. when they left 3D shortly after I exited my life there with them. I realized that as a child in my past life with them—plus as a child in this current life—that every time I watched the sun set, I knew in my deepest heart that the time would come when I had to take their place within the ever evolving spiritual hierarchy. This deep knowing was what caused my intense homesickness and sense of being so alone on Earth as a Wanderer child in this life. Watching the sun sink below the western horizon was always such an emotionally painful reminder that I was on Earth to do many things; one of which was to evolve into a higher frequency being that functioned much as the three of them had for me for so very long.

I also told each of them how profoundly I loved them and how grateful I was to have had them guiding and reminding me for so very long. I thanked them repeatedly for remaining behind for so long to assist me, to help wake me up to why I was reincarnate on Earth now, and to keep me on-track within this aspect of my unfolding soul mission. For me, I did pretty well up to the end but then I got all mushy and the marvelous Sirian reacted the way he always did when I became overly emotional; he rolled his piercing green eyes, pressed his lips together, and gazed off in another direction to collect himself. The Pleiadian smiled his always-perfect *Mona Lisa-esque* smile, while his fifth dimensional High Heart energies literally filled the space to the point of near bursting. Orion was the Elder master teacher and cosmic father figure, and he and I said our farewells to each other last. Then—they were gone.

It was not as excruciating emotionally as I thought it would be and it actually felt correct. I felt like I had reached some level of interdimensional adulthood by our parting. It felt like being entrusted with the family car to drive with no adult supervision for the very first time. It felt good, in a terribly bittersweet sort of way, but I would miss having the three of them constantly at my etheric elbow. I continued having telepathic/clairvoyant meetings with the three of them throughout 1998, but with the start of 1999, they were permanently gone. The Pleiadian was the only one who continued to make occasional contact after the start of my intense physical transition (ascension) process in February 1999.

Fig. 3.11. The 8D Orion

Fig. 3.12. The 6D Sirian

Fig. 3.13. The 5D Pleiadian

February 1, 1999 (thirty-nine days after my forty-seventh birthday) was THE day my life, my body, my mind and my reality changed permanently. This was exactly as if someone had abruptly turned on an invisible switch somewhere and all hell broke loose. I went to bed on the last day of January 1999, and woke up hours later in another reality—one that was unlike anything I had ever experienced prior. If I thought I had felt terrible over the past couple of years, all that was activated within me this day would make everything I had previously been through seem like child's play.

I woke up that morning with a pile of physical symptoms I had never had before. I awoke with nearly constant hot flashes for the first time in my life. I'd had a couple mini "hot flashes" the year before, but this went from nothing one day, to extreme and constant hot flashes only twelve hours later. It was beyond traumatic and a shock on every level. I woke up sick and with amplified pains and all sorts of strange symptoms that made very little sense to me. The worst part of this was that, over time, I would discover that all of these intense symptoms were only going to get worse over a period of many years. I had reached some unknown activation point and nothing would ever be the same again because of it.

It took me a couple months to even think to time how long one hot flash lasted, then clock how long I was not feeling anything, and when the next hot flash cycle began. When I did finally think to time the miserable things, I discovered that one hot flash would last for forty-five minutes with about eight minutes of no sensations at all, then the cycle would begin all over again. This craziness went all day and night for many years. It was a brutal process that just continued on and on and on. (As I'm writing this today in July 2009, I'm still having hot flashes but they're much less severe and frequent because I have transmuted my densest energies already.)

Let me clairify exactly what I mean when I use the term *hot flashes*. Usually we think of some middle-aged woman getting hot and frantically fanning herself and not much more. In my case the hot flashes—which really are kundalini fire rising repeatedly—always came with multiple other symptoms and each was unique and usually unpleasant. No two hot flashes are exactly alike and they are much more than only getting physically hot for a bit. They are kundalini fire rising repeatedly up to different chakras to burn away any and all lower vibrating energies within you and your multiple energy bodies.

When I would have a hot flash from this puzzling starting day forward, my ability to mentally focus would automatically come to a dead stop. My ability to

314

mentally focus and direct my thoughts would immediately stop and be put on hold during the entire duration of the hot flash/kundalini rising. I would also become nauseous from the energetic intensity of the hot flashes/kundalini risings, dizzy, mentally dazed, emotionally imbalanced and usually very angry, freezing cold, burning hot, sweat profusely, sudden intense need to urinate, plus have tremendous physical pains in different parts of my body. This did not seem to me like how typical menopausal hot flashes should be, but I figured, what did I know about it? I had never heard of any middle-aged woman ever mentioning symptoms this extreme or having what energetically felt like what I suspect a NDE (Near Death Experience) feels like! Again, I blamed these severe symptoms on the fact I had probably been horomonally imbalanced ever since age twenty-seven when I required a hysterectomy and never took any hormonal replacement medications.

Eventually I bought a few menopause books written by doctors to try and figure out what was going on with my body. This whole menopausal situation was another mystery because I'd had no menstral bleeding cycles to judge my approaching perimenopause or menopause against as most women do. Of course I clearly remember my Higher Self dream message from five years earlier. Once I had reached this physical activation date (2–1–99), I was shocked at how severe this process actuality was. I believed that I had understood what this D 1 47 lucid dream message really meant five years earlier, and I did, yet I did not realize how literal and powerfully physical it was going to be until it actually started. There were so many times over the months and years to come that I honestly did not think I would physically survive this transformational process.

As it interestingly turned out, I also quit smoking cigarettes eight days after February 1, 1999. How is that for cosmic Higher Self timing? Six months earlier I had planned on quiting smoking but I certainly had no idea that this too would begin during all this other transformational (ascension) insanity. Yet, this is often how our Higher Selves set things up for us; multiple things happen at the same time because they are all interconnected and need to be dealt with while other massive changes are happening. If you are going to feel miserable and be sick anyway, why not resovle multiple issues all at the same time? Energetic transformational efficiency at work.

What I didn't know at this time and wouldn't for nearly eight more years was that on January 5, 1999, humanity entered the *First Day* or *Day One* of the Mayan calendar cycle of *Days and Nights*. (These Mayan Days and Nights unfold from January 5, 1999 through October 28, 2011.) I also didn't know at this time that it was the beginning of what has been called the great "*Galactic Alignment*"; the years from 1998 through 2001 when the Milky Way Galactic equator crosses the Galactic axis and aligns perfectly with the Galactic Center. I consciously did not know about either of these two amazingly important spiritual and energetic activation events, but they were the same information my Higher Self had shown me five years earlier calling them my D 1 47 activation point.

I did know from having read Barbara Hand Clow's book *The Pleiadian Agenda* in 1996, that the Sun's corona would be entering the Photon band of higher dimensional Light around the winter Solstice of 1998, two days before my forty-seventh (D 1 47) birthday. As Clow mentions in her Appendix B that if her theory is correct, then there should be significant changes in our solar sytem or consciousness during 1998–2001 when first the Sun's corona, and then the Sun, enters the Photon band. Because I had already been seeing this Photonic light energy around the Sun, in the air, and throughout physicality years earlier—plus I recognized it from my 12,600 B.C. Egyptian past life—I knew we were nearing the higher dimensional energy of the Photon band again well before 1998.

With everything that had suddenly been activated via the Feburary 1, 1999 D 1 47 process, I was positive something exceedingly important had just begun. I learned much more about many of these cosmic and galactic events seven or eight years later when I first read about them (Mayan Day/Night cycles and the Galactic Alignment) online. This was another clear example of more back engineering I had to do with the numerous unusual symptoms I had had for many years.

February 1999 I was struggling to go into my usually effortless, fast and easy meditational state. Now my mind just changed channels on me continuously. It was extremely frustrating that I could not instantly focus mentally as I always could before. It's like my mental focus and razor-sharp concentration has been unplugged, scrambled, and now I cannot remain mentally focused on any one thing no matter how hard I try. This same problem now applies to my ability—make that inability—to read books. At this point (in 1999) I can no longer read books! I used to effortlessly swim through a good book in a day or two and I could remember it all and even where certain information was within it. Now I have to re-read one paragraph sixteen times and I still cannot grasp what I have read. I am literally loosing my old familiar and accute mental focus because its been unplugged so now I get a lot of mental static and flashes of channel surfing images and disjointed noise!

Eventually I was able to get enough of a grasp to still access some higher level insights and infomation occasionally. In this particular case it was somewhat like I was both awake and asleep dreaming at the same time, which was a new phenomenon for me. It was very pleasant actually, plus great training at becoming increasingly multidimensionally aware on a conscious level.

While in this strange new state of awareness I clairvoyantly saw and underdstood that, *"The five points are about to fold up"*. This meant that humanities 3D physical bodies, their lower, polarized consciousness and egos were very close to expiring. Their 3D expiration date was just around the corner! The *five points* were symbolic of the physical human body geometric pentagram pattern, while the *folding up* indicated our current and highly compressed evolutionary/ascension process. This sentence meant that humanity was currently vibrationally outgrowing its 3D physical body vehicle, so it—the five pointed star—was going to be *folding up,* dying while evolving into a much more energetically complex and higher vibrating geometric vehicle. I knew all of this was time-coded and our physical body patterns were currently *expiring,* but would automatically begin a metamorphosis of energetically evolving into the next higher, faster, and vastly more light-filled phase. I understood this was going to be a slightly modified, non-Lightworker *species version* of my personal D 1 47 transformational (ascension) process.

This higher aspect of me knew this, and much more, and remembering it was completely non-dramatic and unemotional in every way. It was business as usual to this higher aspect of myself. To my lower ego self it was of course endless physical and emotional pain, sickness, mental confusion, extreme polarities struggling desperately to be resolved on all levels, and a literal ongoing slow-motion dying process. It was quite an interesting and polarized point of view between these two extreme levels of awareness I was intimately connected to. The higher ME knew what was happening and why and that it was perfect and right on time. The little ego me was having one very big and horrible time with it all however.

There is more than just two polarized states of being existing at opposite ends of some invisible pole. There is a vibrationally higher third state of being and consciousness, and my becoming aware of it is another aspect of this ongoing metamorphosis. (Years later I would discover that this third point or state of being would be called *quantum* and/or *triality consciousness.*) They are all the same thing—us evolving beyond our egos, our polarized brains and isolated linear consciousness and time awareness, into a vastly more unified higher state and frequency beyond polarity in 3D. Once you resolve the polarities within yourself, this automatically creates a direct third point to your Higher Self.

This awareness of our dense physical bodies and their matching external world reality *expiring* on some enormous cosmic timeline was like going to school for twelve years, and along the way, forgetting that

Graduation Day was a preset date for everyone in school. Years later I realized that this must be what the Mayans and others meant by 2011–2012 being the *end time.* It is, and its impossible for it to not happen thank goodness.

February 1999 I suddenly had a colossal overview hit me like a ton of beautiful, glistening gold bricks. It was breathtakingly wonderful and I realized it must look very much like what some of my Higher Self sees all the time. It was a brief and splendid quantum perspective, and one I was slowly and steadily becoming more familiar and comfortable being within.

From this higher, nonlinear quantum perspective, I clearly saw and felt my multiple past life selves and the different master teachers and other dimensional Starbeings that were present in many of them. This enormous and highly complex geometric picture of my multiple sevles—my so-called *past* life selves and the master teaches in them—were all connected like perfect soul geometry, and the clairvoyant image I saw was indeed geometric. My point of view of this soul level geometric shape was from inside of it, looking outward in all directions simultaneously.

Imagine yourself inside a colossal multifaceted diamond. Each of the facets of this perfect diamond represent one of your many past life selves. Each of the facet lines on this diamond represent the energetic interconnectedness between every facet and aspect of the many past/present/future selves. From this internal perspective within the diamond looking out in all directions simultaneously, you as Higher Self can easily veiw every one of your seeded aspects or individual selves within their different incarnational timelines, both on and off Earth. You are overseeing from your unified Higher Self perspective from the center outward in all directions simultaneously. All is always connected to all even when unaware of that fact.

Next, I realized that so many of my past life selves and the master teachers I'd had in some of them had all intentionally contributed to the building and layering of this version of me, Denise, in my time on Earth now as a First Wave Lightworker at the end of the Mayan calendar. I saw Master Hotei and Jade One from that ancient past life in China. I saw Queen Najet from my past life in Egypt who tried to integrate and house too much too soon in her female body and time and fried energetically because of it. I saw the Egyptian past life male with the three ETs, and so many other of my past or other lives/selves. I saw and felt how each one of them had contributed aspects of themselves to this me, here now, so that I would have all the tools I needed in this life to do this particular job. I saw, felt, knew and wept with gratitude and love over the complete beautiful and perfect creation, the grand plan, the massive and endless love involved and the absolute flawlessness and interdimensionality of it all. I knew that this was what Barbara Marciniak's channeled Pleiadians meant with their great line, *"You are the Standard Bearer of your Soul."*

March 1999 and the thing I had avoided my whole life with my Mom had finally arrived. It arrived— as these things usually do—with decades of past frustrations and anger, and it was finally volcanic erruption time. It was something she and I both absolutely needed to face and move through for each of us individually, but also as a team living and working together through the ongoing (ascension) changes and transformations.

I suddenly errupted one day over some small criticizing crap she was far too good at doing with me and The Battle began for the first time in both our lives. I needed to confront her and she needed to be confronted. We both needed to purge old emotional baggage we had been hauling around for decades. This old emotional crap could not remain inside either of us as we continued growing and evoving at the rate we had been. My issues were with her as my mother, but her issues went much farther back to her childhood and were continuing to be played out, primarily with me. I'd had enough of it all and so I started the brawl with her which I had never done before.

I will spare you all of the ugly, and just say that it was profoundly important for both of us and was just more of the many issues and old stuck emotional energies we each had that needed to be dealt with finally. This is an ongoing process and there are *multiple* layers to it we each must move through. As is usually the case, we have to deal with one issue multiple times over months or years before we have honestly dealt with every bit of it on all energetic levels. I wish these buried emotional issues and energeis could be dealt with in a big oneshot sort of way but they rarely are. We have to work through each of them multiple times before they are totally discharged and completely transmuted.

So far these emotional energetic issues for me had centered around plenty of ex-husband stuff, old boyfriends, my son, my mother and father, my sister, my past lives, my many fears, nightmares, projections, fragmented and monstrous bits and pieces of myself that had gotten cast-off and strewn here and there over the astrological Ages. You would think I'd be making a decent dent in all this inner work by now wouldn't you? I was, but there was more to come.

April 14, 1999 and I had just gone to bed and abruptly did not know who I was! I had about five perfectly delicious seconds of absolutely no identity whatsoever. Zero sense of egoic identity, no name, no personality, no nothing—just pure, unfiltered, naked awareness. It was confusing and perfectly brilliant at the same time. It was shocking and disturbing momentarily to my ego self, yet, it was the most free and complete I have ever felt in this life or any others that I consciously remember.

I had no personality during those few seconds of identity freedom—no personality to filter all the incoming and outgoing information and stuff that we all have running constantly. It was so pure, so vast, so direct and it felt normal despite it being the first time I (Denise) had ever experienced it in this way. It felt like Home and like the real me without any restrictive personality clothing on. It was really wonderful but the cosmic size of it was a bit unnerving. Sense of self means so many different things to different aspects of us and also to where we perceive ourselves to be at the time.

I wondered if it was my Higher Self awareness which was weird and confusing because I didn't know who I was. In the next instant I understood that it didn't matter one little bit and I needed to *get over it*. I realized that this state of no personality, no ego or smaller fractured and filtered self was normal and another aspect of being within quantum consciousness. It felt amazing to not have any filters or identity tags attached to me, but to simply be immeasurably more unified consciousness.

March 1999 came and went and there was nothing but physical and emotional pain, sickness, intense rage, profound exhaustion, uncontrollable crying, kundalini hot flashes day and night, vomiting and nausea, bladder spasms, bone and joint pains, mental static and blurr with no ability to focus, and general *hell on Earth* in just about every sense. I can really only hint at how profoundly severe, how sudden, how horrible, how toxic and intense this entire phase was for me physically, mentally, emotionally and psychically. The worst part was that it simply went on and on and on. As I was to learn over time, there was a very long, difficult and dark road ahead of me and I had to travel it alone and without any medications (pharmaceuticals) or anything else. I had to do it with only my over-the-counter acetaminophen and nothing else—the result of having highly (chemically) sensitive Pisces Rising I suspect.

April 1999 and it is just the same horrific unending sickness, physical and emotional pain, ultra sensitivities to nearly everything, kundalini hot flashes constantly, insomnia because of the constant hot flashes or as they are called when you have them at night *night sweats,* low-grade fevers, chills, bone and body flu-like aches and pains, cyclical ascension related bouts of purging diarrhea, mega headaches, severe and constant abdominal bloating, dizziness, extreme sensitivity to all sounds including my own voice, increased etheric/psychic activities, continued inability to mentally focus, forgetting the names of simple everyday objects and different words, anger and downright intense rage. I had never felt rage in my life prior to the start of my D 1 47 process (which I first discovered in late 2005 was called "ascension"), and I was shocked by my sudden hatred and absolute intolerance of all the assholes n' idiots around the world! Little did I know at the time, that even this disgusting and ugly (ascension) symptom was an exceedingly necessary one I had to move through in this ongoing process of transformation. If we are satisfied and accepting of lower and heartless things, people and ways, nothing would ever improve, so here comes the (ascension) rage and intolerance over them which forces *you* to move on and create those new, higher and better ways.

During this time I had two more teeth abscess which only made me more sick and weak than I was anyway. I spent more money and time in dentists chairs having earlier root canals and crowns extracted because they had abscessed to the point there was no saving them. In these cases I wasn't even given antibiotics by the dentists, and because my mind was not working so great, I didn't even think to ask or insist that I have them. So, I would go home after each tooth extraction and become more sick and weak for a while. It seemed that one body problem was endlessly compounded by another and another and another until I was so buried underneath it all that I couldn't do much physically at all. This was the grand and much needed tearing down phase, the further dismanteling of physical Denise and her ego self and corresponding mental abilities, the literal and symbolic dying phase of this enormous inner and outer process. It was at best, brutal.

June 1999 and I am so extremely and constantly bloated in the diaphragm area that I can't eat solid food. I am even throwing up room temperature water. It quickly reached the point where my body could not cope with drinking ice water, so I had to drink only room temperature filtered water so my gut wouldn't bloat any more than it always was. (This extreme diaphram bloating was another common ascension symptom I learned about seven years later in 2005 while online. At that time it was being called *"Buddha Belly"* which reminded me of Master Hotei, and that at least gave me a smile and some pleasant insights into this uncomfortable ascension symptom.)

During this period where I couldn't eat much of anything, I gained the most weight and in record time! You can just imagine my joy. It was amazing and none of it made much sense to me then. Some of these symptoms were very much like what a couple of the menopause books I had bought were saying was common for women during perimenopause and menopause. However, the majority of my numerous other symptoms were not in any of these menopause books written by professionals, so I knew something else was happening.

I was also occasionally sensing some negative energies and small, lower frequency entities in my bedroom, which, considering all the sickness, pain, rage and weeping I was constantly living with wasn't much of a stretch really. (When one is in their Inner Basement for great lengths of time, cleaning up their lower frequency *stuff* down there, it's not uncommon or abnormal to run into some Dark company.) I was psychically wide open and unprotected most of the time and wasn't strong enough or mentally focused enough then to take the normal psychic, etheric, and astral precautions I normally would have.

At one point I could clearly feel some negative *something* had gotten in because of my own confused, unstable, and ultrasensitive, wide open state. I quickly did a very informal banishing ritual to the four directions and amazingly, I was able to sleep for four hours straight that night. It was a minor miracle for me at that point considering I couldn't sleep for longer than forty-five minutes without having a hot flash that would wake me up and then need to uninate. Hot flashes and frequent urination and bladder spasms seemed to all go together, which meant constant running to the bathroom all night long.

Despite being so sick and profoundly miserable, I understood that whatever all this darkness was, it was territory I simply had to traverse and transmute. It did not matter if this darkness was other aspects of me, other aspects of other people, or other aspects of nonhuman, nonphysical beings or entities. When you are down-and-out energetically and utterly exhausted and cannot mentally focus to save your life, it simply does not matter how dark the Darkness is, or what form it shows up in, or who or where it came from. It only matters that you—as a First Wave Lightworker—survive and transmute it all because that is what you do so well.

July 1999 and I was still having residual, stinky dank bits and pieces bubble up from deep within my inner basement—my lower chakras—as would be expected during this type of ongoing total transformational process. Some long-forgotten mommy guilt came bubbling up one day about my son and needed to be processed and released. In the great cosmic scheme of things this emotional tidbit was nothing, and yet to me—the mommy—it was a toxic monster living in my inner basement that had grow large and ugly, as they all usually do.

There was the remembering and re-feeling of the whole situation with my son, and then my seeing and feeling the guilt I created around the event, and then how I promptly suppressed the whole business and carried on as if it didn't happen! Classic cover-up attempt. However, because this was deep-level inner House Cleaning time, all of these past issues, guilt, fears, angers, wounds and so on all had to be dealt with, healed, transmuted and released. That was the magic formula and there were absolutely no short-cuts to any of this process. None. You simply dove into your own inner dank and toxic emotional and energetic septic tank and cleaned up as much as you were capable of at that moment. Obviously, you would need to repeat this process until all layers of it were cleared and released on multiple levels. This was the procedure and it did not matter that you were dying while it all was happening, because that was another aspect of The Process. I simply had to tidy-up and transmute before I could move on to a higher vibrating level and state of being. There is only one way to the other higher side—and that's right through 4D hell. Deal with it and just keep moving forward.

I was slowly learning that on one level what I was doing was transmuting as much current life issues as I was capable of at the time, plus many of my past live's unresolved emotional, energetic, and polarized issues too. As if all that weren't enough, there were those occasional colossal negative energy-spills left by strangers across time in the form of murders, rapes, tortures, mutilations and so on that I—as a Lightworker—needed to transmute and permanently clear also. Through repeated journeys into these extraordinarily dark and repulsive landscapes where past negative human activities have been energetically festering for years, decades, and eons, I came to intimately understand that to get from 3D to 5D, requires expeditions through 4D—the archetypal astral dimension or *"hell"*. No wonder it was so sinister, wicked, depraved, appalling, enormous and so filled with ancient monsters! Nonetheless, traversing and transmuting 4D was *the* energetic roadway out of lower polarized 3D physicality and into nonpolarized, higher vibtating Heart consciousness and increased unity of 5D. We had to make the frightening and often repulsive alchemical crossing through the forth dimension and deal with many of its terrifying inhabitants and energies first. This alone was the majority of the alchemical ascension process; cleaning up the planetary 4D collective astral sewer system.

August 1999 and I'm sicker than an ugly ol' dying dog. It really was quite amazing how sick I was constantly without having anything a doctor could find, recognize, or diagnose. They never found anything wrong with me, including no hormonal imbalances due to menopause which I found hard to believe actually.

Because I had no medical insurance, I always paid cash for everything, including being told by medical professionals that they couldn't find anything wrong with me. So, I'm more sick and exhausted than I have ever been in my life, yet, there's nothing wrong with me and there are no medical signs or tests reflecting that I am feeling everything that I am. Oh, and I paid cash to find all that out too.

If you knew me you would know how frazzled I really was, because normally, I would have instantly and easily known that all my symptoms were energy related. I knew that anyway because of my D 1 47 heads-up message and I still paid a couple doctors to confirm it for me. So now, I'll just be sick, imbalanced, and repeatedly die at home and not worry that there might be some actual physical thing wrong with me. Here are some of the symptoms I was having.

- Weight gain
- Profound exhaustion
- Insomnia
- Nightmares, weird archetypal dreams
- Extreme dry eyes
- Bottoms of feet burning hot
- Sudden ice pick stabbing pains in certain bones and joints
- Inability to digest food
- Strange food cravings, heavy protein cravings
- Hot flashes and Cold flashes

- Constant sweating from hot flashes/kundalini fire
- Ultrasensitivity to solar energies, transmissions, solar flares
- Earthquakes, magma, weather and pressure sensitivities
- Inability to mentally focus, remember names and common words
- Bouts of Diharrea purgings
- Frequent urination, bladder spasams
- Chills and frequent low-grade fevers
- Flu-like body aches and pains
- Emotional extremes, crying with deep compassion, equally deep rage
- Chemical sensitivities to foods, drinks, clothes, buildings, all products
- Ultrasensitivity to all physical sounds, people's voices, even your own
- Extreme diaphragm and belly bloating
- Burns on parts of face from both chemicals and kundalini fire
- Hips, legs, knees, ankles, feet in pain and often swollen
- Severe pressure in spine when physically in a lower energy location
- Sensation of things touching your skin
- Sudden and severe allergies
- Inner body electrical-like vibrations of the systemic Rewiring process

- Extreme electric static buildup with constant zapping discharges
- Seeing lights, mist or fog, flashes of lights, balls and pinpoints of colored lights, dark shapes, heat mirages, energy portals, seeing physicality thinning and disappearing
- Hearing nonphysical sounds, voices talking, your name being said

I have had all of these symptoms and no doubt some I have forgotten since Feburary 1, 1999 when my D 1 47 business started. Again, I didn't know at the time what all of this was other than what had been trasmitted to me through my dream message in April 1995. It wasn't until late 2005 when I ran across a link online to some very excellent information about ascension, its many symptoms and cycles, that things fell into place. Finally discovering that information was profoundly helpful to me, plus it was wonderful discovering that numerous other people were having these weird and miserable symptoms too. Misery *does* love company, especially when it is ascension related!

October 1999 and Mom tells me about a psychic attack she had the night before. For Mom this was highly out of the ordinary. For me, not so much so I was mildly concerned. She told me that in the middle of the night she had been awakened because something unseen was blowing cold air on spots of her face. She said she just thought it was a bug and wiped her face and hair. At this point I interrupted her and told her that I too had felt cold air being blown on a tiny area of my face next to my mouth last night around 12:30 AM. I continued telling her that moments after feeling this I saw a small light slowly getting brighter in the nighttime darkness of my bedroom.

After hearing what had happened to me, Mom continued with her experience. Her situation had continued and she began feeling bites on her left arm which caused her whole arm, shoulder, and hand to ache for hours. She thought it was a bug and turned a light on to check but found nothing. She said at this point she suddenly began having very negative thoughts such as, *"We are going to die,"* and *"It's going to become very bad,"* and so on. Mom is one of those happy, glass-is-half-full Jupiterian types so this was thoroughly out of character for her. All I could wonder was who or what had been messing with us both the night before? Whatever it was was something I was unfamiliar with.

November 1999 and I cannot believe my condition. My physical body and mental situation only continues to worsen. My usually impressive and faster than the speed-of-light memory is shot and lying dead in the back corner of my brain somewhere. My body has aged so fast, that for the first time in my adult life, I actually looked my age. I am continuing to gain weight despite not being able to eat much at all, and often what I do eat makes me feel like I have been poisoned, which I probably have been at this stage of my ongoing process.

Leaving our property to go to town to shop and run the monthly errands had literally become an agonizing trek through the lower layers of hell. As soon as I drive the car off our property and a few yards down the road, my diaphram bloats even more and becomes harder simply from entering lower vibrating energies. It is very painful and makes taking a deep breath almost impossible. Every time I leave the property and drive anywhere, all of my miserable (ascension) symptoms magnify so much so that I now hate having to do any shopping at all.

After many months of this I finally realized that Mom's house and property was indeed vibrating extraordinarily high in comparison to everything outside of our property. The world *out there* was very much still in the Dark Ages vibrationally, and every time I had to go out in it to shop, it would make me more sick and in much more pain and profoundly beat-up feeling than how I felt at home. I realized that whatever was going on in my body that hurt so badly at home, was incredibly amplified every time I went out into the lower vibrating world *out there*. Eventually Mom started noticing this excruciating change in energies and frequencies when we were in the car driving to or around in town also. The necessary monthly shopping trips out into the lower vibrating world became something neither of us wanted to have to do each month, and this only worsened every month and every year.

The other major event and turning point that happened in late November 1999, was that Rosa and her two young daughters moved out after renting next-door for nearly fifteen years. Rosa had finally had enough of Tessie's (her Landlady) cruelty and abuses. She had saved enough money to buy her and her daughters a house of their own in town and she couldn't move them out fast enough and get permanently free of Tessie and Johnny. Stan, Tessie's barely human abusive, alcoholic husband had died a few years earlier so the house was now her and Johnny's responsibility. Not that any of them had ever been responsible for anything other than getting drunk, high, or both and trying to maintain that state for as long as possible.

After Rosa moved out in late November 1999, the house remained empty for about four or five months, which I thoroughly enjoyed. It was even better having no one live in it at this point and I enjoyed having no people, no noise, no energies of any kind coming from that retched house right next-door to us. I was so sick, so extremely sensitive, and so deep into my transformational dying process at this point, that it would have been best if I could have lived where there were no neighbors for at least a mile in all directions. For now however, just having that rental house empty was a huge blessing and reprieve for both Mom and I.

December 15, 1999 I was outside working in the yard when a wasp buzzed my head, and as I dodged him, I noticed something unusual around the Sun. After the wasp was gone I made my hand into a fist to directly block out the Sun but safely see the space all around it. Doing this I could easily see an enormous pale white mist-like energy slowly moving and undulating far out around the entire Sun. I had never seen this anomaly before and assumed it must be solar flare energies.

I quickly got our sunglasses and called Mom outside to see it for herself. We stared, squinted, pondered and watched this massive solar energy radiating out in all directions off from the Sun. As we watched this new solar anomaly we both saw brilliant silver-white metallic looking UFO *things* flitting and seemingly playing with each other within this solar energy. I don't know what these things were, and I am not saying they were UFOs in the sense of ETs piloting them because I did not get that feeling. Mom and I watched both the solar energies flowing and wafting slowly like some type of massive transparent solar veil, plus these small brilliant dots zipping around within it.

(I have repeatedly seen these same tiny silver-white dot sized *things* zipping and playing around physical airplanes too, so who knows. I don't know if they are just another etheric life-form or if they are indeed some type of UFO craft in the way most people think of ET type craft. Every ET I have ever known never needed any UFO or craft of any type to get from one point or dimension to another however.)

After a few minutes we also saw what looked like a large cloud of dust much lower in the sky and closer to us, suddenly appear and then move upward toward this slowly shifting solar mist energies and merge with it. Mom thought it was a dust cloud from the field to the east of us but there was no wind blowing, plus I didn't feel it could have been that. I don't know what that cloud-like thing was but it made its way into that solar energy so very far away and very quickly.

This solar anomaly was (and still is) there for all to see, and yet, I have heard no one talk about this highly amazing physical phenomenon. From that December 1999 day on, I would always check the Sun and these massively large energies radiating off from it. Year after year, I have done this while waiting for someone else to mention it or suggest what it may be, but I have heard nothing. Solar flares? Our Sun orbited inside the energy of the Photon Band? Yes to both I believe and probably other things I am unaware of.

■ April 2000 the house next-door to us on the west side was rented after almost five months of sitting empty and silent. Because Tessie and her son Johnny didn't come around to clean up the yard, pull weeds, rake, or do any repairs or cleaning to the inside of the house after Rosa moved out, I naively expected the horrible place would just sit empty forever. Dream on! As it turned out, they had rented it to two half-brothers in their mid-thirties. (Mom and I would discover three and a half miserable years later that these two half-brothers were friends of Johnny's.) This change was another monumental turning point in my ongoing transformational ascension process, but of course, neither Mom nor I knew this at the time.

These two half-brothers—one with black hair and the other with blond hair—moved in this day and with them arrived a non-operational pickup truck and van. There was also an assortment of off-road quads, one dirt bike, one camper shell, one female pit bull dog, rifles, handguns, golf clubs, fishing equipment. Immediately after they moved in the continuous drugs and alcohol, nonstop male friends and also male sexual boyfriends, and relatives arrived. We did not sense the day these two brothers moved in, the years of severe misery, pain, and near insanity that would be caused because of these two male friends of Johnny's.

Mom and I didn't know that these two half-brothers—whom I will call Rick (black hair) and Mike (blond hair)—were friends of Mr. Damaged Goods Johnny, and that they had been told a number of lies about Mom from when he had lived there many years earlier. Rick and Mike moved in knowing all about Mom—from Johnny's perspective—but we would not figure this out for another torturous three and a half years. We were definitely handicapped with this entire situation from the day they moved in next-door.

The brothers moved in with their many non-operational toys and vehicles and it didn't take them long to make it known that they had no intention of keeping the house or yard clean. The weeds, dog shit, copious beer cans, trash and household garbage piled up quickly making the dirt bike, quads, and other broken junk look overgrown and as if they had lived there for decades instead of only a few months. The already lowly and negative energy that had always existed on and around that property seemed to spring to life with a renewed vigor now that these brothers had moved in. They were a perfect match for the negative energies that had always been there, waiting for vibrationally matching humans to live there again. That day arrived in early April 2000.

These two half-brothers moved in and our lives changed in profoundly unpleasant ways because of it. Thankfully, they both usually went off to work each weekday morning together leaving the one female pit bull dog on her own for around ten hours a day. Not being a dog person this seemed terribly cruel to me and I thought the poor dog would starve. However, Rick always fed it every morning and evening even if that was very late at night. I learned that this was how dogs ate, which was the opposite of how cats do; cats nibble a few bits of food throughout the day and night whereas dogs wolf down their food very quickly. I learned that *dogs are from Mars and cats are from Venus.*

The brothers settled into their new house and we adapted as much as we could to them and their addictions living only a few feet away. The weekdays were usually better than the weekends only because— like so many people—they believed the weekends are strictly for getting as utterly fucked up as was physically possible and having as much *"fun"* as was possible at the same time. These guys worked harder on the weekends getting intoxicated and/or high than they ever did during the week while at work. It was crazy and destructive, yet it was their version of fun and having a great weekend, and they attempted it every single freaking weekend.

Obviously, we had to listen to the majority of their weekend *partying*, puking, yelling and pissing in the yard outside. Even Johnny would come back over to get high and drunk with the two of them occasionally, and then yell obscenities at us. This situation was as extremely polarized as anything on Earth could physically get and it was overwhelmingly miserable for Mom and me on every single level. Their presence caused Mom and me physical, mental, psychic, and emotional pain that never diminished day or night.

In early June 2000, I had to confront Rick about how his new male pit bull puppy barked the entire time they were gone at work every day. Rick of course did not appreciate hearing anything from me, and I certainly did not want to have to speak to him either, but the situation quickly became unbearable. Rick and Mike would leave for work around eight each morning and would return home any time between 6 PM and 2 AM. This was normal for them, which was fine because the longer they were not next-door, the better. Nevertheless, Rick's new little male puppy did not enjoy being tied up at the opposite end of their yard while the older female pit bull was never tied up and could freely roam their entire yard. He also didn't like not being able to run and play and would become very hungry and lonely out there for twelve to eighteen hours every day. Therefore, he barked and howled continuously, and I mean *continuously*.

After a couple months of listening to this and finally realizing the puppy wasn't barking so much because it was a new environment for him, but because he was really miserable, I tried to talk with Rick about it over the fence one night at midnight when he and Mike finally returned home. The very next morning our cat went missing.

Five long worrisome days later, our cat showed up covered in dirt and weak from thirst and hunger. I was beside myself because this cat had never disappeared like this before. It took a lot of mental focus and psychic work for me to do what normally would have effortlessly come to me psychically, but eventually I was able to clairvoyantly see what had happened to our cat. Rick had caught him sleeping under their mobile, which he had started doing during the five months it was empty, and he had locked him in his broken down Van on the other side of his house. After five days, he just opened the Van's back doors and let our cat out. The cat was lucky that was all Rick did to him.

I fed and bathed our cat and told him he could never go over our fence into their yard again. I can take a lot of negative crap, but when it comes to harming animals, I become enraged. I cannot tolerate animals being abused for any reason. By his immediate actions with our cat, Rick clearly let me know that The Great Polarity War was now on. He made no changes with his puppy and everything remained as it had been, except that he was creating a very unhappy and damaged male pit bull dog. Maybe that was his intention all along or maybe he was just selfish or lazy. Many dog owners want a dog, yet they don't want the responsibility or to take the extra time and energy that dogs obviously require. At any rate, Rick's male pit bull puppy suffered every day and night—as we did—because of his continuous barking, crying, and howling.

June 13, 2000 I woke up at 3 AM from a horrible nightmare. In it, some young crazy unknown man with a gun was hunting Mom, my sister and me, and he actually did shoot each of us, which was a dream-first for me. I had never had a dream before where I had been killed in it so the nightmare was highly disturbing. I woke myself up from it easily, but certainly did not like what it symbolized and I felt as if I were still covered in sticky astral filth.

Unfortunately, my lifelong normal five-mile-wide psychic radar sensitivity was so scrambled and fried that I did not fully catch the potent symbolism in this nightmare. Hindsight answers so many questions and confusions doesn't it? Better late than never I suppose.

In August 2000, another gruesome landmark into our deepening and unending suffering arrived. Rick and Mike returned after a weekend away with what turned out to be Mike's full drum set. Evidently, it had been left behind when they moved in five months earlier. They had now retrieved it however and brought it home so Mike could play his drums at their house—which is so very close to our house. Mike put his drum set in an extra bedroom on our side of their house and pounded away for five hours straight this first day. Mom and I honestly could not believe that the entire horrible situation had made yet another quantum leap into increased misery for us. Mike however was having a grand old time, as he obviously loved playing his drums. I could relate having played Zills, Castanets, and Flamenco heel and footwork for many years when I lived elsewhere. However, I always made every physical effort to not be heard by my neighbors whereas Mike did just the opposite. Mike and Rick used his drums and drumming as intentional weapons against us.

Guess how well my shattered (ascension) nerves and insomnia coped with his nearly daily drumming? My sensitivities to all sounds, including my own physical voice, caused me actual physical pain. This particular ascension symptom became so extreme that I would often have to wear earplugs in stores when I had to do our normal shopping. The noises and voices in the stores made it almost impossible for me to think and shop, besides being physical painful, so I always carried a pair of earplugs in my purse. You can imagine how severe almost daily drumming for five, six, or more hours was with this level of hearing sensitivity anyway.

Mike's drumming constantly interfered with Mom's ability to just relax and listen to her favorite TV programs each day. She also could not rest and nap during the late afternoons when she needed to thanks to his endless drumming. Mike's frequent meth induced marathon drumming sessions almost drove us both over the edge many times.

After a few months of our having to suffer Mike pounding on his drums between two to ten hours a day, I called the police occasionally to complain about the excessive noise. The way Mike and Rick dealt with cops showing up at their door about the drumming noise was to threaten killing Mom and me if we ever called the police again. As the police officer would be driving out there driveway, Mike would just start drumming again and play for even longer as punishment for my having called the police on him. It was an insane, no-win situation for us because the police never did anything other than tell him to stop, which he never did.

September 2000 and Mom and I are driving home from town but we needed to go elsewhere first so we drove past our house. As we did, we both looked at it as we drove past and saw yellow all over it. To me it looked like it had been painted bright banana yellow. Mom said she had seen a huge bright yellow ball of energy over the house. (A year before this experience I had painted the house a darker tan color with white trim. It had never been yellow while Mom owned it.)

The other interesting anomaly was that we both realized we had seen our house minus the six-foot wood fence being there. In those few seconds as we drove past, we both had seen our house down to ground level meaning there was no fence blocking the view of it or the front yard. What Mom and I both saw that day was yet another typical portal house mystery. I speculated that what we had both seen might have been our house possibly many years in the future, when someone else owned it and had painted it an atrocious yellow and possibly removed the front fence. I had no other idea of what it was that we had both seen that day.

September 2000, Rick and Mike's sister, along with her four young kids, moved in with her brothers next-door. Just when you think it can't get any worse.

After a few weeks of Rick, Mike and their two dogs, their sister and her four young kids all living there together, Rick started spending as much time away from the house as he could. Evidently very young kids interfered with his lifestyle. My guess was that he was spending most of his time with boyfriends or other relatives after work, and if he could, he would spend the night with them as well. Rick's absence was only a minor improvement for us however. The sister and her kids were almost as bad as Rick and they were much louder than he was. It was a deeply miserable time for Mom and I and it simply escalated month after month.

One afternoon a month later, Mike and his sister were in the house alone while her four kids played outside. After a couple hours Mom and I heard the two youngest of her four kids (around age four and six) pounding repeatedly on the front door crying to be let in because they were hungry. After listening to the kid's door pounding and crying for about ten minutes, we went to our windows to see why they couldn't get into the house. As Mom and I watched the crying and very frustrated kids, we realized their mother had deliberately locked them outside because they could not open the front door. We could clearly see them turning the doorknob but it was locked so the kids screamed, cried, and pounded on the door as any child would have.

My first thought was that she and her brother Mike were probably getting high inside the house and that was why they locked the four kids outside. On the other hand, something even worse could have been going on in there that they did not want the kids to see or hear. At any rate, this locking all of her kids outside for an hour or longer happened at least once a month. I wanted to call Child Protective Services but I knew doing so would start WWIII. It would have probably gotten her kids taken away from her and possibly gotten both her and Mike arrested for drugs. I just was not capable of that level of negative battle with those types of lowly people and their extended family and friends and all they would have done to our property and us. I did not make the phone call and just hoped she and her damaged clan would move out as soon as possible.

October 22, 2000 Mom has a dream I found extremely interesting and informative. She told me about a dream she had that began with her seeing one large lamp with a smaller one on top of it. The dream shifted and an electrician entered and unfurled a large map in front of her. As he is showing Mom the map, he had his arm around her waist tightly and said, *"We are rewiring the whole city."* She said his hug felt like far too much pressure so she quickly woke herself up. My guess was that was his intention all along; give Mom this important message and then have her wake up quickly so she would remember it.

The second Mom repeated the electrician's sentence I automatically knew precisely what it meant. It was as if I had always known this information but it had been just below my conscious awareness. Having Mom tell me her dream triggered my deeper knowing about what it symbolized and meant at another level. I instantly knew that *"rewiring the whole city,"* meant our entire nervous systems and more were currently in an ongoing process of being *rewired* or upgraded to accommodate enormously higher and faster frequency energies, plus tremendously larger amounts of it running throughout our physical bodies constantly. As I am having this mini revelation about our being *rewired*, I saw a mind's eye symbolic version of an old lower 110 electrical wiring system being upgraded to new and greatly improved 220 lines throughout our bodies. It meant that our ability to house massive amounts of higher frequency Light energies within our physical bodies—our nervous systems, brains, cells and organs plus our nonphysical bodies—were being redesigned and *rewired* on all levels.

This information was extremely important to me because, for many years prior, I had been feeling a strange physical sensation like electrical energy literally vibrating deep inside my body. I would usually feel this sensation when I woke up in the middle of the night. Around 3:00 or 3:33 AM or so I would seemingly get pushed back into my physical body from the etheric level sleep state, and then lay there for a half-hour trying to figure out what that inner vibration I was feeling inside my body was. When I would get kicked out of Sleep Land around the same time each night, I always had the feeling that I'd had as much of this *rewiring* as I could safely cope with that night, and so, was deliberately shoved back into my physical body and not allowed to go back to sleep the rest of that night.

This inner vibrating sensation felt like a mild electrical current running deep inside my physical body. In the beginning years of this rewiring process it would run in perfectly timed increments of about four seconds vibrating or buzzing, followed by three seconds of no vibrating, then four seconds on again, and three off again. I would lay there in bed feeling and carefully counting, trying to discern what exactly it was that I was feeling. If I couldn't fall back to sleep anyway then I was going to lay there and pay attention and try to learn how this rewiring process worked. Thankfully, it never was physically painful but was a definite curiosity until Mom shared her dream. Hearing that one word—*"rewiring"*—made instant sense to me and was a very positive indicator of how much our bodies and brains were actually changing at nonphysical levels, and eventually all the way down into our physical bodies.

Over the years that I have been paying attention to this energetic body rewiring sensation, it has moved slowly from my lower body up into my solar plexus area, then my chest, and finally my head. Sometimes I would feel this inner vibrating only when it would stop. I hadn't realized it had been buzzing constantly until it stopped and went quiet and the sudden contrast almost knocked me over a few times. I have had this ongoing *rewiring* process since around 2000, and I still feel it, although it feels a great deal faster and less intense today. It feels like I am energetically spinning faster and quieter inside now (2009). This rewiring is an interesting sensation and one ascension symptom that actually is not painful.

October 30, 2000 and I had another of those intense dreams about my seemingly endless need to do inner house cleaning. The dirty details of all my personal lower *stuff, junk, wounds, traumas and fears* are not really what's important, only that I still had more inner emotional issues that required further attention. In this particular dream I needed to go back about twenty years and do further inner Denise house cleaning of more lingering emotional issues. I had dealt with much of this particular *stuff* years earlier, but there are multiple layers of it that require us going back repeatedly over the years or decades to get every little speck transmuted. This dream was yet another excursion back into some of my personal past emotional muck still living in my inner basement. This repeated process of excavating my own emotional issues, wounds, fears and angers to transmute every aspect of them was becoming second nature to me at this point. I was becoming an old pro at fearlessly diving in, transmuting, integrating and then releasing my old basement debris, which is the primary feature of our ascension process within Phase One.

November 2000 and the sister's husband in his Van and his male Husky dog arrive from out-of-state and moved in next-door. Now there are four adults, four kids and three dogs all living next-door in a three-bedroom mobile home on a quarter acre lot filled with expanding trash and household garbage that is never removed.

The BBQ grilling and drunken partying around their front door escalates to an even louder level now that the brother-in-law is living there too. Three very low vibrating, low consciousness, alcoholic, drug addicted males and one female, endless beer, pot, meth, and guns makes a volatile combination that you know will eventually explode all over the place. Before that point however, let the weekly outdoor drunken partying and noise increase a few more notches in intensity. These people never had their parties inside their house, but always outside around their front door, which of course faced our house and large windows. It was like witnessing intoxicated cave dwellers around a campfire yelling, grunting, and posturing back and forth with each other endlessly. It was repulsive and depressing and I certainly did not cope well with the lower energies and negativity day and night, year after year during the already most difficult period of my entire life.

Within hours of the sister's husband moving in, I came down with a severe fever and became even sicker than usual. Many times Mom and I would simply feel overpowered by these people's lower vibrating energies. It was often just too much for both of us to cope with or try to ignore. We would become sicker, more frustrated, more exhausted and beat-down feeling over the endless months of negativity so physically close to us, and often directed at us. It didn't matter what I tried, what I did or did not do, how much I and Mom both tried to ignore it all, or how much we did everything in our power at the time to energetically barricade against them and their lowly energies and consciousness. It felt like we were losing the polarity war because I was so sick and we both were so exhausted from the continuous assaults on the physical, psychological, and astral levels.

December 2000 and I am still dreaming about past emotional issues. Just how much icky, dark junk did I have stored down in my basement anyway? Quite a bit obviously! So, back into the emotional body and astral trenches once again to excavate more ex-husband junk, more beloved son crap, more me stuff, and plenty of *I'm a female struggling in a dark and lowly Patriarchal world* abuses and frustrations. Nothing new here except that my basement should be looking damned spiffy clean at this point.

2000 ends with my—unknown to me at the time—ascension sickness or *"ascension flu"* physical pains, fevers, mental fog and inability to focus, increasing insomnia, endless kundalini hot flashes, extreme emotional sensitivity, severe chemical sensitivity, and as if all that wasn't enough, the two very negative brothers and Co. living next-door causing continual noise and monumental misery. I would not wish this constant negative nightmare and never-ending pain and misery on my worst enemy. Just when you think it could not possibly get any worse it always did.

I was already deeply exhausted and in bad shape a full year before Rick and Mike moved in next-door in April 2000. With their constant onslaughts and negative energies, I actually thought at different points that I might not survive this astonishingly difficult (ascension) process under these extreme negative conditions. It was one thing being so dreadfully sick and in pain with no one else around to have to psychically, energetically, and physically deal with while in that extremely vulnerable ascension condition. It was an appallingly different and very dangerous situation having the *Dark Side of the Force* living only a few feet away, aiming at you constantly. The entire nightmarish chaos was nearly unbearable and I came very close during these years with the polarized neighbors to *the brink and falling over the edge.*

It was a situation of being the most physically, emotionally, mentally, psychically and energetically vulnerable and weak that you have ever been in your life, then you suddenly discover you are also within a battle of polarities that is archetypal in scope and size. I can't even digest food every day at this point, let alone do all of this concentrated polarity battling and polarity resolution work at the same time. This entire situation was so much more than just a couple of noisy low-life, alcoholic, sexually distorted brothers with a bunch of trashy junk living next-door to us. This was a highly focused and deliberate marathon Dark verses Light polarity battle over things I was not fully conscious of at that point because I *was* so profoundly sick, mentally confused and extremely exhausted the majority of the time.

Our everyday life and higher vibrating home sanctuary had been taken over by the brothers, and now their sister and her four kids, her husband and his dog, the continuous dog barking and now bloody dogfights, the weekly drunken parties outside until 2:00 AM, and Rick's choking BBQ smoke filling our house every other night. Let us not forget Mike's nerve-shattering, almost daily six hour or longer drum playing and stereo blasting meth-fueled sessions, in addition to their other endless noises and negativity. Just when I thought it could not get any worse, it always did.

Mike's drumming was something he did every time Rick left the house and went to do whatever he did with whatever male he could connect with. Rick would supply Mike with drugs and beer each morning, and then leave because he knew he would get high and drunk and then pound on his drums for the rest of the day, and that it would make our lives a living hell. I am sure this particular torture was something Rick saw to just for us. Mike was a dedicated, professional alcoholic and meth addict and he preferred living alone in the house, pounding on his drum set every day for hours in his intoxicated and oftentimes-psychotic world.

Rick on the other hand was extremely social and preferred being with other males constantly. He enjoyed having recreational fun and whatever else he did with men as often as possible. During the months while their sister and her noisy tribe of young kids lived there, Rick spent as much time away as he could. Once the sister moved out six months later, Rick and his endless stream of adult male boyfriends were back next-door again.

Rick was so damaged and energetically imbalanced that he could only relate to males on all levels. Anything female, feminine or nurturing was deeply repellent to him. Because of this he was addicted to one polarity—one-half of the old 3D battery of life and that was the male polarity—but only the especially low vibrating male side. Rick's primary addiction was sexual and not drug and/or alcohol related as his brother's was.

This combination of very low frequency, dark energy addictions both brothers had, effortlessly opened the energetic door (many years before they moved in next-door to us) to a demonic entity—a *female* demonic entity. Neither Rick nor Mike were possessed by this female demon in that stereotypical Hollywood movie sort of way. This female demon was energetically attached to Rick. He was her primary food source due to his very low frequency male sexual addictions and the specific dark energies they manifested. Mike and everyone else in their extended circle were her secondary level food group because they were not as potent and negatively charged as Rick was. She was Rick's nonphysical parasite who constantly fed off him and his continuous supply of low vibrating male sexual addictions, his violence and cruelty, and his lowly emotions and dark physical actions. This type of demonic parasite attachment is far more prevalent than people would ever guess or believe in the old lower third dimensional world.

Unfortunately for Mom and me, I was to wrecked then via my ascension process to sense or clairvoyantly see that Rick had a demon attached to him. For a year, I did not clairvoyantly see or psychically sense that Rick was a physical puppet for a nonphysical demonic entity and that she was the one who wholly controlled him, Mike, Rick's male sexual partners, their relatives, their friends, and even their two dogs. Everyone believed Rick was a powerful, dangerous and violent man who was lord and master over his lowly tribe of flies. The truth however was that Rick was merely a slave and puppet to this nonphysical female demon that controlled him, his life, and most everyone in it. Rick's ego thought it was all him of course, but it was the female demonic entity who controlled, directed, manipulated and empowered him.

The entire situation was beyond belief and the absolute worst and most dangerous time of my entire life considering my already profoundly weakened and psychically vulnerable condition. Even worse than all this was the fact that I was unable to completely detect or perceive the other layers and polarity issues and the negative entity controlling Rick, Mike and Company and why. I had been a physical and psychic target the entire time because I was a Lightworker and did not realize it for all of 2000. Because I was in a tremendously weakened condition at that time, and my clairvoyant abilities were not what they normally were, I did not sense or see the bigger polarized picture and all that was unfolding and why.

One day in early 2001, I had been outside working in the yard on the east side next to the large empty field. At that time the field was full of dry waist-high wheat crop. It was a quiet, tan colored sea of dried crop swaying gently in the warm afternoon breezes. This particular day I first heard and then saw something moving inside the crop, heading in my direction. I stopped what I had been doing to watch and wait to see whatever neighbor's dog was running through the large field. I stood right at the edge of our property and this large field, watching the tops of the dried crop shake and part from the movements of a dog moving unseen within it. There was a forty-foot bare dirt area around a water pipe directly in front of me in this huge field, and when the dog finally exited into this cleared area of the field I would easily be able to see it so I stood there and waited.

After about a minute the dog reached this open dirt area, trotted out fifteen feet or so into it, and then saw me standing there watching him. He stopped as soon as he saw me and the two of us stared at each other for a good minute. The big shock however was that it was not a dog. I did not know what it was because I had never seen anything like it before.

It was the size of a large dog but it was the colors and shape of its ears that really stood out as unique. It had amazingly large, tall, and rounded ears. I had never seen any dog with such large upright rounded ears like this animal had. My first thought was that it was a Hyena but its back, hips and legs were more like dogs.

It had a very short coat with black, white, and dark orange colored patches all over it. Again, I had never seen any dog with those colors before. Being a cat person these coat colors immediately reminded me of Calico cats, but even that was not correct.

This animal and I stood staring at each other long enough for me to get a clear look at his entire body, head, and coat. He looked very strong and powerful but I knew it was not a dog or a hyena and that he was not from anywhere around here! What that meant I did not fully know at the time and it would take six more years before I discovered what exactly he was and where he had come from.

Six years in the future I would watch a TV program one evening about wild dogs that live only in certain areas of South Africa. These wild dogs were the first and only animals I had ever seen that looked exactly like what I had seen exit the large crop field next to our southern California portal house in early 2001. I learned from watching the TV program that these animals are called, *Wild Painted African Dogs.* I was dumbstruck watching this TV show and seeing many of the identical creatures running wild through the dry South African brush. I could not believe it. We'd had another physical being enter through the portal at Mom's house and land from another continent and possible timeline, and trot right up to about twenty feet in front of me. This experience was exactly like Mom's eighteenth-century man encounter in the 1970s. In these cases, the eighteenth-century man and the Wild African Painted Dog each saw Mom and me as clearly as we saw them. Time, location and distance obviously mean nothing in areas where old 3D portals exist and anything can travel through them evidently.

After about a minute of this dog and I staring at each other, he turned abruptly and headed back along the same path he had come in on. I watched him disappear back into the dried crop and continued watching the tops of the crop shake and part as he trotted back through it. After he was about fifty feet deep into the crop again, the moving and parting crop abruptly stopped. The wild Painted African Dog had disappeared from the middle of a dried crop field in 2001 SoCal, and hopefully returned to his natural home and timeline in South Africa. I didn't move for another ten minutes because I wanted to see if the dried crop moved again or if something else might come wandering through the portal and pop out in front of me. Nothing else happened and the wild Painted Dog from South Africa never reappeared.

It was shortly after my portal encounter with the Painted African Dog that Mom and I heard of a husband and wife's experiences with something similar in another town. We had gone to a metaphysical bookstore in this nearby town and got talking about anomalies, time-slips, and event's bleeding through into other timelines and such with the storeowner. It was then he told us an amazing story a local couple had recently shared with him.

This other couple lived in the same town were the bookstore was located, and one morning as the husband and wife went around opening their curtains to greet a new day, they opened them to see that their 2001 southern California town was gone and had been replaced with something very ancient. The couple carefully described what they both had seen standing in front of their large living room picture window to the bookstore owner. They told him that it was a dense tropical landscape filled with huge roaming dinosaurs!

The most disturbing thing about all this to me was not that it was dinosaurs but that it lasted for a half-hour! Can you imagine watching dinosaurs feeding and tromping around in some prehistoric landscape out your home's front window *for a half-hour?* In both of our portal experiences with another human and an animal, our encounters only lasted a few minutes. I cannot image a half-hour of dinosaurs, but that's just me. Wild Painted Dogs from South Africa, ETs, negative entities, men from other countries and centuries yes—but thirty minutes of dinosaur viewing out my living room window was way too much for me! I would have worried the scene was not going to shift back to my timeline. Funny what we each find frightening and beyond our ability to cope with.

It was very interesting for Mom and me hearing these other people's portal or time-jump, time-slip, ancient dinosaur experience. It told me that not only were there multiple portals open in our SoCal area at that time, but that most likely there were other people experiencing very similar anomalies, timeline distortions and manifestations to what Mom and I had been experiencing over the past two decades in that particular area. I found that possibility exceedingly interesting and telling.

January 2001 and my (ascension process) sickness and pains increased and were made excessively worse thanks to the negative neighbors, their continuous noise, drumming, dog barking and overall darkness. I honestly did not know how I was going to survive another year of what I was living through because of my D 1 47 transformational process plus all of them and their endless negative energies and nerve shattering racket. It was an exceedingly dark and difficult time and one that just kept growing darker and more negative each month.

During 2000, I had to make a few phone calls to the county Animal Control office and the police about Mike drumming for six or more hours nearly every day, and then their dog barking constantly when they would leave. The male pit bull repeatedly got his chain tangled in junk or trash in the yard and would cry and howl because he couldn't move at all. An already bad situation would often become significantly worse because the growing pit bull puppy would get into some type of trouble from being tied up every day. If he was not tangled up in something, he could at least move around between fifteen to twenty feet. If his chain became tangled, he couldn't move at all, and there were many times he came very close to hanging and choking himself as he struggled to get free.

In severe cases, I would call the Animal Control office to have them come out and free Rick's tangled, screaming puppy. The officer would leave them a notice about the excessive barking and that they had a certain number of days to solve the problem. Nothing ever improved no matter what the Animal Control officers told them or threatened them with. Neither did anything the police did about the many other things the brothers did to our property and us. These people did not care about their own dogs or anyone else and they simply focused their energies and hate at us for complaining about their actions and inactions. It was a profoundly difficult, painful, dangerous and frustrating situation.

The brothers had also taken to stacking their household garbage against the fence and as close to our front door as they could get it. Rick and Mike stacked a 5x10 foot pile of trash and garbage against our fence that sat there for about a year. The stench of stale beer baking in the sun came wafting into our house every day, which was nauseating to me. This maneuver to cause us more misery also caused mice, ants, flies, bugs and plenty of wicked stink all the time so I eventually reported him to the Health Department. Rick and Mike's actions did not even make sense and they really only caused themselves more problems and expenses— besides making our lives miserable too. Were they really *that* stupid? Were they that desperate to do illegal things simply to hurt us, yet would eventually come back around to them that they would then would have to pay repeated fines for?

People like Rick, Mike, and Johnny and Co. often have outstanding warrants for their arrest, no Drivers License because of DUI's and other legal situations just waiting to catch up with them. You would think that alone would make them want to be as silent and invisible as they could, yet, they would usually do everything in their power to get you to call the police or other authorities on them. This was often how the police discovered those warrants and other longstanding legal problems. How many actual firing brain cells does it take to figure out how to be a semi-decent Bad Guy anyway? Obviously more than our neighbors had, yet it never solved any of these ongoing problems for us. When you have hidden demonic assistance directing multiple people and situations, much more can happen than would have if the brothers were on their own.

As the years progressed, it had become amazingly physically painful to leave our small property to do the necessary food shopping and other chores each month. While Mom and I were at home or on our property, we existed within much higher vibrating energies so the physical pains were less—not gone, but less severe. However, the second we left our property and drove towards town my body felt like I had instantly gained thirty pounds and was under extreme pressure just from going back into lower vibrating energies *out there in the world.* My diaphragm would instantly bloat making it difficult to even take a deep breath. My entire spine felt like it was being crushed from all angles simultaneously simply because I had *gone back down energetically* into the so-called normal, but much lower vibrating world.

Guess which businesses caused me the most acute body pressure and pain? Banks. The energies inside banks were the lowest, densest energies, and I absolutely hated having to go into any bank. When I did, it felt like I was literally being crushed from the density. The unseen energies and emotions connected to money in general are so low vibrating that it was nearly unbearable to be around if you were energetically vibrating faster.

Our individual (ascension) symptoms would amplify whenever we left our higher vibrating home and property to do the necessary shopping. Body aches and pains, mental confusions, irritability, vision changes and blurring, seeing a fog or white mist everywhere, hearing and inner ear pressure changes, nausea, dizziness, severe headaches, spine pains and pressures, excessive inner heat, emotional sensitivity, severe chemical sensitivity, sudden ice pick stabbing bone pains, and greatly increased intolerance and rage. The bottoms of my feet would become so hot it was painful and nearly impossible to stand in place. Because of this one symptom I couldn't wear closed shoes for many years, not that this was a great loss because I have always preferred going barefoot or wearing flip-flop sandals anyway.

The fun and satisfaction we both used to experience shopping and searching for specific things or buying supplies so I could build something for the house or yard, quickly altered into extreme physical pains and difficulty that literally made me sicker than I was while at home. I had never had any problems with chemical sensitivity prior, but when I started my D 1 47 (ascension) process I instantly became ultrasensitive to all chemicals in nearly everything. Needless to say, at the very end of the patriarchal Piscean Age, chemicals are in just about everything.

The chemicals in foods, drinks, cleaning supplies, fabric softeners, laundry soaps, carpets, furniture, paints, chemicals in woods and building supplies, chemicals in shopping stores and public buildings, tires, oils and all automotive products made me profoundly ill. This became so severe that I hated having to take the car in for oil changes because breathing the toxic petrochemical tire and oil smells would make me terribly sick for days, not to mention swollen, red-faced, and red-eyed too. My physical appearance would worsen because of these lower vibrating chemical poisons and how severely they affected me. People would actually stare at me all hot and red-faced as I hurriedly pushed my shopping cart through the stores struggling to get what I needed as quickly as possible and get back outdoors again. It was insanely horrible physically and emotionally and it lasted for many miserable years.

This chemical sensitivity became so severe that as I entered most stores and my body encountered the chemicals within the thousands of products in it, the whites of my eyes would instantly turn red, not just bloodshot, but entirely red. My face would also turn red and the skin on my cheekbones would actually blister right in front of shoppers and staff while we were talking. (I think some of these shoppers and staff wondered if I was going to spontaneously combust right there in the store before them!) The bottoms of my feet would become so hot and painful that I would have to take my flip-flop sandals off so I could walk barefoot on the cool tile floor. I was also having monster hot flashes constantly. The combination of severe chemical sensitivity and hot flashes seemed to trigger frequent bladder spasms, which is just a polite way of saying I would suddenly almost pee my pants in public. During the cold winter months when the stores and businesses would turn their heaters on, my chemical sensitivity was increased tremendously. The heated air seemed to activate the chemicals inside the stores, which of course affected me even worse. Air condition greatly reduced the chemical situation I discovered over the years.

I would be shopping, struggling to mentally focus on why I was in the damned store in the first place, when I would have a hot flash and instantaneously and uncontrollably almost urinate because my bladder muscle contracted wildly. As if all this weren't enough fun in public, my mental focus would simply stop dead in its tracks also. Because you cannot hide or fake your way through severe kundalini rising hot flashes, I would be reduced to shaking and sweating profusely in a corner of the store, trying to not urinate on the spot, and survive the intense kundalini hot flash while going into a mild state of shock and have my mind literally stop working. I simply could not think or function for a few minutes while this cascade of chemical toxins and energetic transmutations overwhelmed me while in public. Sometimes I would start crying because I could not remember why I was even in the store. In a few cases, I couldn't remember which city I was in or what decade it was. I literally hot flashed my way right out of linear time and consciousness! On top of everything else, the noises and people's energies were so terribly amplified, nerve shattering and overwhelming to me as well. My vanity and desire to be invisible while out in public was shot-to-hell due to these acute ascension symptoms and my extreme psychic sensitivities.

I remember using a lip balm with SPF 15 sunscreen and those chemicals left a rash on and around my lips for well over a month. That certainly taught me to not color carelessly *outside the lines* with my lip balm like I usually did! I was forced to stop using products with chemicals in them and go as natural as I could. I certainly did not do this because I was on some noble health kick—I did it simply because the products and foods where making me more sick and toxic than I was already.

Being a Wanderer I was used to being in stealth mode or energy camouflage mode most of the time. I did not want to be seen or felt by other people, and I was good at being rather invisible and energetically quiet while out in public. With my severe ascension symptoms that lasted for many years, I suddenly became highly visible during the absolute worst and most painful and shattering time of my life, and I hated it. Believe me when I say that I did look *almost* as bad as I felt. It was no wonder strangers in stores stared at me. What a total contrast from having them stare at me as a polished dancer and entertainer. Polarity resolution on all levels.

February, March, and April 2001 were just more of the same. Every other day of Mike's methamphetamine drumming for four to eight hours, continuous dog barking every time the brothers did leave, continuous negative energies, ongoing ascension illness and pains plus exhaustion and deepening frustrations at not being able to solve any of these ongoing problems with these neighbors and noise. There was never a moment's peace or quiet since the brothers moved in. If they were home, it was noisy—when they left home, the male pit bull barked incessantly until they returned, which was usually between twelve to fifteen hours later. The only time it was *physically* quiet was when they were asleep.

It got to the sad point with their barking dog where either Mom or I would go to our back door, open it, and yell at their dog to shut up. He would stop barking for a blessed five seconds, and then start again. I tried feeding him dog treats, giving him dog toys and dog chews in an attempt to keep him from barking constantly. Nothing I tried worked. I must admit that occasionally yelling at the top of my lungs at their dog to shut up was the only release Mom or I had with any of their constant tortures. Yelling at the dog to shut up was stupid to do, but sure as hell felt good at the time.

I remember one afternoon, after a year or so of this one male dog's constant barking, realizing something rather strange. Rick always tied this not neutered male pit bull in his backyard, but he always left the older female pit bull loose. The male puppy, who was quickly becoming an adult dog, would see the female dog doing whatever she wanted, like jumping their fence and running throughout the neighborhood, and he would lose his little puppy mind when she'd leave. He would cry and howl and scream in protest at being tied up while she could run lose and even leave their property by jumping their four-foot tall chain link fence. It was so cruel watching and listening to that male dog's misery and increasing anger. As much as I hated the dog for his constant barking and making our lives profoundly miserable, it was obvious he was deeply miserable too.

One day I discovered something very interesting about this dogs barking however. I had reached my limit of listening to him bark for hours that day and had gotten up and walked to my backdoor to open it and yell at him. As I reached for the doorknob, he magically stopped barking precisely *before* my hand touched the doorknob! This weird anomaly had happened repeatedly for a few months before I fully noticed that the dog would stop barking at the same second my hand reached for the doorknob to open it to yell at him to shut up. Now, how did that dog—tied up next door on the other side of a six-foot tall wood fence—know that I had gotten up from my back bedroom, walked down the hall, into the kitchen and up to the backdoor for the very reason that I could not take his constant barking any longer? How in the world would he know to stop barking at the exact second my hand reached for the doorknob? What was this highly annoying abnormality?

Once I finally made the connections and realized it was something that happened regularly and was not just a strange coincidence, I mentioned it to Mom. She told me she had had the same identical thing happen every time she would get out of her chair in the living room, walk into the kitchen, and just as she reached for the doorknob, the damned dog would stop barking as if he could see or hear her. He could not of course, but this is what was happening to both of us and it made no physical sense whatsoever.

This mystery continued until I discovered that once I had reached the point where I decided to walk outside to either yell at or talk to the dog through the fence, that alone would cause the dog to instantly stop barking. Just my thinking about doing something in connection to him would cause the dog to stop barking briefly. This was impossible and something else was at work than just me thinking something or Mom or I reaching for the doorknob. That dog was not telepathic.

Something else was causing the dog to stop barking at precisely the same second Mom or I would have a thought and/or physically reach for our doorknob. Not actually physically touch the doorknob mind you, which the dog could have possibly heard, but before we physically touched it.

I experimented multiple times and eventually realized that something else was causing Rick's male pit bull to bark constantly, also to stop barking at precisely the correct second Mom or I had reached the absolute end of our tolerance over his barking—then start barking again two seconds after we'd gone back to our chairs and sat down! This happened to both of us dozens of times and it hinted that something else was manipulating Rick's dog to bark, and then to be quiet when Mom and I were doing certain things inside of our house. This happened when there was no one next-door so it was not the brothers or relatives doing anything with the male pit bull. No, *something else* was manipulating that dog and it was not anything or anyone physical or human, but demonic.

At some point in early 2001, I began experiencing another phenomenon in the middle of the night. This would wake me up, and as usual, I would look at the clock. It was always minutes before or minutes after 3:00 AM and this anomaly would last for as long as forty-five minutes.

What would wake me were the very loud sounds of what I thought was a diesel truck engine idling a couple of blocks down the street. I would get very angry that some truck driver had left his truck running while he was doing whatever it was that he was doing. Of course, that was what I *believed* this sound was and that it was caused by some inconsiderate truck driver at 3 AM. After lying in bed listening to this damned noisy engine idling for thirty to forty-five minutes in the middle of the night repeatedly, one night I put my clothes on and went outside and into the street to locate this truck that kept waking me up every few nights. I discovered that there was no truck, no cars, nothing running, idling, flying overhead, or even driving down the road.

After actually going outside at 3:10 AM to see for myself and discovering that there was no truck running down the street, I finally realized this business was not physical. The other anomaly that always accompanied the diesel truck engine idling sound was a sickening burning odor. It smelled like burning tires or rubber, mixed in with some other strange burning chemical odor I had never encountered before. It was a horrible stench and would last for as long as I heard the idling engine sounds.

Typically, the sound would wake me up and I would automatically glance at the clock. Many times, would get out of bed and look out my open window to the west where the sound was coming from. I never saw any vehicles even drive past the house, but by this point, I would smell that distinctive odor of what smelled like burning tires or rubber mixed in with other unusual burning chemical smells. I would lay in bed for a half-hour or longer listening to this sound and smelling the horrible smells and trying to analyze the entire strange business.

One night I realized that it also sounded like this idling diesel engine sound was possibly up in the air and not down on the road as I had first thought. Because I did not know what this sound and smell was or what they possibly indicated, I would simply lay there in bed listening, smelling, and analyzing it all very carefully. I was very aware of a negative heaviness and stillness in the air every time I heard and smelled this particular phenomenon but really did not know what it was. I experienced this sound and burning odors in my bedroom about twice a month for over a year.

(It was about six years later, well after we had sold the portal house and moved, that I happened to watch a movie and a couple of paranormal shows on TV based on true events about certain people who had smelled this same terrible burning chemical smell. The sounds I heard were not discussed, but in all cases, other people who experienced this same horrible burning odor, did so when a demonic entity was present and they were under attack. This movie and TV programs even mentioned that 3:00 AM was significant and indicated the person was under attack from a demonic entity. Live and learn!)

In May 2001, an Asian man bought the twenty-some acre field next-door to us on the east side. Mom and I were incredibly surprised because we never thought that field would be populated with people. Over the decades it had become our field, our empty buffer zone of protection. It was our extended portal area where the wild South African Painted Dog had come through and where many of the sky tubes of light had appeared. In our minds it had become an extension of our property and was a gloriously empty space where humans and noise could not live. It had become a much-loved empty area to us and we were shocked to learn the property had been purchased.

After the Asian man—whom I will call Jake—bought the field, he had it ploughed and a six-foot tall chain link fence installed all around. He then had two massive professional greenhouses built parallel to our backyard area. After the two greenhouses were finished and operational, he had a new mobile home brought in and set up in front of the two large greenhouses close to the paved street.

Over the months we got to know Jake better, and despite our language barriers and communication difficulties, we became polite and respectful friends and next-door neighbors. Jake, his wife, and two high-school aged children did not move into the new mobile home as I thought they would, but remained living in another large city near Los Angles. Jake would occasionally drive down to oversee the set-up of his latest nursery business, his two huge greenhouses, and the landscaping of the empty area in front of his house. Jake was talented in the art of creating more money for he and his family and I learned a lot just from paying attention to his attitude and expectations. He lived and breathed making money, and therefore, that is exactly what he experienced. I suspect kind and gentle Asian Jake was a multimillionaire.

My ancient Chinese past life self, Jade One (see *The Temple of Master Hotei: A Unique Past Life Memory*), was a master gardener himself and those past life talents were both visible and energetically felt at Mom's portal house property. Before Jake bought the field next door I had completely re-landscaped every square inch of Mom's entire property. I hauled countless tons of fill-dirt, gravel, edging bricks, flagstones for walkways, boulders and smaller rocks, and planted numerous flowering vines, plants, ornamental grasses and trees. I had successfully turned Mom's property into something akin to Master Hotei's ancient temple garden and I sensed Jake felt or recognized something Asian, ancient, and sacred in what I had created thanks to me and my past life self, Jade One. Jake had statues of

Master Hotei—the Laughing Buddha—in his house and cars, which made me smile and my heart expand with happiness.

Jake and I always automatically bowed to each other and respected each other very much. I know my female Caucasian self was probably a slight confusion to Jake, but at a deeper level, we both respected each other's love and passion for plants, beautiful gardens, and Master Hotei. To Jake, the Laughing Buddha as a mythical and benevolent prosperity figure. To me, Master Hotei was a fully remembered past life ascended Master and my personal teacher and deeply loved friend. The strange link Jake and I both had to this particular ancient Chinese Master was enough of a connection for us in current time, even though Jake knew nothing about my actual past life with Master Hotei, the Laughing Buddha.

After months of setting up his new nursery business in the field next to us, Jake hired a local man to be the groundskeeper at his new place. This man— who I will call Juan—lived a couple blocks away and he worked six days a week starting at seven in the morning. Juan was married with two young school age daughters. It was a decent situation for a few months, but eventually Juan came under the influence of the female demon attached to Rick on the other (west) side of us. When this happened, Juan instantly became a new tool for her to use to try to get at me—but more about that later.

⭐ It did not take long for the police to turn against me as opposed to honestly and legally dealing with Rick, Mike and Co. It turned out that the majority of times I called the police because of something Rick and Mike were doing, they usually turned on me and dumped the responsibility back on Mom and me for what these neighbors were doing to us. They simply refused to do their jobs and deal with the crazy alcoholic and drug addicted men with guns, and have to fill out paperwork, when they could just kick a couple of older women living alone in the teeth instead. No paperwork that way, plus Mom and I presented no real threat or risk to them whereas the crazy armed and impaired males next-door did. Nevertheless, that is often how this one works in the old lower patriarchal world.

To show just how severe this police situation really was, one time Mike, Rick, and Johnny were all drunk outside having their version of fun when Mike decided he would fire his gun at us. Actually, I was surprised this had not happened sooner. Because we knew they were drunk and/or high and that their crazy actions were escalating, when we heard the loud gunshot sound, Mom and I hit the floor. Mike and the other two were only a few feet away from our house laughing and shooting towards our house over our six-foot tall wood fence. I quickly called the police and told the dispatcher that our neighbors had fired a gun at our house and were drunk. The dispatcher asked me if they had guns, (I kid you not) and I repeated what I had told him the first time. Within minutes, numerous police cars showed up next door. Evidently, the sentence *gun fired at us* is something they have to pay attention to, or so I hoped.

Seeing a small army of police arrive and knowing Mike had fired his gun at our house and that all of them were drunk, I thought surely we would finally see some results from the police. They went inside and we could hear yelling, cussing and more yelling, but amazingly, no one was placed into the back of a police car. No one was arrested—not even Mike for firing a gun at our house. (Very well done Miss Demon!)

Afterwards, three of the police officers came over to our house, commiserated with us and wholeheartedly agreed that we were indeed in a very bad situation having neighbors like them. After that little bullshit speech one of the cops suddenly turned on me and made the whole thing my fault for not getting restraining orders against all of them and for not make a citizen's arrest and so on. There it was in all its lowly glory—officers of the law not willing to do their jobs but shame, blame, and demean the female victims for being victims! That was the absolute last time I called the police for anything. I knew it was never going to get real or honest with them and that I needed to find another way of dealing with the ongoing situation because the officers of the law were simply another aspect of the problem.

I had done what I personally needed to do, which was to face my fears of police and other powerful authority figures and call them a few times over a three-year period. I worked through my personal issues concerning police and having to deal with them, but when Mom and I realized they were simply an extension of the negative neighbors, I was finished with them all. I had faced my fears and learned what I personally was supposed to concerning this dysfunctional and distorted legal system, and based upon how the majority of them treated our situation and us, I was done. Once again, I had to learn that the answers, solutions, and power did not exist outside of me. The only person that was going to *rescue* me and change my situation was me.

☆☆
☆☆ May 4, 2001 there were more ugly threats screamed at us from Rick's boyfriend-of-the-moment and Mike next door. After repeated tries over the past year of calling the police for help, I was absolutely at the end of my emotional rope with the entire miserable situation. I literally wanted to run away and live under a freeway ramp somewhere! I simply could not take much more of this level of constant negativity from such

horrible people living so physically close to us while I was going through the absolute worst years of my ascension process. It was all just too much and I was very close to my real breaking point.

This particular day more threats were yelled at us from another of Rick's boyfriends. This was Rick's modus operandi; he would pitch his hate, anger, and revenge ideas to whoever would listen to him in an attempt to get them to do his dirty work for him. This way, if something went wrong Rick could claim he had nothing to do with any of it and sell-out his friends, boyfriends, brother, sister or other relatives on the spot. Rick often manipulated people into doing cruel and illegal things for him, and they were usually stupid enough or intimidated enough to do them.

For some reason this particular day's ridiculous negativity really got to me. I was utterly spent and could take no more. Later that evening in the dark in my bedroom, I lit incense and finally even thought to get serious about taking back some of my power. My having been so physically sick and psychically open for so long had helped me forget I was naturally a very powerful Lightworker and person that already knew exactly what to do to psychically and etherically protect myself, our house, and property from a higher nonphysical level.

This forgetting business is a common trick negative entities, demons, and energies often use against us, and unfortunately it usually works exceedingly well. Negatively focused beings work on us to forget that we are naturally empowered beings of Light and that we have a way out of the lower frequency Darkness, pain, and chaos we sometimes find ourselves briefly stuck within. I have been taught this painful and dangerous lesson a few times over the decades by a couple different demonic beings. If they cannot kill you or drive you mad, then the next tactic is to wear you down to the point that you forget you even have options or the power to change the situation or even protect yourself. It is a common negative maneuver used by nonphysical (and physical) negative lower frequency beings as well as living humans.

This night I did a simple and old but highly effective etheric ritual of drawing a large pentagram of light in each of the four directions and stating certain things and creating some higher frequency energy borders that simply cannot be crossed by lower negative beings and energies. It was basic Occultism 101 and something I had known for decades, but astonishingly, had never even thought to do from the first moment these demonically controlled idiots moved in next-door. The real con-job was that I did not psychically sense that any of them were demonically controlled, only that they were lowly negative idiots, which was the demon's clever doing.

Demonic or negatively charged and focused entities prefer to do their work unseen, unheard, and in total secrecy because they can accomplish so much more this way and for far longer than if they revealed themselves to humans. Most of these demonic entities or negatively focused beings will not possess humans for this reason. They want to remain hidden to feed and do as much damage for as long as they can, and so, they remain invisible and overshadow certain humans by energetically attaching themselves to them. They do not embody or possess them but remain energetically attached to them like etheric parasites that are able to manipulate and direct their human host's thoughts, emotions, actions, their life and very reality.

The demon feeds off its human host and the host's friends, family, and co-workers if they too exist within a lower range of energies and consciousness. If the frequency range all around is a vibrational match, then everyone connected to the primary human host is also at risk and usually overshadowed and manipulated at some point as well. These demonic dark entities are just like physical viruses, except they are nonphysical, and they effortlessly and repeatedly jump from one human host to another and another and back again, faster and easier than we pass around physical viruses, colds, the flu or other such physical germs and diseases. People can be physically, emotionally, and/or mentally sick. People can also become etherically or astrally infected and sick too but most people are unaware of this level of reality. Clever and determined demons and negatively focused entities take full advantage of this fact.

This particular night I finally became mentally clear enough to realize I even needed to do this old familiar pentagram ritual. I called in higher positive help and assistance as powerfully as I was capable of considering my long-term exhausted and weakened condition. I did this visualization and creating ritual in my bedroom first, then went into the living room, lit another candle and more incense, and did the whole thing again and even more forcefully. It felt magnificent to be doing something energetically creative after a year of dodging bullets and beer cans and negative psychic energies. I had finally reconnected with my ancient warrior self and it felt fabulous.

After doing the two pentagram rituals, I went to bed and had a couple of positive physical body reactions. First, my Heart chakra fluttered open again, which blasted right up into my nasal passage and into my Brow chakra. This too felt grand after such intense and lengthy negative energies beating the hell out of me for over a year.

The next morning when Mom and I got up we both noticed how much better we felt physically. Considering Mom did not even know I had done the pentagram rituals the night before, this was a very positive indication of how severe things had actually been psychically. The night before Mom had a horrible nightmare, which was incredibly uncommon for her. Not so for me however being a psychic sensitive Lightworker, but it told me that Mom was either going through some personal inner house cleaning then too, and/or she was under some form of negative psychic attack as well.

May 5, 2001 I dug out and dusted off my adored twenty-seven-year-old copy of Dion Fortune's excellent book, *Psychic Self-Defense* (1930). I scanned through it again after a decade of not opening it and quickly found her psychic protection and banishing rituals again, scribbled some notes, and brushed up on the rituals to get myself as prepared as I was capable of at the time. Because Mom and I had woke up feeling so improved, I finally realized we both had been under some level of psychic attack since the Brothers Demented first moved in back in April 2000. I did not sense what I was picking up was anything more than my being very psychically sensitive and struggling to tolerate these lowly, negative neighbors living so physically close to us while going through my ongoing transformational (ascension) process. Was I in for one monumental awakening however.

I did a second etheric layer of banishing and pentagram rituals in the dark of the living room on this second evening. I lit incense and one candle and activated my ancient Light Warrior self. I proceeded to build this second night's layer of psychic etheric protections to the four directions, and they were far more clairvoyantly visible and energetically potent than the first night's layer was. I was back, focused again, and was doing the only thing I could at that point which was to create powerful energy borders and *finally* protect myself, Mom, our cats, our home and property.

Once finished I could easily feel the house and property humming with higher golden-white Light and Fire energies and I could clairvoyantly see the four huge pentagrams of light permanently suspended in the air at each of the four directions. I had banished first, then sealed off our property along the property lines on all four sides, and then created and positioned four giant pentagrams of higher Light at each of the four directions. I could clairvoyantly see that this second evening's ritual had built-up substantial etheric energy and potency to prevent any negative energy from getting in or reaching us.

A couple of hours after I finished psychically protecting our entire place, I went to bed around 11 PM. No more than a half-hour later, I unexpectedly experienced a profoundly important face-to-face etheric meeting. I had been laying there in the dark as I do each night for a while, when all the sudden a nonphysical entity deliberately revealed itself clairvoyantly to me. I was not thinking about Rick, Mike, or the psychic protection rituals I had done earlier that evening. Actually, I had been thinking about yard work I was planning to do the next day when this ghastly female demon intentionally revealed herself to me clairvoyantly for the first and only time.

It was female, and yet had no obvious external features to indicate she was. Nonetheless, there was absolutely no doubt in my mind or heart as I viewed, and psychically scanned, the demonic creature that she was indeed female. I saw her clairvoyantly as slightly transparent and superimposed over Rick's actual physical body. It was startling how similar they looked despite Rick not being physically ugly. Rick was semi-decent looking, but this female demon was hideous, and yet they were a perfect match and vibrational fit with each other. She was Rick's nonphysical demon parasite that fed off his endless male sexual activities and addictions, his fears, hates, wounds, darkness and violence. She absolutely controlled Rick in all ways and had for numerous years, long before they moved in next-door to us.

Suddenly, here she was, intentionally revealing herself to me clairvoyantly literally a couple of hours after I finally got my head together enough to think of psychically protecting our home and myself! Rick and Mike had been living next-door to us since April 2000, but it only took two nights worth of my doing etheric protection rituals for this demon to discover I had made it more energetically difficult for her to access our home and me. Her way of dealing with my having done that was to reveal herself to me. It was a very bold move on her part and I was terribly glad she did.

What I clairvoyantly saw was her standing with her right shoulder pressed up against our physical wood fence that separated our property from the rental property next-door where Rick and Mike lived; exactly where I had created and hung a large etheric pentagram on that west side. Her head was turned, facing me directly, while her right shoulder remained pressed against our fence. I could only see her and Rick's right shoulder, partial neck, full head and face above our six-foot tall wooden fence. I am not saying Rick or the demon were over six-foot tall because he/she wasn't, only that that was the image the demon clairvoyantly revealed.

As I mentioned, she was transparent and superimposed over Rick's physical body, but I could clearly see her features and certainly feel her immense hatred and repulsion of me. As I watched her glaring at me, snarling, and flashing her numerous tiny pointed teeth, a thousand subtle mysteries and questions I'd had for the past year tumbled perfectly into place. In that minute or so of her deliberately revealing herself to me clairvoyantly, I finally realized what had in fact been going on with Rick, Mike, their sister, Johnny, the dogs, the many drug addicted and alcoholic friends and relatives, Rick's many boyfriends, the police, the animal control officers—all of them. The entire insane lowly mess and chaos all suddenly fell into place and made perfect sense to me. Rick's female demon was—and always had been—running the entire show with all of them and this was not going to be changing or ending anytime soon. She was letting me know all this and more, and that the Polarity War had just shifted to a much more intense and dangerous level.

All I could think back at her in those outside-of-time clairvoyant moments was that at least the repulsion we felt for each other was mutual. I was glad she found me just as revolting and disgusting as I found her and Rick and Co. She was actually doing me a huge favor by revealing herself after a year of invisible torment and attacks. I telepathed that I was not intimidated by her growling, sneering, and ugly teeth flashing gestures and then she vanished. She did not go anywhere or leave, she simply returned to stealth mode again after intentionally letting me know whom I was actually dealing with. I knew things would become far more dangerous now that she had clairvoyantly revealed herself to me. Just when you think it cannot possibly get any worse...

Fig. 3.14. The Demon

Rick's female demon had numerous tiny, razor-sharp teeth, just a lipless slit for a mouth, large dark eyes that exuded nothing but hate and a dangerous malice, very thin sparse strands of dead looking hair, medium to dark gray skin, and no nose or ears. The most dominant feature was a large round raised brand of some symbol with plenty of scar tissue that nearly covered her entire forehead. It looked to me like she had been branded on the Brow chakra area of her forehead and that brand produced a very large and ugly raised scar of some ancient unknown symbol. The symbol branded into her forehead extended about two and a half to three inches from the surface of her forehead. It reminded me of those unpleasant looking butt or sitting pads that chimpanzee's have, and I do apologize for the repulsive visual I just shoved into your mind's eye! As disgusting as that sounds, it was similar to the demon's scar tissue brand but with some unrecognizable symbol pattern in it.

This same night I had gone to bed around 11 PM, but by 1:03 AM, I was jolted awake suddenly by what sounded to be frighteningly close repeated gunfire. I laid there awake with my heart pounding and frozen from the fear and shock of extremely loud sounds of gunfire all around our house. As I laid there in the dark listening and psychically sensing for all I was worth, I realized that it was not gunfire at all, but more like someone way up a hundred feet in the air, violently pounding on the eucalyptus tree branches with another large piece of wood. This was physically impossible of course, but that's what it sounded like to me in those moments. These sounds were as loud as gunfire, but they were up in the air, above our house and the surrounding blocks of the neighborhood. I had the psychic impression that a nonphysical *something* was throwing a major temper tantrum up in the eucalyptus treetops and it sounded like repeated gunfire going off above and all around our house. It was incredible and very frightening.

Absolutely every dog in the town was barking and howling miserably and they continued doing so for over an hour. You could easily feel serious negativity covering the whole neighborhood like a suffocating black blanket. As I laid there listening, I kept waiting to hear human sounds or people talking outdoors, car doors slamming, police or ambulance sirens, fire trucks or anything. There were absolutely no other sounds except every dog within a half-mile radius barking and howling like I have never heard dogs cry before. Every dog in town except Rick and Mike's two dogs that is! No human sounds, no police or ambulance vehicles arrived that night as I kept expecting due to the loud and repeated sounds of gunfire. I laid there in the dark listening, feeling the livid negativity flying, raging, and thrashing about wildly over the entire neighborhood.

After a half-hour of lying in the dark listening and sensing all of the rampaging negativity flying about overhead, I finally connected all the invisible dots and realized what had actually happened. Because I had regained enough mental clarity to realize I desperately needed to psychically protect our entire property and myself, I immediately created etheric pentagrams for only two nights and one day. That was all it took to cause the demon to reveal itself to me after a one year of incognito misery. This was also all it took for these almost immediate psychic and energetic reactions and repercussions from Rick's female demon. The next layer in this paranormal process was the actual energy break the demon had to Mom and me. The etheric energy break and disconnect manifested as the extremely loud sounds I heard that mimicked repeated gunshots overhead. All of this dramatic reaction because I did only two nights and one days worth of intentional and highly focused pentagram construction on the etheric level.

When most serious and well developed negative etheric energy disconnects are finally made, it usually physically sounds much like hearing sonic booms from aircraft breaking the sound barrier—or repeated gunfire or loud, sharp cracking sounds in the air overhead. This noisy psychic phenomenon happens when a potent negative, nonphysical demon or entity is finally cutoff energetically from positively focused, higher vibrating people and physical locations. As frightening as the loud booming and cracking sounds are, it is a positive indicator that an energy disconnect has happened.

The next week Mike and Rick both hurled verbal death threats at me and things sounded like they were escalating and becoming more dangerous. Fortunately, Mike did not fall over the edge and spray our house or us with bullets. It suddenly was sounding like Rick's invisible demonic controller was trying to get me more emotionally and physically involved with the two crazy brothers. I tried very hard to not fall and take her bait however.

By May 11th, only six days after Rick's female demon revealed herself to me, she jumped from her primary human host (Rick), over to Juan, the groundskeeper who worked for Jake on the opposite side of Mom's property! Six short days and she jumped to the property on the other side of us and began manipulating Juan to continue harassing and attacking me. Juan had never paid any attention to Mom or me prior to this, but suddenly he was now talking under his breath whenever I was outside working and he would sneer hatefully at me the whole time. What happened that day was so obvious because Juan's personality changed so dramatically and so suddenly. That day Juan became openly hateful towards me and he said and did a lot of little things to let me know how he felt about me; he and Rick's female demon that is.

Because I had successfully not taken the demon's baiting me through Rick and Mike over the past few days, the demon simply jumped over to manipulate Juan on the other side of us who worked outside. Now the demon had another human male physically close to us to utilize six days a week while Rick and Mike were gone at work. Juan was an even better tool to get at me than just Rick's barking male pit bull was. This is often how this type of dark energy works in the old lower polarized world.

Suddenly Juan became angry, dark, aggressive, disrespectful and insulting towards me every time he saw me outside working in my yard. He began parking his car as close to our fence as he could and would turn his car radio on loudly and open the four doors so he could hear his Mexican music while he raked and watered Jake's plants and cursed and glared hatefully at me. It was an instant and total transformation and it taught me a lot about how negatively focused entities and demons can effortlessly migrate from one person to another and another and back again *if* all of the people originally vibrate within a similarly low frequency range, which unfortunately Juan did.

The situation with Juan now also being controlled by Rick's female demon never ended for the remainder of years we lived at the portal house. Mom, the portal house property and I, were now uncomfortably sandwiched in between these younger males on the east and west sides that were used, manipulated, and totally controlled by the female demon to stop me in any way she/they could. Because I was a Lightworker on an interdimensional Lightworking Earth mission, it was me the demon had always been after. I knew she would continue using as many people as necessary to try to break me, to stop me from assisting with the interdimensional grid work and higher energy anchoring at the portal house. I honestly thought all of this was too much for me to fight or deal with in my abnormally vulnerable (ascension) condition. I figured all I could do at that point was to not let myself be emotionally manipulated into more hate, rage, and feelings of injustice, which was exactly what I usually would do!

As a Lightworker I have always abhorred lowly egoic people who crave controlling other people and injustice in all its cruel and selfish forms, and all negative, ego-driven situations across the planet. This demonic situation was for me, the epitome of negative beings using certain people to restrict, stop, break, drive insane, or kill someone carrying higher frequency energies. It was the classic Battle of Polarities within old lower 3D, and I was this demon's primary target for the simple reason that I was the only Lightworker doing interdimensional work in that important physical area. Rick's demon desperately wanted to stop all that was happening interdimensionally at the portal house and land via my work and anchoring as a Lightworker Wanderer within physicality. I just had to make sure she did not. It was a test, an Initiation, a severe experience within extreme polarities for me like none other and I did great some days and truly awful other days, but that is what resolving polarity within oneself and the environment is all about during the early stages for many First Wave Lightworkers.

After seeing firsthand how quickly and easily the demon could jump from one human to any other like-vibrating human and manipulate multiple people at the same time, I realized I would have to keep the etheric protective pentagram energies up on our property twice a day. I realized I might not physically survive all I was living through, battling with, and personally transmuting if I was not extremely diligent about this. I also knew I had to be highly conscious of my own thoughts and emotions while within such extreme polarized conditions, doing such personally and collectively important transmuting Lightwork. What a multi-leveled, intense, polarized learning process this whole business was for me.

June 28, 2001 I went to bed and asked my Higher Self for a good conversation and a message came through instantly. It was simple and short but very powerful as they usually are. My Higher Self informed me that, *"Just as the Veil between dimensions is disappearing, so too is the Veil between your conscious and subconscious mind; between your Astral body, the Mental, Emotional, Etheric and Physical bodies."*

The second I heard this I knew what it meant and represented on a massive scale—not only for me personally—but for all humanity. My Higher Self meant humanity when it referred to *"your"* and not simply me individually. It was a great insight into what I had been living through, struggling with and being so terribly sick from.

A few hours later during the early morning hours of June 29th, I had a dream where I was going through an old book that contained a list of all the names of demons and what their individual talents were and so on. In this dream I was carrying on in a perfectly calm state as if this was business as usual and something I did every day. I found whatever it was I was looking for in the book, and so, woke myself up. I have no conscious memory of any of the information within that book in this dream. I didn't care about that aspect of my problem with the demon in the same way I have never been interested about the names of positive, higher dimensional beings and ETs I encounter. Once you have personally encountered one of these nonphysical beings—lower or higher—you never forget them or their unique energies. Their individual energies and condensed personalities are all the name I need or care about.

⬟ July 2001 I was settling myself in bed for the night and I inserted my earplugs (there would be no sleeping at all if I didn't block out the physical noises during the night), then do my nightly pentagrams to the four directions ritual. Because I had been doing it every morning and evening for months, I had built-up the etheric structures considerably and now only had to maintain them by making my visual and emotional contact with them each morning and evening. I could now get away with this lazy and fast method of lying in bed visualizing what I had etherically constructed months earlier. I still went through the ritual each time, but could do it quickly now from my mind's eye instead of actually going through the physical motions and gestures out in the living room or my bedroom.

As soon as I had finished visualizing the four massive pentagrams of light suspended in the air like permanent sentinels at the east, south, west, and north sides of our property, I clairaudiently heard a muffled female voice hissing, bitching, and complaining. There was an instant negative energy feel and I clearly saw a large, blacker than the night, shadow move across my bedroom ceiling.

I jumped out of bed and hurried to the opposite end of the house that was the closest to Rick and Mike's rental house and looked out the windows just out of curiosity. Sure enough, they had just arrived home and were banging around outside, drunk as usual, struggling in the dark to get the key into the front door. Rick and Mike had not been home when I had gone to bed minutes earlier, but they and their female demon were back now and obviously, she was not happy.

The next morning when Mom and I were both up, I told her about what I had heard clairaudiently the night before. She stared wide-eyed at me as I was relaying my experience, which hinted at the fact that she had a story to share too. She informed me that she had heard a muffled female voice last night also, but said she had been for the past few weeks. In that moment, I realized I had too but had foolishly dismissed it as Juan's wife or some other female walking past our house. It is astonishing how quickly I tried to rationalize away having heard a muffled female voice for weeks when I knew all too well that Mom and I both had been under psychic demonic attack for over the past year! How amazingly stupid is that anyway? Incredibly stupid—and yet, it is often what we do in extraordinarily negative situations like this. We rationalize, we intellectualize, and try to convince ourselves it is something physical because having to constantly deal with a negative nonphysical entity is too goddamned much to cope with sometimes! It is a precarious and ridiculous mistake and one that usually brings you to your knees eventually. Moral of the story is to just face the dark scary shit in whatever form it presents itself to you, deal with it as best you can at the time and keep moving forward. It will end eventually.

August 2, 2001 Mom and I have been making repeated trips to the local Animal Shelter to check out the available kittens for adoption. We had almost decided on one particular kitten but discovered that she had been adopted in between our visits, so we were back searching through the many feline cages for another kitten to adopt.

There was a very small ten-week-old male orange kitten who was laying the Love on heavy-duty every time we would walk past his cage. He would talk at us and stick his arm out of the cage to touch us, sing and seduce as best as he could, and he was doing a great job. He was really going after Mom, and I kept glancing over my shoulder at them to see him actually patting her cheeks through his cage bars. I had never seen a kitten act like this before. He was acting as if he recognized us both and was doing everything he could to get our attention. Eventually, I stopped at his cage, bent down to get a good look at him and psychically scan him. He instantly reached both arms out through the cage and put his front paws on either side of my face and meowed at me very intently. He certainly got my attention with that move and I nearly started crying, which wasn't much of a stretch for me with the menopausal ascension intensities I had been living with since February 1999. He hugged my face and talked at me like crazy and I could not believe the determination of this little orange tiger kitten. I called Mom over and he did the same routine to her again.

I opened his cage and picked him up to feel his energies and he immediately started washing my face and mouth like a dog usually does. I have had kittens/cats all my life but I had never encountered one like this little guy. He was different—very intelligent and full of so much love it was shocking. We adopted the little orange male kitten that day and he was profoundly happy because he knew he would not live long if somebody did not adopt him. People think the cats, kittens, dogs, and puppies don't know what's going on in places like Animal Shelters, but sadly many of them know exactly what is coming if a human doesn't adopt them.

After paying for him and doing all the paperwork, we still would have to wait a couple days before we could bring him home with us. During this waiting period I went shopping and bought him a tiny kitten-sized litter box, new toys, his own brush and kitten food. I didn't want to have to go shopping for these things after we got him home, so I got everything prepared for him first.

After all the steps with the adoption where finished, the three of us were finally free of the Animal Shelter and in our car excitedly heading home. I was driving and Mom was holding the orange tiger kitten on her lap and he was not crying or frightened by the moving car or strange noises, which was unusual for a feline. Mom and I were ecstatic and in love with the little kitten already, and he with us I do believe. As I drove us home, all three of us were gushing love and happiness all over the place and feeling great after so much negativity for so very long. It was a very special and happy moment.

All the sudden the little orange kitten started moving in a strange way I had never seen before and Mom and I weren't sure what he was doing. I slowed the car, pulled over to the curb, and stopped. The kitten had his head up in the air as if he was looking at the car's ceiling but he was struggling as if he was choking or could not breathe. Our giddy joy and excitement was quickly stalled by the kitten's strange movements and choking behavior. After about thirty seconds of this bizarre behavior, he stopped struggling and curled up quietly in Mom's lap as if he was suddenly exhausted. We fell silent and just stared at him, then each other wondering what in the world had just happened halfway home? When it was clear he was not going to move out of Mom's lap or struggle in that strange way anymore, I started the car again and continued driving us home. He did not move the rest of the way home.

Once we were home, I carried the new kitten to my bedroom where his personal litter box was in my bathroom. I wanted it and his food and water to be the first things he was introduced to in our house. I put him in his new, never been used litter box and he used it, then jumped out and walked throughout the whole house as if he was intimately familiar with it! Another anomaly. He walked through our whole house and did not smell things, check things out or investigate, or get frightened and jumpy by anything like normal kittens and cats do in a new place. I could not believe what I was seeing. This tiny baby kitten acted as if he was thoroughly familiar with our house already, which of course was impossible. Or was it? He was unique, mature, intelligent, and full of more love than any feline I had ever encountered in my life.

As the first day passed, I fell hard for the little orange kitten and bonded with him in a way I never had with any other kitten or cat. I was a bit worried about why he wouldn't eat anything or even drink water as the day wore on however. I knew he was hungry because he would go over to his food bowls and try to eat, but he seemed to have some trouble swallowing. After trying to eat or drink but having some strange type of difficulty or pain doing so, he would give up and jump back up on me to rest or sleep. This kitten never once sat on my lap but would always walk onto my chest and lay down on my Heart chakra area. He slept there every night, he napped there during the days, and he laid there when he would wash himself. He would always lie on my Heart chakra area and never on my lap.

By the end of that first day I knew he had not eaten anything or even had any water and I was worried. I tired milk, warm milk, and an assortment of other treats just to try to get him to nibble on anything but he didn't or couldn't. The morning of day two, I thought he would eat for sure and watched him closely as he hungrily headed straight for his food bowls. He obviously wanted to eat, and he tried repeatedly to eat, but something was making it painful or difficult to swallow anything. After struggling a bit with it all he would give up and come back to me to rest on my chest over my heart. Let the crying begin.

By the end of day two, I knew he had not eaten or drank anything and was starting to seriously panic. I had never had this problem with any kitten or cat before and the little guy was thin when we got him from the Animal Shelter. He was not round and full as most kittens are but rather thin and small like he may have been the runt of the litter.

I called the Animal Shelter the next day in tears because I really was worried why he couldn't eat or drink anything. They told me to calm down and not worry, as he would eat when he was ready to. To me he looked and acted as if he was very ready to eat the first day we brought him home but he just could not swallow for some unknown reason. Neither he nor I got any helpful suggestions from the Animal Shelter that day.

Our new orange tiger kitten walked around the house as if he had lived there for ten years and Mom and I watched him in utter amazement. Nothing in the house startled him or seemed new or mysterious to him. Nothing! He didn't even smell objects in the house or carefully investigate like kittens and cats do in new surroundings. He was completely at home there and very familiar with the house, its smells and sounds, how to use the litter box and that beds were for sleeping and so on. He was unique and the love he gave us both was almost too much. He was a much higher frequency feline than any I had ever encountered. He had more love and higher vibrating energies in him spilling out all over us than any animal I had ever experienced or seen. And, he could not eat or drink anything and was becoming weaker every day and my heart was absolutely breaking. Just when you think it cannot get any worse, it does.

Because he was not or could not eat or drink, I was very careful to let him sleep on my chest all night because I felt he must feel safest there. Because I wasn't sleeping well and was doing a lot of crying and feeling very emotional about his inability to eat, I was quickly becoming weakened too. Here was a ten-week-old angel kitten that had convinced us to adopt him, and now he is starving to death and we cannot solve this terrible mystery. It was absolutely beyond awful.

By August 10th, he is still exuding as much love and higher energies as he did the first time we saw him at the Animal Shelter. However, I knew he was dying and that there was nothing that would fix him. I just loved him and tried to make him feel as good as I could in between sobbing much of the time. I took him outside to sit in the dirt and sunlight, probably for the first time in this young life. He sat there blinking in the bright sunlight and looked around the backyard and seemed to deeply enjoy that. After a few minutes he looked at me and did the *"I love you"* and *"Thank you"* slow eye blink that feline's do. I burst into tears again.

As I watched him experience Nature and sunlight for the first time in his little kitten body, at one point he etherically left his exhausted, starving kitten body and floated up into the upper branches of a large pepper tree I had physically sat him under near the back of our yard. I clairvoyantly watched him float free of his starving physical kitten body, and knew he was momentarily feeling good and pain-free at least.

Later that evening I tried again to get him to take some water through an eyedropper I'd sneak into the side of his mouth. At this point, he would gag and react as if the water caused him physical pain. I cried and he continued starving to death. That night he slept all night on my chest as he always did and I could feel he had a fever.

The next day I discussed the situation with Mom and we both decided it would be best for all of us if we took him back to the Animal Shelter. I knew I could not continue like this because I wasn't healthy enough myself, and the lack of sleep and constant emotional pain and crying was exhausting me even more than I had been before he arrived in our lives. After deciding that we should return him to the Animal Shelter, I wanted to share Nature and sunlight with him one more time before he died.

I took him outside in the backyard again, and because he was so weak and frail, I would pick him up and carefully set him on boulders, under trees and bushes, next to the birdbath, in the flowers, in the dirt and grass. Despite being so terribly sick and weak he seemed to thoroughly enjoy what I was trying to give to him. Two hours later, we drove our greatly beloved angel kitten back to the Animal Shelter for them to try to help him in some way. There was of course, more crying and confusion followed by further crying. It was so hard to leave him there but I knew he would have the vet and other shelter people watching him carefully.

We returned to the Animal Shelter two days later to see how he was doing, and if the Veterinarian had discovered why he couldn't eat or drink since the day we took him home. It was a mystery because Mom and I both remembered watching him eat dry kitten chow when we first saw him at the Animal Shelter so we knew he was eating just fine there. The Vet told us he found absolutely nothing physically wrong with him and that he had never seen anything like it before. My heart crashed and I started crying again in front of everyone. I gently retrieved him from his cage and held him next to my chest but he and his vast love energies were gone. He was in the final process of releasing from his physical body. I cried some more and told him it was good that he was leaving his body now and to not fight any longer.

That night Mom and I both intended that he would painlessly exit his kitten body so his starvation and suffering would finally end. We both visualized helping him out of his physical body so he could be free of that pain and misery.

August 14, 2001 and I wake up with a high fever and body aches, pains, and general flu-like symptoms and am profoundly exhausted. I have stabbing ice pick-like pains in certain bones and am an emotional wreck over the precious angel kitten. I can psychically sense he has not died yet, and that makes me feel worse knowing he is still suffering. I spent the next two days being very sick with these flu-like symptoms but I knew I did not have the typical "flu". I knew this was all the emotional exhaustion and pain over the suffering and slowly dying kitten.

While I was aching and shivering with chills under my ascension blanket, I suddenly remembered something I had read many months earlier about severe negative psychic attacks by Carla L. Rueckert who channeled the RA books with Don Elkins and James McCarty from 1984–1998. I remembered reading about the years of continuous severe negative psychic attacks all of them—and I believe a couple of their cats— endured from a negative nonphysical entity due to the higher Lightwork they were doing channeling the RA group information to humanity. In those moments, I remembered reading about how they each came under repeated dangerous and life threatening psychic attacks, as did a couple of their cats. My remembering this suddenly made everything the angel kitten and we had been going through tumble darkly and perfectly into place.

I instantly understood what had happened in the car while we were joyfully driving the orange tiger kitten home from the Animal Shelter that first day. When he suddenly started acting like he was choking and looking up at the car's ceiling and crying in pain, that was when Rick's female demon did something to him etherically to make him not be able to eat or drink anything. In those few seconds in the car, ten miles from home, Rick's female demon attacked our much-loved new little kitten, which caused his lengthy and very painful slow-motion starvation and eventual death. In that second I realized that the entire reason the demon did all that was simply to cause Mom and me as much emotional and physical suffering and pain as it possibly could. I should not need to elaborate on how deeply she succeeded in causing all three of us tremendous pain and suffering.

On August 24, 2001, Mom and I went back to the Animal Shelter to check on our little angel kitten. We both were hoping beyond hope that he had died and was pain free finally. Once we got there, we were told that he had died during the night. Twenty-two days of profound suffering and starvation, but he was finally free of the demonic attacks. We talked one last time with the Vet and I asked him if he had any more information or idea as to what had been wrong with our adopted kitten. He repeated what he had said earlier—that he had never seen anything like it before and there were no physical reasons that he could see that would cause the kitten to suddenly not be able to eat or drink anything. I knew why finally but it was good to hear the Vet say this nonetheless. Mom and I thanked him, left the Animal Shelter, and have not been back since.

October 15, 2001 a girlfriend I had known for fifteen years called to tell me about a strange dream she'd had the night before. I listened as Lana told me her weird dream but about halfway through it I became terribly concerned. Despite our being very close friends I had not told her about my problems with the demon because I felt she did not need to be burdened or frightened with that type of information. She did know about our ongoing miserable situation with Rick, Mike and Co., but I had never mentioned the demon to her and never would have.

Her dream consisted of her driving on a local SoCal freeway to try to reach her boyfriend who was at work. While driving on the freeway to reach him, Lana sees a car accident up ahead that has blocked all the lanes so she had to stop and wait. While waiting for the car accident to be cleared away, Lana spotted a young woman who looked very different from everyone else in her dream. She thought it strange that no one else seemed to even see this strange looking woman at the freeway accident.

As Lana continued telling me her dream over the phone, my heart sank and my solar plexus flipped and twitched uncomfortably. Lana described this young woman in her dream as having rows of tiny, razor-sharp teeth, large wild obsessed-looking eyes, and something that looked like a large round brand in the middle of her forehead. I nearly started crying listening to Lana perfectly and unknowingly describe Rick's female demon to me. Just when you think it cannot get any worse, it does, again.

When Lana had finished telling me her dream, I could barely contain myself. I knew I had to tell her about our situation with Rick's attached female demon, and that that is who contacted her in her dream last night. So I told Lana my miserable negative story about how Rick had a female demon controlling him, and that because I was doing certain higher dimensional energy work, I was square in her dangerous crosshairs and always had been. I told her that Rick's female demon wanted to either drive me mad or kill me. Lana had phoned me for council about her frightening monster dream, but I had to lay all this on her instead and inform her it was real and not merely some strange dream from her subconscious.

After Lana had described what this female looked like in her dream, I described what the female demon looked like to me and we compared notes. I could not believe this vile demonic creature had astrally contacted my best girlfriend, plus using Juan constantly now too, not to mention murdering our little orange angel kitten in the absolute worst of ways. She was clearly letting me know this was serious business to her and that she simply was not going to disappear because she had succeeded in breaking our hearts by slowly killing our higher vibrating kitten. There are physical stalkers, but there are also nonphysical stalkers, and this nonphysical demon attached to Rick was clearly letting me know just how determined and far-reaching her multidimensional influence actually was.

I felt responsible for the demon targeting Lana to affect me and I would not allow this to continue, even if it meant ending our long and close friendship. After a couple hours on the phone with Lana that day, I sensed I was going to have to cut her out of my life to keep her safe from this demon and anything the entity might decide to do to her or her family. A couple of months later I did indeed have to break all contact with Lana because she and her boyfriend were both now being influenced and manipulated by Rick's female demon. I cut Lana out of my life then with no explanation to protect her from further demonic attacks and influences. Lana and I did not talk or see each other for well over a year because of this. A couple of years later when I knew it was energetically safe, Lana and I reconnected and I was finally able to fully explain why I had so abruptly ended our relationship. She informed me that she and her boyfriend's unpleasant situations did mysteriously improved shortly after I had refused to talk with her or see her anymore.

2001 completed with Mom, me, our older much-loved cat Toby and Lana and her boyfriend still alive and sane, which was a colossal accomplishment. September 2001, Mike did fire a couple gunshots towards our house again but we just ignored it, him, and the female demon that instigated all these types of physical events. November and December 2001 was just more of the same—daily and/or nightly hours of drumming and stereo blasting by methed-up Mike. If Rick and Mike were not home, then it was twelve to fifteen hours of their male pit bull barking continuously. Same old nauseating daily and nightly torture that pushed one's sanity to the absolute breaking point, repeatedly, but that was the whole point. All I could think of was screaming an ear-shattering, liver-exploding, polarity battle cry of *"FUCK ALL YAWLS!"* I never did physically, but I certainly did silently every day, week, and every year that this monstrous living polarity war lasted. Doing so helped me work my way through so much lower energy and darkness while I was so sick and exhausted and not lose my sanity.

I honestly do not know how I survived another year of this intense focused negativity, chaos, and ascension illness but I did—just barely. Mom coped better than I did only because she is not as sensitive or psychic as I am, plus she was not doing the extensive inner and outer personal and planetary energy Lightworking that I had been since February 1999. Of course she was living through her individual ongoing ascension process at the level she was, while trying to survive the insane, demonically controlled neighbors, barking dog, drunken noise and parties, demonic attacks, plus all of my sickness and ultra sensitivities and all the rest of it. It was the absolute worst of times for us both and the years of it blurred hideously from one into the next, and the next, and felt as if it would simply never end.

January 2002 I had another interesting astral dream experience. It was like an epic soap opera or miniseries that just went on and on, becoming more twisted and unlike my subconscious as it progressed.

The main characters in this dream were people I did know and love in actual physical life, but they were acting completely unlike themselves in this dream. Because I have experienced this particular dream phenomenon many times throughout my life, I have learned to pay attention when the dream shifts into another level where it begins feeling fake or carefully designed by someone else—someone other than my subconscious for the sole purpose of inducing specific emotions within me. I have become rather proficient at recognizing different levels of dreams, when they are someone else's creations, or my own. I can also tell when they are 3D precognitive, or when they are actual events and encounters within another dimension. In addition, I can recognize when I have been astrally abducted and inserted into a staged dream scenario created by lower frequency being. This particular dream was indeed constructed by nonphysical beings and I became ensnared in it for the specific purpose of being milked for certain lower frequency emotions.

Partway through this epic soap opera dream I realized it was not my creation, but that I had been abducted by astral pirates again and was being cleverly herded through their dream maze and deliberately manipulated to produce different emotions; lower emotions such as fear, anger, guilt, a distorted sense of responsibility and so on. I became angry that I'd been astrally abducted and influenced to produce certain lower emotions so that various beings could witness and analyze human emotions. I had the impression these nonhuman, nonphysical beings, could not emotionally feel so they enjoyed witnessing the emotions we in physicality readily exude from being inserted into their carefully crafted astral dream productions.

This is also exactly how lower negative energies, consciousness, and people function in the physical world when trying to manipulate and control the human masses through media distortions and lies. Negative scenarios are designed and force-fed to the masses to control them plus produce specific low-range emotional energies such as fear, hate, and an unending sense of vulnerability and disempowerment. This is a common negative tactic used on both the physical and astral dimensions by negatively focused nonhuman beings and physical humans.

These nonphysical beings had trapped me within another of their epic astral dream creations and it was escalating in ugliness and negativity as they usually do.

It had reached the point where some lowly dark dream actors were trying to push weapons off on me so I would go murder my family, just as they had. I woke myself up at that point and made sure the astral connection was completely broken.

Laying there in bed struggling to remain awake and not be pulled back into the same astral mess, I saw a large circular distortion of swirling, cloudy, vaporous energy above me near the ceiling. It became a real struggle to remain awake and not fall or be sucked back through that astral portal. I looked at my cat that always slept at the foot of my bed and he was staring up at the ceiling watching it too that told me it was very strong this time. I fought for an hour to remain awake and not be pulled back into that lower negative astral rubbish. Finally, the connection and etheric portal broke and disappeared and I could feel that the focus from these heartless beings was thankfully gone.

March 2002 we had another of those marvelous physical ET encounters. This day Mom and I had gone to town because she wanted to have her hair cut at one of those popular haircutting chains. As she and I walked into this well-known hair salon, we both noticed an Asian man in his late forties or early fifties waiting in the lobby to have a haircut. There were no other customers waiting, only him, and now Mom.

For some reason we both were instantly attracted to this Asian man and kept glancing at him sitting there waiting. He was not sitting in the chair normally, but had slid way down in the seat and crossed his outstretched legs and his head was down, as if he was napping or resting. Because he immediately felt different to us both, we kept our eyes on him as inconspicuously as possible.

Eventually an employee arrived and escorted Mom to the back to cut her hair. I had told Mom previously, that once she was back getting her hair washed and cut, I was going to the bookstore right next door to kill some time. Once I knew she was having her haircut, I quickly headed to the bookstore that was literally on the other side of the wall the Asia man, Mom, and I had been sitting against while waiting in the hair salon.

Once in the bookstore, I headed straight to the scant metaphysical section to see what they had. Within a few moments two women in their sixties, and one man in his forties, suddenly had me surrounded. Next, I clairvoyantly saw there was an elderly dead man materialized from the waist-up about twelve feet up in the air off my left shoulder! This is a small bookstore that I've shopped in for two decades and never had I ever run into other people all crowded in around me right at the tiny metaphysical book section. Nevertheless, suddenly here were three people—not to mention one elderly dead guy—that all seemed to need to be right in my tiny space, which as a sensitive I seriously hate. I detest when unaware, self-absorbed people cram themselves into my little energy space out in public and I then get to feel and perceive their energies—that they usually do not even deal with themselves. I certainly do not *want* to psychically see and feel any of their unresolved issues.

Here I am all of the sudden with these strangers crammed in around exactly where I was standing, plus the dead man hovering up near the bookstore ceiling who starts telepathically talking to me. I glance up at the dead elderly man who is telepathically informing me that the one woman in front of me is, or was, his wife and the man is their son. He wants me to inform his wife that he was the one who instigated certain events a few months earlier. He also told me to tell his wife that he loves her and that he is right there near her at home much of the time.

While the dead guy is chattering telepathically at me, I'm discretely glancing at the other three people who literally have me surrounded; the wife and son in front of me, and the other woman slightly behind me and between me and the half-materialized floating dead husband. I am obviously pinned in place physically and not real happy or comfortable with the entire situation. Something about all of it feels off to me.

I have done this sort of thing before when I gave psychic readings many years earlier, but that was a situation of clients intentionally seeking me out for information. This was the complete opposite of that and I was not certain how the three of them would cope with a stranger, in a public bookstore, informing them that she was seeing and talking with their dead relative. This was not how I worked, and it felt increasingly off or strange to me as the paranormal seconds and minutes ticked on around me.

Because of all this, I am trying to discretely and quickly get psychic impressions about all three of them, enough to decide whether or not I want to stick my neck out in a public place and basically do an on-the-spot psychic reading and pass on the information the dead husband just told me. As I am psychically scanning all three of them to discern if they were even emotionally ready for this type of information from a stranger, I could easily hear what the wife and son were saying being only a couple feet away from me. It was after listening to their conversations with each other that I really started to feel that something else was going on than just me finding myself in an uncomfortable public and psychic situation.

If you are psychic, you eventually learn how to cope with what you pick up, what you see, feel, hear, and know absolutely. You have to learn to cope with it all, otherwise it would drive you mad. Here are some examples of random things I have picked up from strangers while I was out shopping, putting gas in my car, opening doors, touching shopping carts, standing in line at the bank, in different stores, and a thousand other common things we all do in our normal lives.

In one previous experience while waiting for the elderly man in front of me in line at the gas station to full his car, I grab the gas pump he had just used to fill up with. The second I touch it I feel he is dying from cancer. I deal with what I have felt, seen, and realized in that split-second and try to not burst into tears and run up to the elderly stranger and hug and cry all over the man. No, just put the gas in your car Denise and keep going. He already knows he is dying from cancer so you do not need to do anything but invisibly send him love.

Standing in line at the bank there is a man in front of me holding his four-year-old daughter in his arms. In a split-second, I clairvoyantly see he has repeatedly molested her and that he sees nothing wrong with what he is doing. I want to call the police on him on the spot—or bludgeon him on the spot—but it is not my call. It is not up to me to interfere with this particular situation because it spans multiple past lives. They have been lovers and mates in more than one past life that I could see, and it is all profoundly complex and distorted in this current incarnation for them both. Dear god just let me get to a teller and cash my check so I can get the hell out of here!

The woman with her two young kids in the shopping cart in front of me entering the store is exhausted, worn-down by her cheating husband, the mortgage, the kids, the bills, and her damned cheating husband who she loves more than any person on the planet, children included. She knows it cannot go on but she does not want to face the pain, anger, and bleeding emotional wounds that have besieged her body and being. Okay, I am just here to shop and I invisibly send her love and strength to deal with her current life lessons. There is no reason for me to say anything to this stranger.

The guy in front of me in the checkout line at the grocery store is a drug addict and thief and he has reached that point where he is about to seriously *turn to the Dark Side of The Force*. He is there, right now, standing at the great-polarized energy divide, teetering, wondering and trying to decide which polarity he wants to commit the rest of his life to. It is not my call to interfere with his profoundly important life decision, standing there in the checkout lane in the grocery store. Free Will and all that. I send him invisible love, strength, and clarity so hopefully, he will at least ponder his situation a bit longer. I already know which way he will go, but it is not up to me to interfere or guide. It is up to me to learn from what I perceive, feel and know.

I could go on and on but I'm sure you get the idea from these past examples that seeing a dead man half-materialized in a bookstore with his wife, son, and the wife's female friend surrounding me is not as weird sounding as it may have been at first. For a clairvoyant it is not weird or unusual at all. The real trick is discerning what if anything I should do or say in that moment and location to the person or people present. That is the real gift of being a psychic in my opinion—knowing when to open your mouth and when not to and why in both cases.

I am standing there in the bookstore with this dead husband frantic to get a message to his wife standing directly in front of me—the psychic—but I'm also picking up some serious strangeness with the three living people surrounding me. As I am listening to them talk, it becomes more obvious that this whole situation is feeling and sounding like a setup—a carefully designed and crafted theatrical production—which is blowing my mind because how in the hell do you get a dead guy to partially materialize right on cue in front of a psychic clairvoyant anyway? How exactly does this unique and clever paranormal trick work?

The wife and son were saying too many strange things only two feet in front of me knowing I was easily hearing every word they said. That just felt wrong. On top of that, there is the dead husband pleading with me—the convenient clairvoyant—to urgently pass along his messages to his wife. The talk between the wife and son was progressing into a conversation that just sounded like the whole situation was an amazing arrangement and I was the target. Because of all this, I made the decision to not tap the wife on the shoulder and as gently as possible inform her that her dead husband had a message for her. Nope, I was not taking what was increasingly sounding and feeling like the most elaborate paranormal bait I had ever encountered in my life! I am walking away and letting this one play out without my assistance thank you very much.

After reaching my decision over this ultra weird psychic situation, I just walked out of the bookstore and headed back to the hair salon to see if Mom was finished yet. As I reentered the hair salon, I noticed there was no one else in the waiting area. I sat down again and only had to wait a couple minutes before Mom appeared from the back with her new haircut. I got up and joined her at the counter as she paid for her shampoo and haircut. It was at this point that the Asian man who had been waiting when we arrived, came out from the back of the salon too.

He walked slowly around the corner, then stopped and stood about three feet away from Mom and me, and this is when the fun really started. Mom had finished paying, so thankfully we were done with all that and could just experience what the Asian man began doing for us. In that moment the Asian man deliberately went into a pose for Mom and me to see and feel, and when this happens with certain people who appear to be normal humans but are not, linear time and physicality simply disappears. You instantly find yourself outside of linear time and polarized physicality, and within a delicious spherical-like space and state beyond it. The exact moment the Asian man struck his pose, the hair salon, cashier, the other two beauticians and the entire third dimensional physical world quickly and silently dissolved. It is better than sex—better than chocolate— even better than warm fuzzy angel kittens, and you know me well enough by now to know what that means to me. This Asian man's induced experience is grand, perfect, and blissfully normal and feels like how some of greater reality beyond 3D feels.

There Mom and I are, standing in and on nothing but brilliant white light, watching this wonderful little Asian man posing for us and radiating beautiful pastel colored lights like stiff wires out of absolutely every hair on his head! Yep, every single hair on his nonhuman and probably stellar, other dimensional head had light flowing out of it. Mom and I floated and observed, felt and absorbed, admired and appreciated every nonlinear second of it all. We watched, felt, and grinned widely as the Asian man slowly shifted from one pose into another, making sure we noticed every single hair with a beautiful bright light streaming out of each tip. The image I saw looked like nearly three-foot long lines of gently waving pastel mint green, pink, baby-blue, pale pastel yellow, brilliant white, silver, and gold light pouring out of each individual hair on his entire head. Every one of these lights was stiff like wire however, and radiated out in all directions out of every hair as if he was weightless and free of gravity. (Later, Mom and I carefully compared notes about this whole event and she said she saw the same things at the same time that I did.)

I remember while staring at him and his individual light radiating hairs, also peripherally observing the surrounding space. It was nothing but brilliant white light with no walls, floor, or ceiling at all. Mom and I were in a higher vibrating space filled with white light and this fantastic Asian man—or whatever he really was—was posing his super slow-motion, Interdimensional Tai Chi-like moves and exuding different colored lights from each strand of hair on his wonderful head just for us. His delight over radiating this hair lightshow for the two of us was absolutely fantastic. It was fun, comical, and deeply moving as these physical interdimensional meetings with ETs and Others usually are.

Fig. 3.15. Asian Man Lightshow Pose

I have no idea if five seconds passed or twenty-five minutes. When you are in an expanded state, there is no linear time and physical 3D reality usually disintegrates. Reality then becomes only what you are experiencing and feeling in those *now* or quantum moments. Once you have tasted from the Expanded Reality menu, life on little 3D Earth with polarized consciousness is never the same, and never ever enough.

Ever so gently, the Asian man ended our higher dimensional vacation, and in a harsh and terribly rude manner, lower physicality and linear time flooded back in filling everything up again. It felt like what dropping down out of light-speed must feel like. The physical hair salon reappeared and all the mindless, endless, repulsive human noise of 3D did as well. It was insulting and mildly nauseating after where we had just been. It was going from playing with Angels, to suddenly standing naked in a world of shit, continuous noise, sickness, horrific imbalance, and monumental insanity. These fully conscious, expanded adventures and travels are sometimes difficult transitions indeed. The contrast was vulgar and harsh and I desperately wanted the entire asinine 3D human population to experience a few moments of higher dimensional freedom, beauty, and quiet. That has always been my primary desire; to have "*normal*" humans directly experience higher consciousness and a vastly higher reality outside physical 3D. Wars, greed, corruption, religions, governments, negative planetary systems, lies, manipulations, money, murder and all the rest of it would end immediately if others could experience higher energies and realities beyond lower frequency and linear 3D for themselves.

With more composure and grace than I thought I had at that moment, Mom and I turned and silently walked out the hair salon to our car. Thankfully, I had parked the car directly in front of the salon so once we got in it, I could continue carefully watching the Asian man who was now paying for his haircut—if he even got one. I started the car and Mom and I just sat there for a few moments watching him pay his bill and then walk out of the building, around us, and into the parking lot. I was determined to not let him out of my physical sight. I wanted to see where he went and what was coming next, so I carefully watched him and I knew he knew Mom and I were watching him leave. We could still feel each other, and Mom and I knew this event was not over yet. The air was still taut and snapped, crackling with higher vibrating energies and I was not about to miss his grand finale, whatever it was.

The Asian man walked out past, our car, and deeper into the huge parking lot behind us and the further away from the stores he got, the less parked cars there were. I watched him in the rearview mirror while Mom watched him in the mirror on her visor. We watched his back walking away from us, and when he reached the empty open area in the middle of the vast parking lot where no cars or vehicles were, he physically vanished as we both watched. I knew he had waited to reach an open, empty area where there was nothing blocking his view so Mom and I would see him physically vanish and not wonder if he had just disappeared behind or into a vehicle. He wanted us to see him exit this dimension, and I smiled and thanked him for that parting gift as it was the cherry on the top of a wonderful, higher dimensional vacation Mom and I both desperately needed right then.

After reviewing this entire event, I realized that everything I had seen and experienced in the bookstore were created by the Asian man in the hair salon! I believe it was a sort of test for me to see if my ego self would take the bait. Because I sensed something else strange was going on with the entire bookstore event and did not take the bait, I feel that then Mom and I were gifted with the Asian man's posing and higher dimensional hair lightshow event. I have discovered that just because someone looks human and normal in every way that certainly does not mean they are physical humans. This is another reason why developing your discernment and ability to honestly read energies and situations is so very important.

June 2002 and I had another in a series of the most horrendous lucid dreams I have ever had. I did not realize at the time I had the first two of these intensely negative lucid dreams that they were about me viewing, feeling, witnessing, and living through actual physical events that have happened to other people. As a psychic, I usually clairvoyantly saw and felt actual and/or precognitive events while fully awake. Encountering them while asleep in a lucid dream state was not my normal and familiar method. I eventually unraveled this mystery too, but it was one of the most horrible and dark aspects of being a Lightworker, and it took me a few repeated trips to hell before I discerned what exactly was happening and why.

In this particular lucid dream I suddenly found myself somewhere in Los Angles with two young women in their early twenties and one male in his early thirties. He, whoever he was, had picked up the two young women in some nightclub in the city and convinced the two of them to *party* at his expensive house up in the hills. The two young women thought it would be a fun sexy time, so off the three of them went.

Once he got the two young women up at his large and expensive house in the hills, the women discovered there were four other men at the house waiting for him to return with the evening's entertainment. The two very young women were these males prey, and after all of them had played sufficiently with both women at that beginning level, they were ready to move to the next much darker level. Up to this point, I was an invisible witness whose viewpoint was up near the ceiling of this man's house. As all of them moved through his house, I did too, and I saw and emotionally felt what each of them was feeling throughout the night.

The original man has gotten the less intoxicated young woman tied up on the bed and a couple other men were busy with her. The original man, plus two others, started torturing the other young woman, who thankfully was very high and drunk. Not drunk enough however to not know what was happening to her and that it was incomprehensibly painful and frightening. She suffered long and horribly as they cut, tore, and mutilated.

The second young woman on the bed was screaming and injuring herself just trying to get free, but all she could do was listen to her girlfriend being tortured and finally murdered. Once she was dead, the focus turned to her and she suffered the same horrendous hours of torture, repeated rapes, and finally being murdered.

What was the worst for me was that not only did I witness an actual physical event, but also that I had to physically and emotionally feel what each of them— victims and perpetrators—felt during the entire evening. That was the important part for me; that I felt all of the women's fears and pain, plus all of the men's rage, bloodlust, and lowly darkness. It was important that I both psychically and empathically lived through this event from each person's perspective and that I was a witness to the entire dark and ghastly event.

Once the men were finished with the second young woman, I could finally wake up. I had witnessed, experienced, felt and lived through the monstrous event and now my real Lightworking job was to transmute and permanently clear all the residual negative energy that remained from their horrible actions and the women's fear and pain.

The quickest and most thorough way for me to do this level of energetic transmuting and bulldozing Lightwork, was through the dream state. Because I would feel the whole event from each person's body and consciousness, I could more quickly and easily transmute the entire dark energetic mess through my High Heart. By doing this type of Lightwork through the Lightworker's body, his/her consciousness and being, we directly experience what darkness feels like and how it functions within lower frequency humans within polarized 3D. In addition, because much of this type of Lightwork is done while we are asleep and out-of-body, we can access more, feel more, then transmute and clear much more, much faster.

This type of severe negative scenario is far more common with Lightworkers than you would guess—at least it was in the first many years of the ascension process. I will never forget a few years after I had repeatedly experienced this type of physical torture and murder by other people in a lucid dream state, another Lightworker, a young woman living in New Zealand emailed me about an awful lucid dream she'd had a couple months earlier. Her letter moved me so and validated what I sensed was actually happening and why, that I want to share her story also.

I will call this young woman from New Zealand, Rose. Rose wrote me about a lucid dream she'd had recently with a Guide at her astral side. He told her they needed to go somewhere so she could see and feel for herself, some very unpleasant energies created by other people a very long time ago. Rose followed beside her nonphysical Guide within her lucid dream and they quickly reached the entrance to a very old castle in Europe somewhere. Rose wrote me that she followed her Guide down many narrow stone steps farther and farther into the dark, dank, negative energies that were the dungeon below the enormous castle. As they descended further into the dark stink, Rose said she could hear many people screaming in agony down there.

The Guide led Rose through the massive dark dungeon so she could view and feel the men, women, and children being tortured and murdered down there. Eventually, the Guide stopped in front of one man's cell and Rose had to feel and know what horrific tortures had been done to him. He lay there in the dark filth, broken and dying slowly and painfully. It was up to Rose to feel and live through what he and a couple other people had gone through down there at the hands of their tortures and executioners. Rose told me she cried and pleaded with her Guide to not make her have to feel what those people had lived and died through in the Middle Ages. He reminded her that she had asked to do exactly this type of Lightwork before she incarnated in this current life. Rose was a Lightworker, and this was simply another aspect of the work many Lightworkers on Earth have done repeatedly over the past decade or so to transmute both ancient and current residual lower vibrating energies.

As soon as her Guide reminded her of this fact Rose knew it was true and turned to once again view the broken, dying man in the dark cell radiating fear, hate, tremendous pain and much negativity before her. Rose did what she needed to do for the Collective, the planet, and herself. She felt what that innocent man had felt being tortured to death for something he did not do. Rose then cleaned what she had personally felt and lived through and permanently removed that particular negative energy from the planet and the Collective. Once she had accomplished this her lucid dream ended. Rose was profoundly affected by her experience for many days afterwards, as would be expected.

Lightwork is about transmuting Darkness and so-called evil, polluted, horrid, dark and lowly energies that remain in places and timelines all over the planet and within the 4D astral dimension as well. Lightworkers work with higher frequency Light in very Dark places to transmute lower frequency or negative, stuck energies and consciousness so that vastly higher vibrating Light replaces it. Lightworkers are much like Cosmic Janitors and there is nothing romantic or special about any of it. It is brutal, shocking, horrific, and traumatic work cleaning up not only your own personal lower vibrating emotional issues from this life and all others—but it is really hard clearing and transmuting other people's longstanding energetic murders, tortures, rapes, sexual perversions, hate, fears, pain, misery, brutality, wars and insanity. Nevertheless, this is polarity resolution work and how we achieve it in our bodies, hearts, minds, and current lives. Lightworkers repeatedly dive into the massive energetic septic tank—the 4D planetary Collective—and swim around in it so we can transmute those lower residual energies and permanently remove them.

In spring of 2002, we risked getting another kitten but this time from a woman who used to breed cats. All went well and Mom and I got an adorable flame point kitten from her that we named Reggie. It turned out that Reggie was the second kitten I would encounter that was one of the new, higher vibrating felines incarnating on Earth at that time. (Years later when I first heard about "Indigo" humans, I thought of the tiny orange tiger kitten and Reggie because they were like Indigo cats. These two cats were much like Indigo humans in that they were higher vibrating beings that were extra sensitive and loving with expanded awareness and feelings.)

Toby, our elder cat, loved his new Reggie kitten and it was a grand and happy time for all of us. As Reggie grew, he and Toby would chase each other through the house, which Toby thought was just the absolute best thing ever. They were very good for each other, and with Reggie being a higher vibrating cat than Toby, it was easy to see and feel the vibrational differences between them. We loved them both dearly, but Reggie was certainly something else.

One day when the two of them had been playing the chase game of running from the living room, down the long hallway and into my bedroom, I noticed that only Reggie would jump as he crossed the threshold into my bedroom from the hallway and vice versa. Toby would run as usual, but all the sudden Reggie would jump in the same exact spot every time while running in either direction. It looked like Reggie was jumping over something invisible positioned right at the entrance into my bedroom.

Mom and I both watched Reggie repeatedly jumping over the unseen something in my doorway when he and Toby chased each other through the house.

When Reggie was just walking, he would walk around this invisible something, both coming in and going out of my bedroom. It was yet another portal house mystery.

A week or so after first seeing Reggie jumping and walking around that area of my doorway, I clairvoyantly saw something very strange in that same spot and knew it was the object Reggie had been jumping over and walking around. It clairvoyantly looked to me to be an etheric box about two feet square. It was transparent with massive amounts of what looked like thin, multicolored laser lights crisscrossing each other within the etheric box of light. I immediately went into psychic scan mode to discern what it might be, if it was negative or positively charged, and who or what placed it there and why. It felt neutral to me, which was a huge relief. It felt like it might be something etheric to keep lower negative things—like Rick's female demon—from being able to enter my bedroom. Because Reggie never acted as if it was negative, just some obstacle in his way, I was not too worried about it being there, but it certainly was strange looking. I saw it only a few more times and then it was gone. As soon as I could not see it any longer, Reggie returned to walking and running through my doorway normally.

♂ July 2002 Rick and Mike's father showed up and stayed for a couple of weeks and it was very telling. When Rick and Mike went off to work in the morning, dear old Dad would stay there alone with the two dogs watching TV and drinking beer all day. One morning a couple hours after his sons had gone off to work, he opened the front door and turned on porn movies very loudly, no doubt for our listening entertainment for the rest of the day. The same thing happened the next day, and the next, and on into the second week. What's that old saying about the apple not falling far from the tree?

At first I just figured good old Dad was doing the same lowly crap his sons did, which was to try to make us miserable in whatever ways they could. I started psychically seeing certain things about Rick and Mike's Dad and one of his brothers—the boy's uncle—and sexual abuse with Rick when he was a young boy. What a family line of ongoing sick, twisted, dark negativity! In the end, we just ignored dear old Dad and his loud porn movies grunting out their front door and whatever he was doing and why. I was not playing The Game anymore because I had learned the hard way that it simply did not work.

August 2002 and my inner body electrical vibrations and shaking—the rewiring process—has become rather extreme. Every night I would wake up and lay in bed carefully observing and analyzing how this energy felt physically. It has gotten to the point where I can lay there for forty-five minutes and count the seconds on and off that this electrical buzzing sensation does running deep within my body. It does not hurt at all but feels rather strange and coded in its perfectly timed intervals.

Over the months and years that this rewiring ascension symptom continued, I tracked it moving gradually throughout my physical body. It first began low in my body and slowly moved up into my trunk or core (solar plexus chakra) where it remained for the longest period, which makes sense actually. Eventually it moved up a bit more into my heart and upper chest area. After this, it entered my neck and the base of my head for a while, and lastly, it entered my head where it is not as intense as the first couple of years.

I have noticed over the years that this energetic rewiring process started out feeling like a mild electrical current vibrating and buzzing deep inside my body. At its most intense, it felt like I was shaking slightly inside. Over the years however, it felt like it increased its spin or vibration to where now it feels like a super fast hum that I can barely feel any longer. Again, this rewiring process has never caused me physical pain but only felt rather strange.

A new phenomena started sometime during 2000, and I am sorry I didn't take notes and date this exactly as I usually did with the more interesting anomalies. There was a cluster of the worst of the worst years of my ascension process where I was so wrecked and sick that it was all I could do to get through one minute, then one hour, and then deal with the next hour, and the next, and so on. I spent a lot of time under what became my *ascension blanket* in my chair in my bedroom shivering and shaking, sweating and aching, burning and freezing, puking and crying, seeing lights and strange new nonphysical beings and energies so thick I could not see my TV behind them! It was so extreme and I just tried to survive each hour and then each day of those beginning years of my ascension process. In other words—there were phases where I did not journal or even scribble down notes about some of my strange experiences I was having only because I was far too ill to do so.

At some point during these extremely difficult early ascension years, I noticed a new physical event happening often when Mom and I would venture out to do our necessary monthly grocery shopping. My sense was that it was just time for this particular phase of interdimensional ET actions with Mom and me. Actually, nothing would have surprised me at that point because the Veil had huge gaping holes in it and all sorts of beings and energies where crossing back and forth over the normally monitored and closed off dimensional borders. It was a chaotic situation from my sensitive psychic perspective for many years. It was fun and exciting on the one hand, yet dangerous, wildly busy, and very peculiar on the other.

One of the times this anomaly happened we were in a Super Wal Mart store doing some shopping. Because I was familiar with certain positive ETs and their energies, it was easy for me to feel them even before my eyes physically or clairvoyantly located him, her, or them. This day in Wal Mart, the store was busy and packed with lots of extra (human) shoppers. That in itself was torture for me because being in large groups of lower vibrating people caused me physical, emotional, mental, and psychic pain. However, suddenly I energetically felt an ET nearby and started scanning the human Wal Mart crowds for anything unusual. Mom felt her too because I saw her staring intently in the same area of the shopping crowd that I had been.

After a couple of seconds, I spotted an unusually tall woman who looked to be in her late twenties or early thirties. She was wearing a Wal Mart vest indicating she worked there, which I thought was a humorous touch on her part. I could easily see her head above the crowd of shoppers as she popped in and out of sight heading directly towards us. Mom and I stood unmoving amidst the sea of human shoppers and waited for her to make the first move. No one else acted as if they saw her of course, so we just calmly waited to see what was coming next.

As she got within about six feet of us, she stopped and did this weird physical gesture or *posing* as I have come to call it. When she knew Mom and I could see her body fully, she stopped walking, struck a weird pose like an actor from a cheesy forties movie, and held it for about fifteen seconds for us. I could feel she was deliberately exuding specific energies for us to feel and be affected by. Her physical pose meant nothing to me symbolically and it actually looked a bit ridiculous, but nonetheless, there she was right in the middle of Wal Mart of all places, posing in this weird position grinning and staring at us as if she was having a ton of fun doing this to, and for us.

Mom and I did not move during this whole time and our eyes never left her. While watching her I did what I always do, which is to psychically scan and feel or read the entire situation energetically as best I can. I did not sense any other ETs around, only her. I also tried to sense or read her pose and what it might mean if anything. I got nothing with that other than her and her weird pose was what caused Mom and me to intensely focus on her and easily slip out of linear time. I suspect that was her point with her *posing,* because linear time and all the painful physical noise and human crowd melted away as if someone had quickly turned the 3D dial all the way to the off position. Nothing but the three of us existed in that wonderful quantum state, and we were powerfully connected to each other in that potent triangular energy and stance.

When she ended her pose and began walking again, linear time and all its extensive rude noise and chaos came screaming back in at full speed like some dirty bastard had released the third dimensional pause button. In these interdimensional transitions, you step out of linear time and physicality to find yourself within a blissfully silent and pristine higher dimension where light and gestures or postures done by higher vibrating beings hold tremendous coded energies. In this particular higher frequency state, the lower dense world you had been focused within seconds before is delightfully gone, and linear time-space is instantly forgotten. Being *in the moment* in a state of quantumness like this is being Home again, and a person only needs to experience this transition once to be changed forever. Mom and I have experienced it dozens of times, and doing so makes it much easier to become consciously familiar with making these vibrational transitions to higher frequency layers and dimensions that are constantly all around us. All of this is really about energies, different frequencies, layers of consciousness, and your current focus or where you believe this aspect of yourself to be at that particular moment.

Mom and I watched this young female ET being, pretending to be a human Wal Mart employee, walk a few feet away from us in the crowd of shoppers and literally vanish before our eyes. Some ETs thoroughly enjoy doing this luxurious and dramatic exit maneuver for us Earthly Wanderers/Lightworkers. I think they enjoy reminding us about their ability to step into and out of different dimensions and timelines. I know that in some cases with me, certain higher dimensional ETs used this as another clever teaching tool to trigger, jolt, or shock me into an altered state of consciousness. They are so great at kicking us right where we live, only to remind us that we really do not live there at all.

2002 completed with December being an extra emotional month with more family and neighbor issues. It really was just more of what had been going on for years at this point; constant physical pains, sicknesses, new allergies, severe chemical sensitivities to seemingly everything, severe solar flare sensitivities, endless dog barking, neighbor noise and negativity, Mike's endless drumming, demonic energies and unrelenting pressures and so on. It was exhausting and intensely frustrating never having any peace and quiet while I was so sick and constantly going through so much all on my own.

By this point, the extreme contrast of polarities was nearly too much for me. On the one hand, I and often Mom too had nonphysical and physical ET and other dimensional contacts with certain beings, interdimensional insights, teachings, journeys and adventures that were much like being Home again. All of those higher dimensional energies and contacts against a backdrop of constant negativity and demonic and lower human assaults, ascension illnesses and pains, mental fog, emotional extremes, ultra sensitivities to the world I was living in and profound, unending exhaustion. It was certainly an ongoing polarity battle and the most difficult and dangerous thing I had done in many lives.

April 2003 arrived, and despite my current inability to mentally focus or retain much for very long, I suddenly had a burning desire to buy a computer. I had never *ever* used a computer before and I did not even know how to turn one on or off, but I suddenly wanted one more than anything else in the world. I had also never been online or even sat next to someone and watched over their shoulder while they were online. I did not know what the Internet was, because I had never seen it at this point! Nonetheless, I suddenly was obsessively focused on buying myself a desktop computer despite not being able to remember my first name half the time. It was not a pretty sight, but somehow I gradually figured it all out.

I first educated myself by watching different TV shopping channels selling computers and taking notes about things I had never even heard of. I figured it didn't matter that I did not know what all the technical terms and things meant, I would learn what I needed to from the people pitching computers on these TV shopping channels. It helped a lot actually, and once I had my computer-buying notes organized, off I went to purchase my very first PC.

You have to keep in mind that not only was I severely handicapped from my ongoing ascension/menopause symptoms, mental fog and inability to mentally focus or retain much of anything, but I had never touched a computer before. I was attempting to do the seemingly impossible by buying a computer then, and yet, I simply had to have one and as soon as possible for some unknown reason.

I bought a computer and printer/scanner and hired a PC tech guy to connect it all and get me online— whatever in the world that meant—and then began the ugly process of teaching myself, all by myself, how to operate my new computer. Everything was abnormally difficult and confusing for me due to the ongoing ascension symptoms, constant hot flashes, solar flare symptoms, demon attacks, neighbor noises, lack of decent sleep for many years and constant exhaustion. I will confess there was plenty of sweating, cursing, freaking-out, major confusions, note-taking, and buying How-To computer and Internet books. Did I mention there was plenty of cursing and crying? The thing with hot flashes is that every time you have an emotion— especially lower emotions like frustration, fear, worry, confusion, embarrassment, or any self-induced pressure of any kind—it automatically and instantly causes an intense long-lasting hot flash. It was a case of me getting frustrated and confused over something with the computer or the Internet and that would automatically trigger a super-sized hot flash, which usually caused further brain shutdown and quite often frustrated crying and very serious cursing.

I spent every day reading pages of crap I did not need to, but because I was so mentally fried and confused, I read every page believing they were important and that I needed to. Eventually I got online and found myself in a truly alien landscape that reminded me a bit of the astral plane to be honest. The more I wandered around in my miniscule, newly discovered corner of cyber space, the more I read endless pages of even more useless crap. It took me one year before I felt safe enough *not* reading every damned word that popped up on my computer screen! It was a very hard, very frustrating and extremely confusing time for me, but somehow I got myself through it without blowing my computer up or becoming seriously lost or stuck online, or having a breakdown! To me, that alone was a major accomplishment considering my physical, mental, emotional, and psychic state at that time.

Seven years later, looking back at this it is obvious why I was compelled to buy a computer and teach myself about the Internet in early 2003. I had important things to write about; knowledge, memories and experiences to share that required a computer and basic knowledge about how to function online. At that time I needed to discover online spiritual, astrological, and ascension related forums and share some of what I knew and was experiencing at then. I eventually did find a few different forums and always used the same username of *Lapis* on them all. I also needed to discover blogs, and eventually, have my own as a safe online place to write and freely share what I knew, what I was living and discovering every week, month, and year with people interested in ascension, ETs, past lives, multidimensional consciousness, astrology, Mayan cycles and other related topics. (See TRANSITIONS at .deniselefay.wordpress.com) I also needed to discover online book publishers so I could self-publish a couple of books yet do so in the way I wanted and needed.

(It wasn't until late 2005 that I first discovered a link left at an astrology forum about *"ascension"* and followed it back to Karen Bishop's website. That was a very important day for me because it was *the* first time I had ever heard there was a term for what I had been living through since February 1999. This ascension process produces numerous symptoms, and once I had read through much of her previous *alerts*, I finally felt like I wasn't so miserably alone in what I had been calling my D 1 47 process.)

June 2003 and Rick and Mike's sister and husband and their four kids and dog are back again. Just when you think it can't get any worse it does, yet again. The noise and negativity is increased a few more notches again, and to make matters even worse, Johnny is spending more time there getting drunk and loud with the rest of them outside in front of their front door.

The other thing that started at this time was Rick's two pit bull dogs figured out how to escape and run throughout the neighborhood, hunting. Every couple of days his dogs would bring home a dead rabbit, and eventually, other neighbor's dogs too. Someone called Animal Control about Rick's pit bulls killing other people's dogs and I hoped that finally something would actually happen that would force Rick to deal with both of his dogs. The only thing Rick did was brag to everyone about how his dogs were killing other people's dogs. Typical...

Animal Control went to Rick's house to see the dead rabbits taken from a neighbor's rabbit hutch and left lying dead around his yard like chewed up dog toys. Amongst the dead rabbits and trash, the Animal Control officer also discovered another neighbor's expensive dead dog. Did anything change because of this? Hell no. I think Animal Control threatened Rick about letting his pit bulls run loose but nothing came of any of it. It was amazingly sad that such negativity could continue causing so much pain and misery to so many people for so long. Rick's dogs killing spree continued throughout the summer months and the neighborhood was becoming afraid to go outside because of it. It was obvious that his male pit bull had changed now that it had killed a few animals. He had finally become dangerous to both animals and humans, but of course, nothing was done about any of it.

I came close one day to having Rick's male pit bull attack me as I went to my mailbox to collect the mail. His dog had taken another rabbit from a neighbor's rabbit hutch and was in the process of playing with its dead body next to the road. I didn't see or hear him when I went out to get my mail, and he charged me. His normal light brown doggie eyes were completely black and he looked and acted as if he was possessed. He probably was. I punched out as much higher light energy in that split-second as I could produce just to keep him from touching me. By the look in the dog's eyes he was deep in the middle of bloodlust and no doubt being manipulated by Rick's female demon as well. It was a very tricky and frightening moment, but the male pit bull only charged me with bunny blood all over his ugly mouth and face, and acted as if he was going to eat me. I called Animal Control once I got back in the house, but again, nothing came of any of it.

August 2003 I had another lucid dream experience that affected me deeply and for a very long time. It was another Lightworker dream mission where I had to witness and feel very dark and negative events that actually happened physically. In this dream experience I suddenly found myself somewhere in Mexico. At first, I was an invisible observer to what was going on, then as usual, it switched and I felt what each of the perpetrators and victims individually felt.

The lucid psychic dream went on and on and it had to do with a group of Mexican males who would kidnap Mexican girls, young women, and middle-aged women for the sole purpose of torturing, raping, and then murdering all of them. The males would bury their victim's bodies in shallow graves out in the desert or set them on fire out there. What was truly ghastly about all this was that it had been going on for many years. People knew it had been happening, but nothing much was being done to stop it or track down the murderers. In a low vibrating patriarchal world, females are highly expendable.

As usual, I perceived these horrible events first from the point of an invisible observer overhead, then as each of the male perpetrators, then as each of the female victims. It was obviously horrific and the negativity and fear was sickening and extensive. It hung permanently like invisible fog in the whole desert area where these numerous tortures, rapes, and murders had taken place over the years. That was what I was supposed to clear; the dark energies and emotions that remained in that remote Mexican desert area from all of the people—males and females—that had been involved over the many years.

This particular Lightworking dream-clearing event was extra difficult for me because it was so evil, so violent, so totally lacking in any higher energies that the whole thing was alien to me. It was foreign in its purpose and extreme negativity, but nonetheless, it all had to be energetically transmuted and permanently removed now.

Seven years after this astral clearing Lightwork, I watched a new movie on TV based on a true story about a group of Mexican males who had been kidnapping, torturing, raping, and murdering females out in the Mexican desert for numerous years.

⊕ October 2003 I had experienced another astral abduction. It was slightly different from previous staged epic soap opera type dream scenarios. I recognized early in the dream that it had been carefully designed and created, and now that I was in it, I knew my reactions and I were being observed. I played along because this astral abduction had a different look about it. Its creators were obviously trying a different tactic with me and I was curious to see what was around the next crafted corner.

This dream setting was in some diner in a mountain community. The place was full of regular people happily eating and talking. As I entered the scene, I saw a young man holding a baby in a corner near the front door of the restaurant. He was dirty and his clothes were filthy and torn. He looked like the classic *homeless or street person.* What got my attention was that as I first noticed him, he immediately went into that familiar *posing* routine I had experienced while awake in shopping stores. It was this posing and holding it move that really drew me in to the staged setup.

I walked up to the nineteen or twenty-year-old young man to get a better look at the baby he was holding. It too was filthy and in an old dirty smelly diaper. He and the baby were revolting in that it was so over-the-top nasty and an obvious ploy to invoke emotions in the viewers. I looked at his filthy baby, who was also holding a perfect full-diaper pose for the whole dinner to see. It really was a cleverly staged scene.

I laughed aloud at the ridiculousness of the scene and handed the filthy young man a ten-dollar bill in this emotional astral panhandling dream. As soon as he took it from me, he and the baby transformed into a six or seven-year-old boy who did not feel right either. This new boy grins but avoids direct eye contact with me and I get the sense it is time for me to exit this astral con job, so I easily woke myself up.

I laid in bed thinking about the symbolism of the dream and another one I'd had twenty-five years earlier that felt very much like came to mind. In this much earlier dream, I learned about being on The Path and about stepping off The Path because someone appeared to need assistance. Once I stepped off The Path in this earlier dream, the small child that appeared to be alone hiding in fear in a hole in the ground crying out for me to help it, automatically morphed into a demonic creature that then tried to drag me down its dark hole in the ground. So much for the old Piscean Age religious distortion of *helping thy neighbor.* Stepping off your individual and important spiritual Path is not the answer or way to go—spiritual lesson learned.

As I laid there contemplating both of these astral teachings, I realized that these particular shape-shifting creatures could insert themselves into both the 4D astral dimension, and less easily into physical 3D. These lower-level interdimensional beings trolled for humans and they used elaborate astral dream props and emotional manipulations as their bait to trigger specific emotional reactions within the dreaming human viewer. I got the impression they did it out of curiosity over human emotions and as energetic food created from our emotional dream reactions. They found it amazingly easy to trigger fear, guilt, compassion, hate, lust, greed and many other low human emotional responses in us through their staged dream scenarios and other elaborate emotional manipulations.

I came to the conclusion that night that in the end it doesn't really matter who or where or why, but only about our ability to discern energies for ourselves and take the power and control over what we want and do not want to interact with. The Dark is not only a great big pain in the heart and ass—it is also our great educator within polarized physicality. I have learned even more thanks to the so-called evil, negative Dark endlessly trying to derail me decade after decade in this life. If you are in lower vibrating, polarized 3D world and consciousness, there is going to be plenty of this type of lower negative energy, entities, and beings all over the place. Use them to learn about polarity, which simply helps you to resolve polarity and finally vibrate into a higher state beyond it. Use the perceived Bad Guys in whatever dimension and form they present themselves to you because they are profoundly important to our individual and collective spiritual growth, especially in highly polarized lower physical 3D.

October, November, and December 2003 ended with the same miserable and unending neighbor noise and dog barking. Animal Control was next-door again, hanging green warning tags on Rick's front door, but he simply ignored all of them and would do something cruel to us because that was how he dealt with his problems—attack us.

I feel I should apologize to you, the reader, for repeatedly bringing up these neighbors and their constant negativity, noise, dog barking, death threats, female demonic assaults and all-around ongoing misery and ugliness. I am almost embarrassed to have to keep mentioning all of it and how insanely miserable the entire situation was. Nevertheless, it is what happened and it lasted from the moment they moved in April 2000, until we sold our home and moved out in June 2004. Realize that words cannot accurately describe how truly horrible, dangerous, painful, frustrating and devastating this entire situation really was at the time. I have actually left out certain unpleasant and difficult events because I cannot stand thinking or focusing on them again now as I write about all of this these many years later. Going back down and over those last four horrific years at the portal house to write about them now, years after I have changed so much, has been a great deal harder than I thought it would be. I am very glad you and I both are almost through it all and can soon happily move on.

I did have another profound and horrible insight into how demonic, nonhuman, nonphysical negative beings operate and affect some of us however. One day after three years of unrelenting assaults from both Rick, Mike and Co. and his female demon, I was outside doing yard work when I noticed that my normal silent, inner mental talk was not sounding like *me*. Being a sensitive, psychic, clairvoyant, and empath—as well as becoming

463

increasingly multidimensionally aware—I have learned to become more consciousness of my own consciousness. Because of this, I have become intimately familiar with how my Denise mind works, how my Denise emotions work, and how I personally talk to myself silently inside my head. I know me, and I honestly know how I function, and only because of this was I able to recognize that I was having foreign thoughts playing inside my head on this particular day. As horrible as this next information is, I feel it is extremely important to share. As dangerous as this demonic battle was, I am grateful I had the experience because I intimately know from personal experience, what it sounds and feels like being mentally manipulated by a demon or profoundly negatively focused being. I intimately know what it feels like not only being the target of a demon's focus and attacks, but I also know what it sounds and feels like having a demon attempt to mentally influence me.

This one particular day while outside raking in our yard, I became increasingly aware that the mental dialogue playing in my head were completely flat and monotone, which is the total opposite of how I think and feel. As I continued raking, I started paying closer attention to the thoughts playing inside my head and began analyzing them. They were indeed flat and monotone and repeated endlessly. Because I do not think or mentally talk to myself in this manner, I quickly realized that what I was hearing being said inside my head in what sounded to me to be my own inner dialogue, was in fact the female demon trying to mentally manipulate me into doing something.

I was not possessed but I most certainly was being manipulated in this very intimate way by Rick's female demon. It was an amazing insight and realization for me and in those thirty minutes I observed this phenomenon playing out inside my own head—disguised as my own thoughts—I absolutely knew how some people are so easily influenced to murder other people. They too heard voices inside their heads that probably sound exactly like their own inner mental voice talking to them just as we all naturally do. The only difference between them and me was that I was already exceedingly familiar with how I personally think and talk to myself inside my head. My internal mental dialogue is the complete opposite to flat and monotone! I am very emotionally colorful, and when I am thinking about people or situations like these horrible neighbors, my inner thoughts and emotions are flaming red-hot and intense with plenty of colorful cursing and ranting all over the place. Flat and monotone is the total opposite to how I talk to myself mentally and how I emotionally feel about difficult and frustrating situations and people.

The inner voice I was hearing inside my head that sounded exactly like my own mental voice, kept repeating this sentence in a very flat and utterly unemotional and monotone way.

A LIGHTWORKER'S MISSION

"Get a gun, go over there, and kill them all. Get a gun, go over there, and kill them all. Get-a-gun-go-over-there-kill-them-all.   Get-a-gun-go-over-there-kill-them-all."

During my darkest and most frustrated moments with these neighbors sounded like this: *"Track down a rocket-launcher and flamethrower and savor every second of blowing that lowly negative place to hell n' gone!"* See how colorful and emotional *my* thoughts are in comparison? Grin. I would never physically carry out any of my personal dark, frustrated fantasies, but I admittedly did have many colorful and highly satisfying fantasies about dispatching them to another dimension. Rocket-launchers and flamethrowers were my extravagant and colorful fantasies, not monotone *"Get-a-gun-go-over-there-and-kill-them-all."* My fantasies were emotional venting therapy and a psychological survival tactic at that time. *"Get a gun, go over there and kill them all"* was demonic brainwashing and manipulations to do the deed physically.

This was Rick's demon doing her best to hammer me into submission through what sounded like my own inner dialogue running inside my head. One huge advantage we have over negative, nonphysical beings is that we have a wide range of emotions, and for the most part, they do not. They experience emotions only within a minuscule frequency range way down in the lowly *hate, kill, pain,* and *do harm to others* end of the emotional spectrum.

How many *"crazy"* humans have you heard or read about who said they heard a voice in their heads telling them to do specific things? Things like *get-a-gun-go-over-there-and-kill-them-all?* The main thing I have had to learn repeatedly over lifetimes—and decades in this incarnation—is that just because a thought rolled through my head does not mean it was created by me! Our egos love to believe they do it all of course, but it is important to learn to discern and read energies, thoughts, emotions, visions, and sensations to know who and what it is that's really chattering away and/or flashing images to you via your inner mind's eye and inner dialogue. This is another very important responsibility that goes along with being a sensitive, psychic, clairvoyant seer, and it takes complete self-honesty, time, practice, and dedication to fully master. Being conscious of one's consciousness is exceedingly important.

Moral of my story is honestly and intimately know how *your* mind and emotions work and feel to you. This is how you learn to discern and read other energies, other thoughts and emotions that are not yours but other human's or nonphysical being's. Before reentering higher dimensional increased unity, we must know and master our individuality within physicality.

467

January 11, 2004 as soon as I crawled into bed and turned off the light, I could feel I was not alone in my bedroom. Once my eyes adjusted to the darkness I saw some different shaped etheric objects hovering a couple feet below the bedroom ceiling. One of these etheric objects looked like a four-foot long metallic tube or cylinder and there were two or three other shadowy circular objects. I didn't know what these etheric objects were, but I did recognize the energies and pale luminous light that was present in the nighttime darkness. As I laid there viewing and feeling the energies, I remembered all the many times throughout my life that higher dimensional energies, objects, and beings had manifested like this to me. I had seen and felt them dozens of times starting from early childhood, and this night was an important moment of recognition for me. I realized that this type of interdimensional information exchange was normal for me and had been all of my life.

After a few moments of my consciously connecting some more of those invisible cosmic dots that spanned my lifetime, my forehead or Brow chakra area suddenly went icy-hot. It felt exactly like someone had rubbed one of those over-the-counter creams for muscle pain that feels both ice cold and very hot at the same time on my physical forehead.

I thought it wise—despite my recognizing all of the familiar ET energies and strange nighttime light luminosity—to do some super fast discerning to make sure I wasn't about to be demonically attacked or abducted astrally or anything else. I easily discerned that it was not negative, but positive ET energies. There was not any ET presence as I was used to, only these etheric shapes hovering silently in the space above me over my bed. It had that familiar feel of an ET meeting, but without an ET actually being present etherically. I had the impression they needed to make some more etheric adjustments inside my head—through my Brow chakra—and that was why my forehead suddenly went icy cold and hot at the same time. I felt no pain or movement inside my third eye or brain, only the surface of my forehead being extremely icy-hot.

I telepathically asked a couple questions but got no answers. I sensed it was another etheric adjustment inside my brain and that there was not going to be a meeting or any intimate ET interactions this time. At this point, I also realized that both the cats were not asleep at my feet on the bed as usual. They were spooked by this particular close encounter and decided to sleep elsewhere, which was unusual. The next day they both were still very jumpy and cautious and stayed outside on the now screened-in backyard deck. Obviously, they only enjoyed when the ETs themselves etherically manifested and not these strange etheric devices that looked like tubes and spheres or circles. Persnickety felines.

February 2004 I woke up around 1:15 AM to see a brilliant white light pouring in through the opening in my bedroom doorway from the hall again. In only a couple of seconds the light vanished and it was normal middle of the night darkness inside the house again. I did what I always do which was to discern the energies for all I was worth and as quickly as possible. It did not feel negative at all and I have no other memory of anything else happening that entire night. No dreams, no higher dimensional travels and no teachings or meetings. There was nothing I could sense or discern other than the brilliant light waking me up. Mom was asleep and there were no physical lights left on in the house. It was them again, doing something that evidently wasn't anything I needed to be consciously aware of so I went back to sleep.

March 2004 and Mom and I are in a busy grocery store doing our shopping. While standing in the checkout line we both noticed a tall woman in her late sixties with a large teased and sprayed strawberry blond-colored coiffure standing in a checkout line a few rows down from us. Nothing unique here except she was doing that strange alien *posing* in front of everyone! Mom and I glance at each other to make sure the other one is seeing this too, and then we quickly scanned the rest of the men, women, and children in the grocery store to see if anyone else was watching this woman posing and radiating energies all over the place. No one else even noticed her that Mom or I could tell.

She was a tall, attractive, well-dressed woman in her late sixties with hair and freshly painted nails that looked like she had just stepped out of a beauty salon. (Just stepped out of a beauty salon? Read on.) She was wearing multiple gold necklaces and drop earrings, multiple gold bangle bracelets and a gold watch on the other wrist. There she was all dressed up, meticulously colored, painted, buffed, polished, and posing for the whole grocery store to see! It was funny in a silly way— terribly obvious and out of place and we could not take our eyes off her. I suddenly thought of that song by Madonna, *Vogue* and nearly broke into laughter hearing the opening lines and finger snapping *"strike a pose"* playing on cue in my head. The entire theatrical and very Leo-like scene was that humorously over-the-top but fun and funny in a wonderfully weird sort of way. The whole event is so strange that for a second you wonder if hidden cameras are rolling somewhere, aimed at you, and not at the obvious and unusual person you are watching.

After a few chuckles, giggles, and questioning *"...are you seeing her too?"* moments, I switched into psychic scan mode to try and energetically read the situation. We knew she knew we both were watching her which I felt she really enjoyed but not in that typical lowly ego sort of way. This situation with her Leo-like energies, hair, clothing, gold jewelry and *aren't I fabulous* humor and theatrics reminded me of the Asian man in the hair salon event. He acted very much the same as this elderly woman in the grocery store, just minus all the bright Leo trappings and colors. She was doing something deliberately to capture our attention and show us something energetically—I just had to discern what that was. Mom and I continued staring at her, not worrying about how rude we might have looked to anyone who saw us unashamedly staring at her. Heck, in otherworld interactions such as this, Mom and I were not within physicality and linear time either so the other shoppers were not seeing us as well.

I remember thinking she just had to be a Leo, then smiling to myself because she was not even there physically. I also had the thought that she was unusually tall—just as the young woman in Wal Mart had been—and wondered if that too was something to catch certain people's attention. I also suddenly had the memory of a great line from the movie *Rain Man* when the Dustin Hoffman character said that the prostitute in the Las Vegas casino was *"very sparkly"*. My next thought was whether she was creating these thoughts and impressions I was having. It was funny to me that I was having all these seemingly random thoughts instantly popping into my mind as I watched her posing for us. Flashy, sparkly, Leos? What is she insinuating or symbolizing anyway?

She was holding that soft smile that seemed mischievous to me, and she kept her eyes from looking directly at us, exactly as the Asian man had. I had experienced this direct eye avoidance thing many times over the decades of my numerous interactions with different higher dimensional stellar beings. In some cases, they would deliberately avoid direct eye contact because they wanted me to pay attention to information they were giving me and not them. They often do this for us so we do not become sidetracked or mesmerized by how they appear. In other cases like this with the posing Leo woman in the grocery store, her avoiding our eyes directly was something different. It was another aspect of her posing and part of the message and drama of the entire staged event.

Because I had been a professional dancer for seventeen years, I had learned the importance and techniques of aligning and holding certain poses, angles, and bodylines for the best dramatic and visual impact upon the viewing audience. I knew exactly how I needed to position my entire body—fingertips to toes—and at what angle for each dance step or move I was going to do. You rarely just danced the steps and moves without considering where your viewing audience was and how best to display specific dance movements to them. Dancing and performing dance is highly technical and geometric, and if you can easily visualize lines, angles, and multiple points-of-view, then you know exactly what dance steps and positions need to be done at which angles facing the audience. It is much like aligning multiple mirrors facing the audience so you can project as much energy to them as you are capable of through the dance moves and angles. When you are in perfect alignment with the correct dance steps and your audience, it is like plugging in an electrical plug into an outlet and you instantly have energy flowing directly to them. They feel that flow of energy because it is a part of your performance. What this tall Leo woman and the Asian man did was very much like this. They were transmitting energies and symbolic messages to their audience, which happened to be Mom and me.

These particular higher beings that appeared to us as normal humans were either ETs, time-travelers, or something else and they obviously had something to say via their posing and highly specific energy radiating. I never could fully discern or read what this tall Leo woman in the grocery store was conveying to us that day in March 2004. It seemed she wanted us to see she was there and that she was not human in the same way we 3D humans were. It seemed she wanted us to feel her and the energies she was emanating while holding slightly different poses, lines, and angles. There were no beautiful pastel lights emanating from each hair on her head this time as with the Asian man however. It was just her looking and posing like a great big brightly colored and sparkly Leo woman in her late sixties. Hum, what am I missing?

As Mom and I continued staring at her in the grocery checkout line, she abruptly vanished just as the other two (Asian man and tall female Wal Mart employee) beings had. That too was an aspect of their revealing themselves to Mom and I (and no doubt many of you reading this) that helped confirm the whole event was indeed well outside so-called normal linear reality and consciousness. It was the clever and dramatic finale at the end of their interdimensional quantum performance for us, their small but highly appreciative audience.

As I am writing this page today (in early September 2009), I just had an insight about these two strange events with the Asian man in the hair salon, and the archetypal Leo woman in the grocery store. I cannot believe I just got the punch line to these two events today, five years later! I don't think this is a wild stretch either but a very clever interdimensional pantomime lesson given to Mom and me five years earlier by them both. On the other hand, it very possibly could have been only one being manifesting as two separate and opposite sexed humans. I am leaning more in that direction at this point.

The Asian man was in a hair salon and his unique message was transmitted symbolically to us through every single lighted hair on his head. Amazingly, they had colorful lights and tiny sparks coming out of each of them. Being a child of the Sixties, one of my favorite songs was *Hair*. I have always loved how long and wild hair was like Aquarian antenna pulling in higher frequency energies and consciousness to expand the mind.

The opposite sign to Aquarius is Leo. The decorated and brightly painted woman in the grocery store looked and felt very much like a Leo woman in her sixties, and that I believe was her symbolic message to Mom and me. The two of them with their very different symbolic posing events, was I believe, an attempt to remind me about the new astrological Age energies of Aquarius/Uranus and its opposite sign energies of Leo/Sun. I cannot believe it took me this long to connect those two particular symbolic and otherworldly messages. I hope I just gave the two of them, or however many of them there really was, a good giggle wherever they are.

March 19, 2004 and it is the spring Equinox. On the Equinoxes and Solstices I usually sit alone, get quiet and ready to receive any incoming cosmic and astrological messages or insights that I can. This Equinox I got a very nice loud and clear message and it said, *"You have been doing Alchemical transformations."* I knew instantly that this one sentence was referring to the past six years of my ongoing D 1 47 (ascension) dying, integrating and transmuting process. I loved the perfect and profoundly accurate symbolism of what I had been living and dying through as actual physical alchemy; turning my personal polarized 3D Lead into higher dimensional unified 5D Gold.

I also questioned about how Aquarius and Leo are intercepted in my natal chart and if that too was another sign about my needing to clear, clean, transmute and resolve all of my lower vibrating aspects, energies, projections from the past Age of Leo through to now at the beginning of Aquarius. I got a big affirmative on that question which did not surprise me because I had sensed that was the case already but wanted validation nonetheless.

I also received deeper insights into all of the compressed dark and unpleasant polarity resolution work I had been going through since February 1999, and how it was both personal and collective, extraterrestrial and planetary, and most importantly covering a time span from the beginning of the Age of Leo all the way through up to now. It was literally half a precession of the equinoxes—about 12,500 years. No wonder I was so exhausted!

This year's spring Equinox gift was my seeing the miserable and very difficult things I had been living through for six years, but from a slightly higher perspective. The second I understand the whys to all the misery, darkness, suffering and chaos, it becomes a non-issue to me personally. It becomes The Mission, The Job, and The Work and suddenly does not hold all the sting and pain it did when I could only see it from lower and much closer ground level. The 2004 spring Equinox was an overview about much of what I had been enduring for six long and very difficult years. I also understood that because I had cleared, cleaned, and transmuted the worst of the worst of my own personal energies, polarity, karma, wounds, fears, projections and issues over the past 12,500 years, that much of these lower frequency energies were now primarily outside of me—like Rick and Co. and his female demon. Those lower energies were still there outside and all around me, but I now understood that I had completed the majority of my own personal inner polarity resolution work at this point. For the most part my personal basement was now clean and clear and the planetary collective septic tank was much brighter than it had been in the past six astrological Ages.

In addition, some of the major Earth changes or terrible planetary disasters that were most likely going to happen wouldn't because the First Wave Lightworkers had done so much inner and outer alchemical energy work already. What we had done up to this point had lightened the massive dark planetary load enough that the numerous potential physical catastrophes—like that incomprehensibly large tsunami I had clairvoyantly seen for years—would not need to happen physically. The preverbal shit was going to hit the preverbal fan on physical Earth if we Lightworkers did not get enough of the lower energies transmuted before a certain time. According to what I perceived on the 2004 spring Equinox, we had.

I was not surprised at all because I have always known deep in my heart-of-Hearts that I am not reincarnate now to die in some catastrophic planetary disaster or insane war. Been there, done that, as the saying goes and it is not what is going to happen on the new higher vibrating Earth.

Thanks to these expanded Equinox insights, I finally realized that because I was now carrying more Light than I ever had in this body before, Rick's demon still had me carefully targeted. I would have been an important and rare achievement if she could kill me, cause me to go insane, or even just go to prison for killing Rick and Co. She would have been extremely pleased in having destroyed or stopped a First Wave Lightworker from doing interdimensional planetary energy work with positive higher dimensional Starbeings. It was quiet an important insight and realization for me that day after so many years of feeling as if I may not survive the process plus the constant negative assaults.

March 22, 2004 I had another in a series of dreams about seeing volcanoes erupting and the Earth breaking open and vomiting up red lava everywhere. After I woke up, I knew this was not a prophetic dream at all, but was about what was happening within me via my ongoing transformational ascension process. I was the thing erupting, I was breaking and spewing hot magma blood all over. I was the thing being born out of the violent transformations and deep, inner changes. These symbolic and fierce dreams were about what I was going through, not precognitive dreams about actual physical volcanoes erupting or other Earth changes. They were about *me changes* and not strictly physical changes to the planet.

April 11, 2004 and I am again hearing what sounds like thunder or deep booming sounds. The strange thing is that these thunderous booming sounds seem to be coming from below ground. I have the sense that it is magma flowing deep underground and that another earthquake is coming soon. I have heard this same deep booming sound repeatedly for years now, and in most cases, a few days or weeks after hearing it, there will be a substantial earthquake somewhere on the planet. Over time I learned that what I was hearing was indeed magma flowing, moving, pushing or doing whatever it is magma does underground and that it usually precedes a decent sized earthquake somewhere.

I used to believe that because I could actually hear it that that meant the coming earthquake would be somewhere here in California or Mexico, but I have learned it does not work that way. Just because I am hearing magma moving doesn't mean the earthquake is even going to happen on this side of the planet. It just tells me that a quake—or cluster of quakes—is coming soon and that they could happen in multiple locations around the planet and/or the Pacific Ring of Fire within a few days or weeks of each other.

Because I have been an *Earth sensitive,* I become nervous, agitated and abnormally jumpy and in a tremendous amount of additional physical pain weeks or days before most earthquakes physically happen. Simply hearing booming sounds of magma moving is a physically painless treat in comparison to feeling the very real building pressures within the Earth prior to quakes. Seconds after the earthquake stops I am usually euphoric and feel as if I've just had some much-needed Earth energy orgasmic release! The second the quake is over, I feel 100% physically and emotionally improved as if the weight of the world has been lifted off me—until this cycle starts building again that is.

Because I have long remembered a past life in 12,600 B.C. Egypt, about 1,100 years *prior* to the fracturing planetary disaster, I have always remembered when Earth was naturally in vertical alignment and there were no seasons whatsoever. As a young child in this life I clearly remembered how amazing, beautiful, and stable life on Earth was prior to the disaster that caused the planetary axial tilt we still have today. That ancient memory was a shocking contrast to the mysterious weather and season changes of this life and time. Because of this old planetary wound and enormous imbalance, I sense that it too is another ancient Earth trauma that is currently being transmuted along with everything else. This ancient tilted axis needs to be corrected and aligned now and I sense many of the larger earthquakes are somehow part of this rebalancing of Earth as she too transmutes and ascends.

May 2004 I had another one of those deeply disturbing and exceedingly negative lucid dream experiences where I had to witness and feel actual events that have happened already. In the Lightworking dream event, I found myself in a well-known city in southern California in an underground club for certain gay males. It was an extremely secret, exclusive place, and catered to a very particular group of homosexual males who preferred their sex with plenty of darkness, violence, and deviant behavior. They also occasionally enjoyed male children. I will not give this event anymore focus or energy by saying much about it all, and I am only sharing this particular dark event to express a point.

In this lucid dream event, I again witnessed and personally felt some different actions from an invisible overhead position first. I then had to experience directly from the different perpetrators themselves, and then from within the victims' bodies as well. By experiencing these horrific events from all three of these points of view, I gained a full perspective of the entire event and the different energies and emotions. I would have much preferred to never know that these types of lowly people, places, and dark sexual desires even exist. Even so, it was something I needed to know did exist and that those past physical, emotional, and etheric or psychic energies needed to be energetically transmuted and permanently removed from 3D and 4D.

There was one more thing that happened in this event that was unimaginable and incomprehensible to me. It was that a father took his two very young sons with him to this evil, retched, deviant place to be sexually used by other adult males strictly for their pleasure. I am sharing only glimpses of this particular event to give you a sense of other aspects of what certain Lightworkers have needed to personally witness, intimately feel, and then transmute and permanently remove physically and astrally.

It is so much more pleasant to read about sitting on a beautiful beach or mountaintop somewhere, praying or meditating to heal the oceans or manifest world peace and such than it is to hear about the darkest and exceedingly worst side of humanity and its negative actions across time on Earth. Nevertheless, certain Lightworkers had to do this particular level of energetic Lightwork (that is rarely discussed or even realized), cleaning up the absolute lowest and darkest residual negativity produced by certain human's actions upon other humans across time on Earth.

There is Lightworking, and then there is *Lightworking.* There are numerous layers, levels, and stages to this planetary and collective transformational Lightworking mop-up process, and different Lightworkers were obviously needed to carry out the different jobs. Meditating with others in some beautiful location to help the whales, stop wars, or spread love has obviously not been my personal mission or talent as a First Wave Lightworker functioning with Phase One of the ascension process. This primarily unseen and rarely ever discussed level of intense transmuting of the darkest and most repellant portions of humanities actions across time had to be transmuted first.

The first five months of 2004 was business as usual with the deranged and demon controlled neighbors next-door. When Rick and Mike where gone, the demon would jump to the other side of us and manipulate Juan the groundskeeper. Rick's male pit bull dog continued to bark when he was tied up, and if he and the female dog escaped, they would run loose through the neighborhood killing other dogs and neighbors pet rabbits. It was more of the same lowly negativity and no one did anything about any of it. God knows I was finished confronting, fighting with, and struggling to get the so-called authorities and professionals to do the jobs they were paid to do. I had finally reached that exhausted, beaten-down point where I just wanted to be free of it all. I realized later that my reaching this point of release or seemingly giving up was a huge and important aspect within the ongoing ascension process.

Even though I'd had some higher insights and perspectives into what all was happening and why on the 2004 spring Equinox, I still was deeply involved in my ongoing alchemical ascension process and was not in great shape physically. I told Mom that at this point I knew if we continued living at the portal house I probably was not going to survive for much longer. I had to let her know that I was at the absolute end of my rope with the demon and horrible neighbors and that I had to move out to save myself.

I had desperately wanted to move out of California since 1992, but lack of funds and other unknown

Lightworker obligations held me in place at the portal house. As the years unfolded, it became increasingly obvious why I was seemingly stuck in SoCal. I had plenty of personal, collective, and planetary Lightwork to do in the location of the portal that Mom's house existed within. As I mentioned earlier in my etheric meeting with Si-Re-Ah in September 1995, some Starbeings/ETs had been building etheric interdimensional devices that somewhat resembled large rotating gyroscopes. One of these etheric gyroscope-like devices had been constructed in the space directly above our house. I could clairvoyantly see it and other things up there, but I did not fully understand what all it did.

From 1995, I was slowly unraveling that this device I am comparing to a gyroscope, even though it was vastly more complex than that, was a higher vibrating device that helped anchor the connecting points of the new more complex grid system around Earth. I still do not understand all the details about this new higher planetary grid system and I don't believe I need to. I certainly may have misinterpreted the gyroscope-looking device I clairvoyantly saw, or not fully understood the higher dimensional complexities of the new planetary grid system project. I did sense these gyroscope-looking devices would not be necessary once the new higher frequency grid system was capable of running higher dimensional energies through it. Once it is running constantly I do not believe these etheric devices will remain because they are simply no longer needed.

I did know that this etheric device was needed in the early stages at certain physical areas like Mom's property where multiple new and much more complex grid lines met and connected together. I also knew that this higher and more complex planetary grid system was exactly the same energetic business that many humans are going through with their body rewiring process for the same identical reasons. Both humans and their multiple energy bodies needed to be radically rewired and upgraded to be able to safely and comfortable house and maintain vastly higher and faster vibrating, more light-filled energies and Heart consciousness. The Earth these humans live on is no different. The Earth also needed to be radically rewired and upgraded to be able to carry tremendously higher and faster vibrating light energies as well. The two things are not separate nor are they two different events for different reasons. It is the same process happening within humans' bodies, brains, consciousness and hearts, as is happening within and around Earth.

I absolutely knew that I was a Lightworker Wanderer who had chosen to return to 3D Earth in this incarnation to help build and anchor a new higher frequency planetary grid system, amongst other things. Mom and I were some of the early ground crew members Lightworking the 3D side of the Veil along with some Starbeing friends and family building from their nonphysical, higher frequency side. I also finally understood why Mom had originally been impulse to buy this portal property and place her house in it. By early 2004, I understood a lot more of the mysteries to the many seemingly strange anomalies we had experienced over thirty-two years of living in the portal house and property. I understood why Mom's house was in this portal and why the next-door demon controlled neighbors-from-hell were the polar opposites of us. They and their invisible demonic instigator lived next-door to stop me in any way they could. I was there to do all that I was capable of as a Lightworker, which at that location was to help anchor that grid point from the 3D side. Obviously, the two energies and missions were in opposition with each other and it would not be a pleasant or easy task.

I believe that because Mom's house and property was within a portal area where an old Earth grid point existed, it was an important and valuable location energetically. It makes sense that this was probably why the west side neighbors were such lowly evolved types. When Rick's demon revealed itself to me, I began realizing that was why she existed next-door to us only a few feet away for four years. She was dedicatedly trying to destroy my interdimensional Lightworker mission within the portal house and property in any way she could. After all, we Lightworkers were breaking up the planetary energetic Darkness and replacing it with higher, faster frequency Light. That was as revolting and devastating to the lower focused life forms as it had been for me to live my whole life within that darkness as a being that carried higher Light within herself. In other words, I could relate.

I had been talking about my enormous desire to move out of California for years, and for years, we couldn't for a number of reasons. When Rick, Mike and Company moved into the rental next-door in April 2000, I became desperate to move. After four continuous years of torture at their hands, I knew Mom and I had to get out of there especially now that the new higher planetary grid work and the majority of my personal polarity resolution work had been completed around 2003. The more elaborate planetary grid system had replaced the old, simpler 3D grid system, which meant great amounts of galactic, cosmic, and multiple stellar Light energies will be what the newly rewired and higher vibrating Earth will be about. The new higher Earth—and the newly rewired, integrated and ascended humans living with it—will be more stellar than old solar and planetary as it had been for so long. Mission accomplished, now let us get the hell outta Dodge as fast as possible please because it's killing me!

After endless discussions and considerations, speculations and home and land fantasies, Mom and I painfully realized we could not yet leave California but we could certainly move. I knew at this point that I had to move just to get away from Rick's demon and their constant negativity and noise. It was crushing me and I would have to move no matter what. After many long discussions, I finally got Mom to understand that I was not going to survive if I remained there, and with the portal house mission finally completed, we could and should move into the nearby city. If I could not figure a way to move us out of California and into a quiet, safe and higher vibrating rural area somewhere, then this move into the nearby city would have to do for the moment. Mom finally agreed, at age seventy-five, to sell her home of thirty-two years with a mortgage paid off many years ago and move into a place in the city where we would have to pay rent. Not the perfect solution for us at all but we had to move.

Early May 2004 I called a realtor to come out and talk with us about selling the portal house. Two days later, she was there with papers in hand. She talked, I asked plenty of questions, and Mom slowly became increasingly excited about moving. It was understandably hard for her to give up her house and go through the difficulties of moving when you are in your mid-seventies and disabled. At that point we both were disabled! Nevertheless, after much careful consideration Mom and I decided to have this realtor put the portal house on the market now that our long-term interdimensional higher grid-anchoring mission was completed.

At some point during the realtor filling out dozens of pages of paperwork, I excused myself to go to the bathroom. My bladder was still having those nearly uncontrollable spasms and I needed to urinate every ten minutes or when another hot flash caused another near-death-like sensation. I ran back to my bathroom quickly while the realtor was still filling out paperwork. When I was finished, I noticed something strange in my bedroom window and windowsill area and went over to get a better look. To my shock and horror, the immaculate room had about fifteen or more large black flies buzzing in my window and windowsill. All of our windows had screens on them and both the front and back doors had screen doors. We had never had flies or other flying insects get into our house and I was mortified these huge black flies were suddenly in my bedroom when this realtor was going to be going through the whole house any minute. How in the hell did they get inside the house all of the sudden?

As I stood there watching these oversized, all black and very large round flies buzzing around my bedroom windowsill, I took a swipe at them and three of them fell down dead instantly. I had barely touched them but they dropped like, well, like *flies!* I also noticed that all of them looked like no flies I had ever seen before. They were too black and too large and too round and plump, not to mention they looked like clones of each other. I realized these were not actual physical flies at all, but a clever creation and theatrical tactic created by Rick's female demon. She had created these cloned, barely physically alive flies that stopped working if you breathed hard on them. As ugly and weird as the incident was in that moment, it reminded me of different horror movies I had seen many years earlier and how numerous flies were always a sign that great and serious "*evil*" was at work. I thought what a cheesy tactic the demon was resorting to over the threat of us selling our house and leaving them with no Light to assault continuously.

After the realtor went through the house room-by-room and then the yard and porches, she called a man to come out and place a For Sale sign out at the street for us. I don't know if the realtor saw the many flies or not, and if she did she said nothing about them. I had the sense she did not see them however. Demonic cloned flies or not, after the realtor left I did my *Oh my freakin' god we've just put the house on the market* dance. I did my exclusive version of the Great Dance of Relief throughout the house because—for the first time in four long horrific years—I could actually see the exit door at the end of my severe, intense, polarity resolution ascension process. Not the end of my personal ascension process, but the end of the portal house higher grid anchoring and demonic polarity wars.

The next day these same large black cloned flies materialized in the living room windowsills too. We never saw these flies actually flying around inside the house from room-to-room as normal flies do, but only suddenly appearing in one room's windowsill, and then another room's windowsills, and so on. These black cloned flies kept manifesting for about a week before they all disappeared permanently. That was the last event, the last symbol, the last gesture and attack that Rick's female demon manifested in our lives.

The portal house, which was no longer a portal but just a higher vibrating house, sold for our asking price only three days after we put it on the market. Some man driving past saw our For Sale sign, stopped and instantly fell in love with the place because he was a professional landscaper and gardener and loved what I had done with the yards. He also valued having Jake's two huge greenhouses and wholesale plants and orchid business right next door.

We asked for a thirty-day escrow, and by late June 2004, we moved out of the portal house and into our new (used) house in a small nearby city. It was, without doubt, the end of an era. Mom had lived in the portal house and property from spring of 1972 to early summer of 2004—thirty-two years. I had lived there with her continuously from October 1991 until we sold the place in 2004—thirteen years. My son and his wife were sad to see the place go because they loved it and the special meaning it held for each of them. However, they knew nothing about all that Mom and I had been through at the portal house and property and why. They will for the first time when they read this book.

I had successfully anchored higher dimensional energies through my physical body, my expanding consciousness, and the portal house and land. I had also transmuted substantial amounts of dark, residual Collective energies in 3D and 4D, and I had completed extensive personal polarity resolution work. Because we accomplished everything we had planned on doing at higher soul levels at the portal house and property, it was finally time for us to move. Mom's portal house and property had provided me with an already higher vibrating place to live during my years of repeated ego deaths, polarity resolution, and very difficult transformations that the ascension process naturally creates. It was a special place for our family, but when the intricate physical and interdimensional energy work was completed there, Mom and I needed to move on to our next phase within the ongoing ascension and dimensional shifting process.

EPILOGUE

Completing Phase One
2004–2009

Around 2003 the Starbeings/ETs working from their nonphysical side of the dimensional Veil departed once the new grid system was completed in our area. Because of this, I knew the old 3D portals connected to the old lower 3D planetary grid system were no longer functioning. There will now be new portals that vibrationally match the higher planetary grid system, the ascended planet and nonpolarized, Heart-based conscious ascended humans living on it. Eventually these new higher (grid system) portals will be for us and different Starbeings, ETs, and other-dimensional beings to use. The old lower 3D portals were primarily for 3D humans and animals and not immensely higher frequency Starbeings. Because of the long ascension process and tremendous polarity resolution work, the vastly more integrated, nonpolarized and light-filled humans will slowly begin reentering *Universal Society* and these new higher dimensional Earth portals will be another aspect of that process for us.

Like most First Wave Lightworkers, I worked very hard excavating from deep within polarized 3D darkness, creating higher energy tunnels up and out of it many years ago. It was the *get the boulder rolling uphill from a dead stop* phase within Phase One. I knew I had completed the absolute darkest, most difficult, painful and dangerous phase of my personal ascension process when the Starbeings/ETs left after the completion of the planetary grid rewiring in our area in 2003. That difficult phase was finally finished and it was time for me to move—physically and energetically—to the next stage within the ongoing evolutionary ascension and dimensional shifting process.

Since late June 2004, Mom and I have lived in our new (used) home in a small city even more isolated than we were at the rural portal house. I've had the sense we are in this house now because it is a transition house; a home in the middle of a still lower vibrating old world, yet we exist just vibrationally beyond it. With this next step of exiting a bit more from the lower vibrating world in June 2004, I entered another phase—living in our new transition house within no-man's land in a slightly higher vibrating layer of reality outside the lower 3D one Mom and I reincarnated into. These are the unseen energy stair steps we each travel—step-by-step—pausing every few stairs because it is still exhausting transmuting more of your dense inner energies and physical body, followed by repeatedly integrating and adapting to each more light-filled, higher energetic level.

After the heinous 2000–2004 portal house Polarity War, Mom and I certainly enjoy our new home and quiet privacy very much. I definitely needed a couple of years to recuperate from my severe ascension and polarity resolution process and Lightworker mission. I realized after we moved into our transition house that I had a type of Post Traumatic Stress Disorder. Seriously—I believe I had a mild form of ascension related PTSD for a few years. Not because of the old 3D portal or house within it, but because of Rick and Co. and everything that transpired due to my lengthy and severe polarity resolution work and constant demonic assaults.

I was shell-shocked, worn-out, and still profoundly sensitive to everything, everyone, every sound and smell. I desperately needed to convalesce and release these ascension related traumas and polarity battle wounds—not to mention the anger and hatred I had accumulated during those last four years at the portal house. That alone was more polarity resolution work and it took me some time to process, move through, and then finally release it too. It is interesting how many of us old entrenched and heavily armored First Wave Lightworkers have had *additional* polarity and emotional issues to transmute and release, merely because we are First Wave Lightworkers! We have spent more time in the lower Dark 3D energies and reality, while being more awake and carrying higher energies than most, and that naturally had consequences that we *also* have had to transmute and adjust repeatedly.

When my highly compressed physical ascension process began in February 1999 at age forty-seven, my lifelong nonphysical Starbeings, ETs, and guides were permanently gone. As I mentioned earlier, the Pleiadian has been the only one of my old familiar ET kinfolk who has come through a few times after my ascension process started. I mention this again because it is important to know that we eventually reach a point where we are able to access higher information on our own—which is the whole point. We absolutely will not have guides or Starbeing and ET interactions in the same way we have been used to throughout our Lightworker/Wanderer lives within the old lower polarized 3D world. One aspect of the evolutionary ascension process has pushed us to vibrationally reach the point where we can access our own Higher Selves and Its immense wisdom directly. That in combination with our new High Heart consciousness means we no longer *need* guides, ETs, and other dimensional, nonphysical beings to assist and guide us as we did before. All of these interdimensional relationships have evolved and dramatically changed due to our moving through the ascension and dimensional shifting process.

Because of these many changes, our ESP abilities will naturally evolve as well. Because I was clairvoyant, clairaudient, claircognizant and empathic since early childhood, I could more easily recognize when those ESP abilities were evolving into something even better. Because I have something to compare third dimensional ESP to, I can tell you that having more of a conscious connection with your Higher Self is infinitely better. It is so simple, so calm, so natural and less dramatic and intense than being psychic. Being psychic is rather external; being in closer conscious contact with your Higher Self is altogether internal. It is you and YOU interacting in a new-to-you higher way and it is tremendously easier and more comfortable than being a third dimensional psychic.

Because we have reached the pre-set expiration date for this system, because we have stopped seemingly journeying away from Source, turned around, and are now evolving back towards Home, we are soon going to be experiencing a profoundly different sense of self and corresponding reality. For the past few years, I have come to understand so much more about what the new 5D astrological Age of Aquarius is about.

This understanding or knowing is exactly that—a marvelous higher, spherical knowing as opposed to the old egoic linear intellectual thinking, contemplating, speculating and pondering we are used to from our earlier (past) lives within polarized 3D.

I clearly see how ascended Leo/Sun—the opposite sign and Age to Aquarius/Uranus—represents our lengthy soul journeys and how we developed important and individuated ego's and a sense of separated self from Source. Eventually, this process would reach its expiration date, its grand completion end date and we would stop, turn around, and begin the first phase which is picking up after ourselves and cleaning up the campgrounds we have been camping in for so long—our time learning and creating within polarized physicality on Earth. With the start of our physical ascension process in 1999, we entered the phase of cleaning up and transmuting our many polarized and projected messes and monsters across time on planet Earth. These messes and monsters were the natural results of our acquiring egos and reaching such an extreme sense of separation from Source and everyone and everything else.

With the Leo/Sun separated ego aspects of ourselves thoroughly established over eons of seemingly linear lifetimes on Earth, we finally reached this current phase where we needed to transmute our little individuated Leo ego selves, into the exalted and integrated aspects of high vibrating Leo/Sun. We needed to transmute our fragmented ego selves, plus the many polarized messes they created throughout our physical human incarnational experiences and lessons within 3D, and ascend. Once we accomplished this difficult stage of the grand integration and polarity resolution process, we are, or soon will realize that we have already become very different beings; that we are currently, and rapidly, evolving into a new species. The recently integrated and transmuted 3D human has (is, and will) reached higher 5D Leo/Sun Heart consciousness, which automatically sends these non-polarized and like-vibrating beings into the opposite Aquarian side energies.

With our lower 3D egos and numerous fragmented selves now integrated and transmuted, we vibrationally become ascended/evolved individual humans that are non-polarized and unified within themselves. Once we transmute our baggage in all its diverse forms, we naturally become more than our past numerous and separated parts. We become whole or unified *individually.* This higher frequency state automatically thrusts us into the Aquarian energy side where everything is about *the Group.* However, this Group is comprised of non-polarized, integrated and ascended/evolved Leo individuals. Because of this, we now have a Group (Aquarius) where every individual (Leo) is an ascended and unified being, which obviously indicates that the entire Group is going to be rather spectacular! When combined, the Group also energetically becomes much more than its many integrated, ascended, and individual parts. This is what fifth dimensional beings and communities are. The early evolutionary levels within 5D consist of polarity resolved and integrated individuals, who are each a unique and important piece of a much larger Group puzzle. This is exalted Leo—still an individual even within 5D—fitting and functioning perfectly within the fully ascended 5D Aquarian Group. Together *the Group* is capable of creating and sustaining a very high vibrating world and reality from their High Hearts (evolved Leo) and individual conscious connections to their own Higher Selves (high Aquarius).

Over the past ten years, the ascension process has compressed greatly, creating much shorter periods in-between each of the different stages or phases within it. In the decade of the 1990s and the first four years of the twenty-first-century, these ascension symptoms and phases would last for multiple months and years, whereas by early 2005, they were cycling through in much shorter periods. What used to take months and years to move through—by 2005—was only taking a few weeks or a month. (Today in late 2009, it takes only days or a week or so to move through each new phase.) Everything, including our ongoing ascension process within Phase One has been increasingly speeding up over the past decade.

From 2003 on, I encountered my share of people online who had not even begun the ascension process and had no problems attacking me for what I was sharing at certain forums about the process. It is easy to understand why certain people would naturally think those of us who were, and still are, living the alchemical ascension and dimensional shifting process are wildly delusional nut-jobs! After all, it takes a higher level of discernment and knowing beyond the ego self to even be able to sense if someone is speaking higher truth or not. The difficulty was that many of us living the ascension process could understand their doubts and disbelief, yet they absolutely refused to even consider what those of us living it were merely sharing. It was still a horribly polarized mentality in the majority of these (new age, spiritual, metaphysical) online forums, and it often turned into polarized debates between those who were not experiencing ascension vs. the handful of people who were; between the old Piscean Age consciousness people vs. the handful of new Aquarian Age consciousness people. It was an ugly and frustrating time for me because—as an Elder First Wave Lightworker—all I have ever wanted to do was share information from outside the 3D box.

In 2007 and 2008, I encountered a couple rather serious free-floating, negative energy psychic attacks in the middle of the night. As a lifelong psychic, what I found so interesting was how drastically the polarity had actually changed. All of my life I had lived within a world reality that was very Dark (much lower energies and consciousness). There were no higher vibrating Light energies within the lower third dimensional world I grew up and matured in. That was why, as a child, I was not happy at all about having to be back on Earth now! Reincarnating on Earth then was vibrationally descending into hell where there were no higher frequency, awake or empowered beings and I felt very alone in a Dark and frightening, dangerous world.

By 2007, I could easily clairvoyantly see and psychically feel that this lifelong Dark planetary energy situation had changed dramatically. More accurately, I had evolved/ascended energetically to a level where the higher frequency Light outweighed the lower frequency Dark. It was an epic experience for me after living for fifty-six years in a completely Dark and controlled world. I knew this was what I had been Lightworking towards my entire life—and a few others—but to finally see and feel the lower Dark energies shattered into large, free-floating chunks with massive Light everywhere was a truly magnificent event. Now, after all the difficult Lightwork, dangerous polarity battles and personal polarity resolution work, Light is the majority, and Dark the shattered minority on the run, desperately searching for places and people to grab a hold of again before it finally goes extinct. I have clairvoyantly seen and felt this Darkness pierced by Light, and then over the past ten years, increasingly broken up, dismantled, cleaned and transmuted into pure Light once again. After a lifetime of being a sensitive, clairvoyant Lightworker, aware of and continually affected by lower frequency Dark energies, actually seeing and feeling the Dark being broken up and increasingly replaced with higher Light has been enormously satisfying. My old Lightworker polarity battle wounds and scars do not ache and sting as badly now, and soon, they too will be gone.

By fall of 2008, it was finally time for those of us who had *gone back down* numerous energy stair steps to assist any who honestly desired to begin the ascension process, to float back up to our current levels. The end of 2008 was an important transition for those of us that had spent 2005, 2006, 2007, and 2008 within lower vibrational levels in an attempt to assist anyone who was showing signs that they were ready to leave the lower world and get with the ascension program. However, by fall of 2008 it was unbearable being in that lower energetic state for another minute. By late November 2008, I (and many others) were finally released and catapulted back to a higher level that energetically matched us at that time. It was literally like coming up for air after four long and painful years being deep underwater.

During 2008, I rewrote *The Temple of Master Hotei: A Unique Past Life Memory* and it was finally published in the fall of that year. I had planned to take some time off in 2009. What I obviously did not consciously know, was that when 2009 started, a second book was preparing to surface! The first week of March 2009, I started writing *A Lightworker's Mission* and the three spring months flowed effortlessly and quickly. Then the summer solstice arrived and I—and most everyone and everything else—entered super ascension warp-speed it seemed! From the 2009 summer solstice on, we have literally been climbing one massive energy stair step after another with zero breaks in-between. 2009 was an intense and highly compressed year of moving through numerous energy stair steps and portals to reach a very specific level so we could then make the complete separation from the old lower 3D world starting in September.

After the 2009 summer solstice came a series of potent summer eclipses or astrological portals. These were followed by the September 9, 2009 separation of worlds, which many Lightworkers had been silently waiting to arrive for numerous long and highly painful years. A couple weeks later the fall equinox arrived. Then, on November 8th we entered the Mayan period of *Night Six*. November also presented us with the annual 11-11 portal, and then in December, we reached the annual 12-12 portal. Shortly after this, we will energetically travel through the always-potent winter solstice or 12-21 (2009) energies. Days later, there will be a lunar eclipse on New Year's Eve. What a profoundly intense and shockingly high-speed year 2009 has been.

Interestingly, I finished writing PARTS One, Two, and Three of *A Lightworker's Mission* on September 9, 2009. I also felt the long-awaited release and separation of worlds very intensely that day. My finishing this book on that day was a clear symbol to me that it was time to release my difficult First Wave Lightworker past now. With the separation of worlds that September 9, 2009 brought, the difficult and lengthy Phase One was finally and completely finished. With that, the First Wave Lightworkers and numerous other forerunners entered Phase Two, which we will begin experiencing with the start of 2010. What is Phase Two you may be wondering? It is the enjoyable phase where we gladly design the New Aquarian Earth reality we desire from our ascended and creative Leo High Heart Consciousness.

About The Author

Denise Le Fay is a lifelong sensitive clairvoyant and interdimensional traveler who has remembered many of her past lives from early childhood. She currently lives in southern California where she enjoys writing, blogging, being creative, and thoroughly enjoying the company of her cat. Visit her site TRANSITIONS at deniselefay.wordpress.com/ Denise can be contacted at: deniselefay@gmail.com

About The Artist

Yasmeen Harper has been drawing and painting since early childhood. Her favorite subject matter has always been the human face and figure. Today, she focuses mostly on commissioned portrait art of people and pets. She currently lives in Las Vegas where she also creates hand painted lettering, graphic art and mural art for businesses and private residences. You may view Yasmeen's work and contact her at:

www.FaceValuePortraits.com and
www.JasmineSigns.com

mythical culture of Palestine. This is their awkward age; one cannot watch even their gaiety, though it is genuine enough, without feeling that it lacks true cohesion. Like adolescents, they have not yet developed a style—or, rather, the style is a hastily assembled surface, and they remain frozen in form-lessness underneath: what is their constant singing but an *attempt* to achieve form?

But the spectacle of normal adolescence is made tolerable by its character as part of a social whole, one stage in a more or less determined life-history; we think we know what the adolescent is likely to become. These people are not adoles-cents; their "awkwardness" springs precisely from the fact that they have been wrenched from the normal social and historical context and have become a world to themselves. And therefore their personalities take on a certain fixity and abstraction, just as their own image of the world, contained as it is in a number of symbols and ceremonials referring to a mythical future, is necessarily fixed and abstract. They are like figures in some pageant expressing a meaning that must remain ultimately unclear simply because this particular spectacle is the only means of expressing it; and the crudity of the figures who enact this spectacle—their archaicism, so to speak—is a part of the meaning: they exist, one might say, for this occasion only, this moment of history, deprived of the past and therefore deprived also of the future, which can have meaning for us only as a development out of the past. It is almost impossible to think of them as moving back into what we regard as the normal stream of life without at the same time denying the significance of what has happened to them: this is what makes it so difficult to confront them clearly, and why so much that has been said about them seems mere rhetoric, whether the rhetoric of optimism or that of despair.

It is possible to ask whether these figures can ever really become anything else than what they are. The film has no answer to give and it makes a bad mistake in trying. Mr. Levin identifies himself very closely with the people in his film (he himself plays one of the few "acted" roles), and much of the film's documentary value comes, no doubt, from its having been made so completely from the inside. But this necessarily leaves it with no perspective beyond those scattered elements of life and culture which the fleeing Jews themselves have hastily collected, and which they employ less as definitive ways toward any clearly defined state of "health" than as temporary psychological expedients to protect them from an intolerable past. Perhaps one cannot expect that they themselves should at once face and assimilate their experience—though if there is any way to health for them, it must require this sooner or later. But if we are to understand what they represent (I assume it is important to try), then we should not too readily accept their own version of the meaning of their behavior—more especially because in their desperation they have seized upon certain cultural elements that are likely to be accepted as automatically meaningful.

These elements consist, on the one hand, of the more or less official symbols of a Zionist future—Hebrew songs and dances, the Jewish flag, the word "Shalom," the word "Palestine"—and, on the other, of certain "fundamental" concerns (also connected with Zionism): the conception of Palestine as a "soil" in which to strike "roots"; above all, a fierce concentration on children—the expected baby who *must* be born in Palestine, the child of the new "generation," who is to represent victory, happiness, life, everything that Europe is not. There is a profusion of children in the film, but the camera rarely lingers on them for their own sake—as if they were not interesting because they are not survivors. And the Jews carry them across Europe like so much necessary furniture to be used in setting up their homes in the new land. As the ship

248

sails into Haifa harbor, escorted by a British warship, a child is born. In another shot, the camera moves in for a close-up of a child at its mother's breast. And as the film ends, Sara looks hopefully to the future, expecting her own child.

For these Jews, it is the mere fact of survival that counts most. Perhaps Palestine itself is sometimes no more to them than a symbolical embodiment of their survival, a name to be written on the earth as they write their own names on the walls of their stopping-places, to prove that they have lived. How much more than this Palestine can be will be determined only in the future—the real future, not the future they create as a protection against the past—and for each of them separately. (Even the obvious analogy between the modern exodus from Europe and the biblical exodus from Egypt, which is immediately suggested by this film and has become almost a standard formula in journalism, requires examination: the Jewish awareness of a *long* history often masks a refusal to be aware of history at all.) And those children, too, born to be a new generation in the new land, must be recognized for what they are: a psychological expedient, one more *evidence* of survival and thus, perhaps, a way out of the real problem, which is not survival but the re-establishment of humanity. The fact that the children are also real children only makes the problem sharper. In the context of the events that stand behind this film, is a picture of a baby at its mother's breast *necessarily* a symbol of hope?

(*1948*)

Paisan

THE FORCE of *Paisan* is in certain images of danger, suffering, and death that remain in one's consciousness with the particularity of real experience. Like the stacked dry corpses of Buchenwald or the clownish figure of Mussolini hanging by the heels, these images have an autonomy that makes them stronger and more important than any ideas one can attach to them.

In the Sicilian episode, a few American soldiers pick their way in the dark along some vague path beneath a wall, crouching slightly, talking in whispers; one of them chews gum rapidly. Various qualities belong to the men: they are young; they have a certain motor efficiency that makes them appear in general well trained, courageous, and intelligent; they exhibit a solidarity that is practical rather than emotional, resting on a common-sense acceptance of their situation; they are in innumerable ways "soldierly," masculine, and American.

In an American film, these men would be "GI's"—the rough and serviceable vessels of democracy; their personal qualities would be expressed through contrived and carefully differentiated patterns of symbols and ideas (one of the group might be a little comical, and another "spiritual" or "cultured"; one might be named Rosenbloom, and—at the very best—one might be a Negro); and their presence on the coast of Sicily would be given some specifically "universal" relevance (probably the episode would begin with shots indicating the scale of the invasion, and then move in to pick up this "representative" group). But here the qualities of the men and the nature of their situation are inseparably contained in the particulars of their physical presence—for example, the way the large and ungraceful helmets diminish the faces beneath them, forcing one to see each man as a whole body, with his "personality" expressed in movement and in the details of his clothing and equipment; or the astonishingly flat and metallic voice of the leader, at once childish and self-assured, suggesting a lack of sensitivity that may be appropriate to his function; even the chewing gum is for once not a symbol of value but simply a fact of nature. And the situation of the men—removed from the elaborate political, moral, and military framework that an American director would use to give it "meaning"—becomes also a part of the screen image, a visible fact of experience: these moments of tension are among the possibilities in a man's life.

This quality of "existential" truth is vitiated later in the episode, when an attempt at communication between one of the soldiers and an Italian girl is used (in a typically "American" manner) to draw vague populist sentiment out of a purely accidental limitation, as if there were some great truth still to be discovered in the fact that one person speaks English and another Italian, and yet both are human beings. But the earlier quality is regained in the treatment of a group of German soldiers and in the image of the Italian girl herself, whose large and somehow undefined body—to an American eye almost repellent in its lack of physical charm, and at the same time disturbing in its persistent suggestion that charm is irrelevant—becomes the leading visual element of the episode. At the end, when this body is seen for a moment dead and sprawling on the rocks, hardly more ungraceful than when it was alive, it contains in its visible presence the dramatic meaning and conclusion of the episode (the product of war is always a corpse, but always a *new* corpse)—though Rossellini's fundamental lack of taste permits him to spoil this effect with a final scene of cheap irony.

In the Florentine episode, there is a moment when a group of partisans captures two Fascist snipers. A confused knot of men bursts around a corner into the sunny street and moves rapidly toward the camera, growing larger and clearer. One man is dragged along by the shoulders, kicking and struggling; another, erect, is propelled by blows that force him to move ahead as if he were part of the group, rather than its object, and shared the general desire to bring matters to a quick conclusion. Just in front of the camera, the men are thrown to the ground and left for a moment inside a small circle, the camera pointing downward at their backs. One of them cries, "I don't want to die!" There is a burst of machine-gun fire, and the scene is over.

This scene moves so rapidly that the action is always one moment ahead of the spectator's understanding. And the camera itself remains neutral waiting passively for the action to come toward it and simply recording as much of the action as possible, with no opportunity for the variation of tempo and the active selection of detail that might be used to "interpret" the scene; visually, the scene remains on the same level of intensity from beginning to end, except for the increasing size and clarity of the objects as they approach the camera—and this has the effect of a "natural" rather than an interpretive variation. The speed of the action combined with the neutrality of the camera tends to exclude the possibility of reflection and thus to divorce the events from all questions

253

of opinion. The political and moral distinctions between the snipers and their captors do not appear (even the visual distinction is never very sharp), and the spectator is given no opportunity to assent to the killing. Thus the scene derives its power precisely from the fact that it is not cushioned in ideas: events seem to develop according to their own laws and to take no account of how one might—or "should"—feel about them.

The final episode, which describes the defeat and capture of a group of Italian partisans and American OSS men on the Po River, is full of these strong images: a corpse floats down the river, held up by a life preserver, with a crude sign —"partigiano"—stuck behind its shoulders; a baby walks among the unresponding corpses of its family, crying as if it will never stop—only the baby and a dog remain alive; a hanged man sways and turns quietly in the wind, while the other prisoners, lying on the ground below him, talk in whispers ("What will they do to us?" "I have wet myself like a baby."), and the legs of a German guard move back and forth in the foreground; a row of prisoners stands at the edge of a boat, and the Germans push them off one by one to drown (but in this there is perhaps too much contrivance; Rossellini slows up the tempo a little, and one is allowed to become aware of the beauty of the shot).

Again there is no room for ideas. All questions have been decided long before the episode begins, and to reaffirm the decisions would be as irrelevant as to reconsider them. All that matters is the events themselves in their character as recorded experience: not why these things happen, but the fact that they happen, and above all the particular forms of their happening.

I began by suggesting what might have happened to some of Rossellini's material in the hands of an American director.

Since the film is concerned throughout with relations between Italians and Americans, this contrast is particularly
relevant, and I should like now to carry it further.

American culture demands victory; every situation must
somehow be made an occasion for constructive activity. The
characters and events in serious American films are given a
specifically "universal" or "representative" meaning in order
to conceal the fact that there are situations in which victory is
not possible. The idea survives—that is a victory; the man dies
—that is a defeat; the "GI" is created to conceal the man's
death.*

But *Paisan* is the product of a country that has known itself compromised and defeated for (at least) twenty-five
years. In the presence of Mussolini, Victor Emmanuel, and
the Pope, no public myth could survive; all action and all
ideas of action become contemptible, and the sensitive Italian was forced into idealist philosophy or into the cultivation
of personal experience—that is, into a passive and aesthetic
attitude to life. (See Guido Piovene's remarkable article in

* A typical figure in our culture is the "commentator," whose
accepted function is to make some "appropriate" statement
about whatever is presented to his attention. "Grim evidence of man's inhumanity to man," he remarks of the
corpses of Buchenwald. "The end of the road," he says as
we stare at dead Mussolini on the newsreel screen. (And
what can one do but agree?) Even in its most solemn and
pessimistic statements, this voice is still a form of "affirma-
tion" (its healthy tone betrays it); at bottom, it is always
saying the same thing: that one need never be entirely passive, that for every experience there is some adequate response; at the very least, there is always—there must be—
something to say.

the March *Horizon.**) Even an active political figure like Silone reveals in his novels a distinctly masochistic relationship to the very political realities he opposes; in the United States, only Southern and Negro writers (for obvious reasons) ever approach the utter self-abasement represented by Silone's portraits of the peasants with whom he identifies himself.

Rossellini neither requires nor dreams of victory; indeed, it is only defeat that has meaning for him—defeat is his "universal." (Even *Open City* is conceived in terms of passivity: heroism is presented not as the capacity to act but as the capacity to suffer; the priest and the Communist are one, and the activity of the underground leads not to victory but to sainthood.) From this hopelessness—too inactive to be called despair—Rossellini gains his greatest virtue as an artist: the feeling for particularity. In the best parts of *Paisan,* it is always the man who dies, and no idea survives him unless it is the idea of death itself.

One more point may make this contrast clearer. In the three good episodes of *Paisan* (Sicily, Florence, the Po River), there is very little effort to individualize the characters; each displays only as much of himself as his situation requires (the most important exception to this is the conversation I have already mentioned between the Italian girl and one of the Americans in the Sicilian episode). And since the situations are abnormal, the activities of the characters do not in any full sense represent them: they remain strangers. Certain of them stand out because they are more continuously prominent in action, but there are important characters who appear only momentarily—for instance, the German soldiers in Sicily or the partisan leader Cigolani in the Po

* "The Italian Church and Fascism," by Guido Piovene, *Horizon,* March 1948.

River episode. But the reality of these figures does not depend on "characterization"; they come to the screen full-grown, and are as real in ten seconds as they could be made in half an hour—they are *visibly* real. (The stranger one sees on the street is no less real and no less individual because one does not know him.) In American films, on the contrary, the characters are likely to be emphatically individualized, and precisely because they are basically abstractions: without character traits and personal histories, they would disappear.

But the rejection of ideas is also a rejection of principles. Rossellini has no intellectual defenses, and when he attempts to go beyond the passive representation of experience, he falls at once into the grossest sentimentality and falsehood. The monastery episode, in which three American chaplains (one Protestant, one Jew, one Catholic) are taught some lesson—humility, perhaps; certainly not tolerance—by a group of Italian monks, is so outrageously vulgar that it must surely be the product of a calculated dishonesty, probably for political reasons. And the dishonesty is made all the plainer by the fact that a view of the Church such as no politically sophisticated Italian could seriously advance in his own name is here presented through the eyes of three simple-minded Americans (what little intelligence they display among them is all given to the Catholic); by this device, Rossellini tries to preserve his "neutrality." (A similar tenderness for the clergy appears also in all the other Italian films I have seen: *Open City, Shoeshine,* and *To Live in Peace.* Piovene suggests that the key factor in Italian "bad faith" is a refusal to deal honestly with the issue of the Church.)

But the sentimentality goes beyond any single issue. The "message" of *Paisan*—after all, it does have a "message"—is that the whole meaning of war (indeed, the whole meaning

257

of history) is suffering and death. Moral and political differences are obscured: the death of a Fascist equals the death
of a partisan, and, as Siegfried Kracauer points out, the
American liberators look much like the German conquerors;
even the German officer of the Po River episode is presented
sentimentally (and therefore with relative success; Rossellini's complete failure with the sadistic German officer of
Open City is evidence of his inability to deal with real moral
distinctions). This view of war is always valid: Falstaff is
more nearly right than Prince Hal, and Thersites than Ulys-
ses. But it is also a view that has a special attraction for a
defeated Fascist nation, and Rossellini cannot restrain himself from taking a special advantage of it; there must always
be one more push—and it always destroys his position, for if
death and suffering are not *in themselves* the greatest of mis-
fortunes, then we are back in the field of politics and morals,
and it is Prince Hal who is right. Thus, in the Sicilian episode,
after the Italian girl is dead, there must be the final scene
to show how cruelly she has been misunderstood. In Naples,
it is not enough that the Negro and the Italian child are both
suffering; it must be shown that *even* an American Negro is
shamed before Italy's misery. In Rome, it is not enough that
the prostitute and the soldier are both unhappy; the prostitute must be the *very same girl* that he remembers from his
first days in Rome and has looked for in vain; and at the end
we must see him throw away her address with a sneer: "Just
the address of a ——."

A number of Americans collaborated with Rossellini on
this film, and their influence is apparent—not least in its sentimentality. But the strength of this American element is a
sign not so much of the corrupting influence of America as
of the accomplished corruption of Italy: only the fact of defeat is Rossellini's own; beyond that, he must nourish himself
at the table of the victors. And there is a significant difference

258

that betrays the nature of this relationship. American senti-mentality is rarely without a note of aggressiveness: I am a small man *and* I shall inherit the earth (this must be one of the things that impress Europeans as hypocrisy). But Ros-sellini transforms this into complete passivity: I am *only* a small man and I have suffered terribly.

From this point of view, the six episodes can be plausibly interpreted as representing the fantasies of the eternally de-feated as he tries anxiously to read his fate in the counte-nance of a new master. In Sicily, the Italian girl is rejected: the American does not know that she was really his friend, and the one who could testify for her is dead. In Naples, the American finds his heart overflowing with pity: he *under-stands;* he, too, has suffered. In Rome, the Italian girl is re-jected again: she is a whore; she has not waited. But in Florence the American nurse presses the dying partisan's head to her breast; and in the monastery, the arrogant victor is humbled before the simple goodness and wisdom of those who have chosen to exempt themselves from history (see Pio-vene again). Finally, on the Po, the American is at last both loved and loving, directing the Italians in their struggle and then losing his life in a protest against their murder.

(*1948*)

Day of Wrath:
The Enclosed Image

CARL DREYER'S basic problem as an artist is one that seems almost inevitably to confront the self-conscious creator of "art" films: the conflict between a love for the purely visual and the tendencies of a medium that is not only visual but also dramatic. The principle that the film is a medium based on movement has often been used to justify a complete preoccupation with visual patterns, as if the ideal film would be one that succeeded in divorcing movement from content, but it is this principle itself that raises the problem, for the presentation of human beings in movement necessarily leads to the creation of drama; thus the maker of "art" films, unless he limits himself to complete abstraction or to generalized poetic symbolism, tends to raise aesthetic demands that he cannot satisfy within the framework he has set. Only in the earlier parts of *Day of Wrath* can Dreyer be said to have solved this problem. And the solution, though brilliant, is essentially unstable; the weaknesses of the film's later parts grow out of the virtues of its beginning.

The film opens with the playing of "Dies Irae," a dreadful, insistent hymn prolonged to the point where it comes to seem a kind of outrage; it is music that does not aim at the listener's pleasure or require his consent. In effect, this music establishes the existence of a world whose graces pretend to no connection with the needs of human beings, a world that may find it proper in the realization of its designs to burn a woman alive for being a witch.

There is only the most unemphatic indication that such a world is supposed to have existed in Denmark early in the seventeenth century. It is not a historical world—though it exemplifies certain historical ideas—and the primary tendency of Dreyer's direction is to keep it from becoming historical, to preserve it self-enclosed and static. Everything leading up to the execution of the witch Marthe is presented like a pageant: each movement is graceful and dignified, each figure in some particular fashion beautiful, each shot "composed"; and the camera focuses always on the leading figures of the pageant itself, following their slow and predetermined movement with an entranced solemnity that permits no glance at the actuality which has brought them into being. Not a single shot is spent on documentation, and though the whole "issue" is between good and evil, these concepts, too, exist only as parts of the spectacle: "evil" is the figure of an old woman whose function is to be thrown upon a fire after completing certain movements of flight, suffering, struggle, and despair; "good" is the process by which this ceremony is carried out.

No dramatic conflict surrounds the witch herself—her one mistaken effort to bargain for life remains no more than an expected stage in her destruction—and there is only the barest beginning of the drama that is to take place after her death. Her very sufferings are given an explicit quality of formality: three screams mark the three decisive moments—capture, confession, death; when she lies bound to the ladder and impotently shaking her fist, one's attention is drawn to a pattern of leaf-shadows that moves across her face. And all problematical aspects of the subject—questions of justice and authority, the reality of witchcraft, the existence of God and the Devil—are avoided or postponed: it is shown, for example, that the pastor Absalon, who is the leading figure in the witch's condemnation, is himself in an ambiguous situation, but this is not permitted to become a dramatic problem until after her death; and the activities that constitute the witch's crime, though formally indicated, remain vague—only later on is it shown that she might have been regarded as actually dangerous.

Yet this formalized and narrow spectacle creates a degree of excitement beyond anything one experiences during the later, more dramatic portions of the film; by the time the witch falls screaming upon the fire, the tension has come close to a point at which it might be reasonable to leave the theater. The chief source of this tension seems to be in the interplay between Dreyer's general approach to art and certain of the specific tendencies of his medium.

Dreyer's initial impulse, in his deliberate exclusion of the historical and dramatic, is to deprive events of the quality of reality; it is this, indeed, which accounts for his concern with the past: since the past can be contemplated but not changed, it exists from one point of view as an aesthetic object ready-made—one can experience it "pure." But he practices his aestheticism on events that possess *a priori* an unusual emotional importance, and in one of the most realistic of all mediums. In the screen's absolute clarity, where all objects are brought close and defined unambiguously, the "reality" of an event can be made to inhere simply in its visible presence; so long as the internal structure of a film remains consistent, all its elements are in these terms equally "real"—that is, completely visible. Thus at his best—which means, in this film, when he is creating his own images and not imitating the creations of seventeenth-century painting—

Dreyer is able to give his aestheticized vision of the past all the force of reality without impairing its aesthetic autonomy; in the absence of a historical-dramatic reality, the purely visible dominates and is sufficient: the witch is an object of art, but she is also—and just as fully—a human being (she is *there*), and she is burnt; the burning is so to speak accomplished by the camera, which can see the witch without having to "interpret" her.

The effect is something like a direct experience of the tension between art and life. In a sense, the image *as* image becomes a dramatic force: the issue is not, after all, good against evil or God against Satan, but flesh against form; stripped as it is of all historical or social reference, the spectacle is of a woman burnt to serve beauty. It is a spectacle not to be understood—the image itself is all the meaning—but to be endured; and the enormous excitement that surrounds it, the sense almost of a prolonged assault on one's feelings, results largely from the exclusion of all that might be used to create an appearance of understanding. Even to see the witch as a victim of injustice would provide a certain relief by placing the events on the screen within some "normal" frame of response. But no such opportunity appears, nothing *in* the film is allowed to speak for the audience or to the audience (two of the characters cannot bear to watch the burning, but this is not what is wanted: it is merely a sign of their weakness). It is as if the director, in his refusal to acknowledge that physical movement implies dramatic movement, were denying the relevance of the spectator's feelings; one is left with no secure means of connecting the witch with reality, and yet she is real in herself and must be responded to; as responses are blocked, the tension increases.

In this blocking of responses, it is again important that Dreyer's aestheticism leads him to the past. The historical past, being real, embodies a multitude of possibilities; the aesthetic past is created by eliminating all possibilities but one, and that is the accomplished one. Thus time becomes fate: the image is distant and untouchable because its form was fixed long before we come to see it; the witch *will* be burnt because witches *were* burnt. The feelings of the spectator really are in a way irrelevant: he is watching what has ceased to exist, and there is no one to "care" what he feels. He has his feelings nevertheless.

In the later parts of the film, in order to relieve the tension that has been established, it became necessary to permit a reassertion of those historical-dramatic elements which have been so rigidly suppressed. But the basic style of the film is already fixed, and this need to introduce new elements results in incongruities, passages of boredom, and dramatic incoherence.

The dramatic plot which begins to work itself out after the witch's death concerns the adultery of the pastor's young wife Anne and his son Martin; Anne becomes a witch, ensnaring her lover and later killing her husband by the power of evil. The ambiguity of the pastor's position, too, is involved with witchcraft: his sin was to conceal the fact that Anne's mother was a witch. Thus witchcraft is no longer pure image, it is a way of behaving, and the question of its reality is no longer to be avoided. A psychological answer is impossible: Dreyer is already committed to keeping the past *in* the past. But the supernatural answer, which is the one he chooses (and with a hesitation that only makes matters worse), is just as bad: once the question of witchcraft is raised, no one can be expected to believe in its reality.

The attempt to impose belief by purely aesthetic means is inevitably a failure, both dramatically and visually. There is a scene in which the pastor walks home at night through an "evil" storm that is the height of visual banality; then his wife, at home with her lover, is shown saying, "If he were

265

dead—"; then back to the pastor, who suddenly straightens up in the howling wind and says to his companion, "I felt as if Death had brushed me by." And there is a continual effort to use the camera for symbolic comment that eventually becomes clear enough but is never convincing: when Anne first tries her "power" in order to call Martin to her side, Dreyer repeats on her face the shifting pattern of leaves that appeared on the face of the old witch before she was burnt; when the lovers walk in the fields, the camera keeps turning upward to the trees above their heads. In general, there is an attempt to equate the outdoors, the world of nature, with evil (the pastor's mother, who is the one firm moral pillar, is never seen outside the rigidly ordered household she controls); but the camera cannot create a religious system.

The purely dramatic failure is most obvious in the film's conclusion, when Martin turns against Anne and thus leads her to confess her witchcraft. Martin's defection is not made to seem an adequate reason for Anne's confession, and Martin's action itself is entirely without motivation: the very skill with which the director now tries to transmute visual patterns into drama (as earlier he had tried to make dramatic patterns purely visual) becomes a kind of irrelevancy. But even in this later section of the film there is still much that is successful. When Anne resolves to kill her husband, a virtual transformation of character is accomplished by the manipulation of lighting. And whenever the aesthetic image does not come into direct conflict with the dramatic structure, it can still take on some of the purity and completeness of the earlier scenes—for example, in the procession of choir boys at the pastor's funeral—except that now the image is felt as an interruption of the action.

At bottom, the film is an aesthetic paradox: out of the pure and enclosed image Dreyer creates a sort of "pure drama," in which the point of conflict is precisely the exclusion of drama; but this in turn creates a tension that the image alone cannot resolve; the dramatic nature of the medium must reassert itself in the later portions of the film, and Dreyer is involved again in the initial contradiction.

(1948)

damnum fon this branch... that a person that shall maintain...
an action... that the one acre of ... machine and...
... finally it ... portion of ... that said law was
... made as to the ... called ... mitigation.

(587.)

Re-Viewing
the Russian Movies

A curse on all Marxists, and on all
those who want to bring into all the
relations of life hardness and dryness—
LEV DAVIDOVICH BRONSTEIN
(1896); quoted by Bertram D. Wolfe
in *Three Who Made a Revolution.*

SIX of the famous movies of the Russian Revolution have been shown recently in New York. Five of them are among the most celebrated products of what we have all agreed to call the great age of the Soviet cinema: Pudovkin's *The End of St. Petersburg,* Dovzhenko's *Earth,* and Eisenstein's *Potemkin, Ten Days That Shook the World,* and *The General Line.* The sixth, *Tsar to Lenin,* is a collection of authentic pictures of actual people and events taken by perhaps a hundred different photographers—newsreel and military cameramen and amateurs, including the Czar himself and members of his circle.

I had seen most of these movies at one time or another, but none of them for at least fifteen years, and I went this time looking very consciously for the pathos and irony of that

269

enormous historical failure which now weighs so dangerously on us all. Irony, God knows, was easy enough to find; every glimpse of the enthusiasms of that revolution brings forth all at once the whole wearisome joke of human aspiration and wickedness—we shall be having it dinned into our ears, in just this form, until we die. There was more irony than the most avid of paradox-mongers could possibly want. Only to see the word "comrades" or the word "workers" in a subtitle was enough. Before I was through I could no longer even understand why our age insists on finding the idea of irony so attractive. I would have given up all ironies, and the sense of tragedy and the sense of history along with them, just to have stupid, handsome Nicholas grinding his heel once more into the face of unhappy Russia.

Pathos was another matter. For pathos there must be victims, and in five of these six movies the glare of triumphant righteousness is so blinding that one can't see any victims at all, only a few martyrs of the working class, their lives well expended, and a few bourgeois or monarchist anachronisms, swept properly into the dustbin of history. No death is without meaning; even that baby hurtling in its carriage down the Odessa steps in *Potemkin* is part of the great plan, and the spectacle is exciting but not saddening. Of course it could be said that Eisenstein and Pudovkin and Dovzhenko were the real victims, ultimately betrayed by the revolution they celebrated; but that idea, if it is important at all, becomes important only on reflection. It is hard to feel the pathos of their lives when you see them playing with corpses; if they had got the chance, they would have made a handsome montage of my corpse too, and given it a meaning—their meaning and not mine.

I do not say that these films of the famous Russian directors left me unmoved, but what I felt was all the wrong things, anger more than anything else. And it is just the best

270

elements that arouse the greatest anger. When Eisenstein photographs the slow raising of the bridge in *Ten Days That Shook the World,* with a dead woman's hair stretched over the crack between the two sides as they come apart, and a dead horse hanging in its harness higher and higher above the river as the bridge goes up, the whole slow sequence being further protracted by the constant cutting in of other shots in "rhythmic" contrast, these controlled elements that once marked Eisenstein's seriousness as an artist become now the signs of an essential and dangerous frivolity which, one suspects, was a part of what made him an artist in the first place (and which is exhibited also in the intolerable pedantry of his theoretical writings). And when Pudovkin in *The End of St. Petersburg* cuts rapidly back and forth from scenes of fighting at the front to scenes of excitement in the stock exchange, one's anger is mingled with shame: this sequence is mentioned with honor in the histories of the cinema.

To be honest, I must say that I had come with some hope of finding that the pretensions of the great Soviet cinema were false. Since I had never, in fact, quite accepted those pretensions, it may not count for much to say that these films seemed to me, in aesthetic terms, as successful as ever. But I do mean that they belong with what we are accustomed to call great films, which is to say that they are crude, vulgar, often puerile, but yet full of sudden moments of power. The scene of the Odessa steps, for instance, deserves all the praise that has been given to it, and perhaps even justifies a recent attempt by Timothy Angus Jones (*Encounter,* January 1955) to establish *Potemkin* as an "epic," especially when one recalls that epic is often an expression of barbarism and superstition. It was not at all an aesthetic failure that I encountered in these movies, but something worse: a triumph of art over humanity. It made me, for a while, quite sick of the art

271

of the cinema, and sick also of the people who sat with me in the audience, *mes semblables*, whom I suspected of being either cinema enthusiasts or Communists—and I wasn't always sure which was worse. (In fact the audiences were unusually silent at most of these movies, and for all I know may have been suffering the same emotions as I was.)

It has been said often that the great achievement of the early Soviet cinema was its grasp of the impersonal, of the drama of "masses" and "forces." It was a new art, for a new age, in which the individual was seen to have his truest being as part of the mass. The real hero of these movies is history. But if there is one thing we should have learned from history—and from the history of the Russian Revolution above all—it is that history ought to be nobody's hero. When it is made into a hero, it is not even history any more, but falsehood. There is something peculiarly appropriate in Eisenstein's and Pudovkin's fondness for architectural and statuary symbolism. Eisenstein represents the rising of the workers, for instance, with a famous montage of three stone lions, one asleep, the second with its head lifted, and the third rising to its feet; by projecting these images in rapid succession, he creates the impression of a single lion stirred into action. This is another example of montage that is mentioned with honor in the textbooks, usually with the information that the three lions were not even photographed in the same city, a fact which is supposed to cast light on the question of whether the cinema is an art. The use of the stone lion is, indeed, a clever and "artistic" idea, but it is also fundamentally cheap, and in both respects it is characteristic of Eisenstein, and of the Soviet cinema generally. What we want most, that cinema rarely gives us: some hint of the mere reality of the events it deals with. The important point about the lions is that all the "art" of their use depends on the fact that they are not alive.

Against the films of Eisenstein and Pudovkin, *Tsar to Lenin* has at least the advantage of not being a work of art or even, in the usual sense, a documentary. This is not to say that it is completely artless. The material, gathered over a period of years from a multitude of sources, was carefully arranged and, no doubt, carefully selected. The sequences are presented as much as possible in chronological order, and there is a spoken commentary by Max Eastman (the pictures themselves, of course, are without sound). At one point there is even a rudimentary "montage," contrasting the homely and unassuming Kalinin with the aloof and splendidly uniformed Czar. I don't suppose, either, that the process of selection rested solely on the objective interest of the material. It is notable, for instance, that the only pictures of an execution show the shooting of Communist prisoners by soldiers of Kolchak's army; on the Bolshevik side there is only a photograph of the room in which the Czar and his family were killed, and a brief glimpse of the head of the Cheka, identified by the commentator as "the incorruptible Dzerzhinsky." (What can it mean to call a political mass murderer "incorruptible"?) Again, in contrast to *Ten Days That Shook the World*, where the existence of Trotsky is never even acknowledged (except for a brief shot of an unnamed figure with the familiar pointed beard shown vaguely "plotting" against Lenin), this film takes perhaps special care to document as fully as possible Trotsky's role as a Bolshevik leader and as commander of the Red Army; the face of that "bloody-minded professor" is the most persistent image in the film. Nor are we spared the ineffable vulgarities of Communist rhetoric; indeed they are more oppressive here than in the other films because the commentary is spoken and we must endure to hear Max Eastman express-

273

ing the sentiments of 1937 in the very tones of 1937. "Kerensky had completely ignored the fundamental demand of the masses." "Lenin explained his purpose to the masses." "Kolchak was totally incapable of understanding the situation." "Trotsky proclaimed: 'Kerensky is a tool of the landlords and capitalists! All power to the Soviet!'" This is the language we once listened to with patience. I would have felt sorry for Max Eastman—who after all made no montages of corpses—if I had not been feeling more sorry for myself. Still, perhaps it would be no better if the sentiments were those of 1955. The commentator is one of the diseases of our time and must be endured; he will be there at the end of the world to say into a microphone: "This is the end of the world." But his greatest power lies not in what he says but in his tone of healthy intelligence; Max Eastman has at any rate a certain nervousness in his speech which makes one wish to forgive him.

What matters chiefly in *Tsar to Lenin* is simply that the pictures it presents are in the most primitive sense true. This is not "history" any more than it is art: it is no more than a fragmentary record of appearances. But after all the ideology and all the art, that may be the best we can hope to have; if it does not contain the truth of history, whatever that may be, it does allow us to know the pathos of history, the mere fact that enormous things have happened and human beings have been involved in them. The crowds that throng the cold Russian streets in this movie are the crowds that really saw the Czarist government fall. They are not "the masses" and they do not enter upon the screen in pleasing and meaningful patterns established by a director seeking to express "the masses." Watching them, it is easy to accept the remark of a British observer, quoted by Eastman: "Nothing like these crowds was ever seen before in Europe"—whereas Eisenstein's crowds make you think most of how brilliantly he has "handled" them. You can look at a face in these crowds and say: that man was really there. Is this important? It must be important.

There was even a brief shot of a man I had met: Victor Chernov, a member of Kerensky's government. When I was a child I sat once at the dinner table while the exiled Chernov talked in Russian with the grownups. He seemed to me a wonderfully big and strong man, with a great voice and beautiful white hair. I knew nothing, really, of who he was or what he had done, and I could not understand a word that was said. I stared at him for that hour or so and thought: he was there, he was part of it. Chernov died only a while ago in New York—by then, I suppose, a commonplace figure among the Social Democrats—but I never saw him again except in this movie, where he looks still like a big and strong man. Kerensky himself is still alive somewhere in New York and no doubt I could arrange to meet him if it were important to me. Maybe it ought to be important. He "completely ignored the fundamental demand of the masses," we are told, and so played his part in what has happened to us; one could ask him what he thought he was doing. But he has already written his answer, I believe, and I have never bothered to read it. What answer he might give could bring us closer to the thing we want to know? It is enough to have him fixed on the screen; a small, not quite handsome man smiling down upon a crowd in St. Petersburg, or holding a bouquet that some admirer has pressed on him, or finally, an exile in Paris, composing his features for the camera in an absurd pose of depth and resolution. The selection of pictures is manifestly unfair to him, but what we see is Kerensky nevertheless—another man who was there. (With Eisenstein, in *Ten Days That Shook the World*, he is portrayed—by an actor—as a

275

posturing fool who dreams of being a dictator; once he is shown brooding at his desk below a bust of Napoleon. He has had the last laugh on Eisenstein at any rate.)

There is also Nicholas II. Rather short, it seems, but very handsome with his neat features and beautiful beard, dignified, clean, inhumanly composed. My mother was born on the day his grandfather was assassinated, and eight or nine years later she was taken to America; my father, a young man of twenty or so, left Russia two or three years after Nicholas came to the throne; but Czar of Russia is still the name of an enemy, upholder of superstition and maker of pogroms. And yet he was not always thinking about how to oppress the Jews, or even about how to oppress the Russians. We see him here at play with his friends and his family. Once there is some kind of romp in a field, with the young man trying to catch the girls and making them fall down in the grass; the Czar does not himself engage in this sport, but looks on, one hand behind his back. Another time there is an incomprehensible ball game, with innumerable balls lying about on the ground; now and then somebody picks up one and seems to throw it at somebody else, but there is a certain awkwardness about the whole thing and it looks like a very dull game. Once the Czar goes swimming with his men friends; they are naked and when the Czar stands up in the shallow water, exposing his behind, Max Eastman says, "This is the first time in history that a king has been seen as he really is." At other times the Czar is shown in his imperial role, reviewing his guard; walking in solemn procession with a robed priest; visiting the front. In a number of these scenes the Czarevich is beside him, a thin pinched boy, learning how to be a Czar. Once the Czarevich appears by himself, perhaps no more than nine years old, dressed in a Cossack uniform with a little sword; an officer lifts him onto a horse

276

and he is allowed to ride around a little; Max Eastman remarks, "The Czarevich was probably the best-spoiled child in the world." Well, the Bolsheviks did not spare the rod: a little later there is a picture of the Czar with his whole family—four daughters, the Czarina, and the Czarevich—and Eastman announces in the loud flat tone of one who has understood and assimilated all: "Eighteen months later all seven of them were shot in a cellar in Ekaterinburg!"—he calls it "Yuhkadderinburg." The Czar and his family, like Kolchak later on, were "totally incapable of understanding the situation," and history exacts a penalty for such incapacity, even of young boys with hemophilia. Though Eastman does not mention it, the Bolsheviks also shot in that cellar in Ekaterinburg the Czar's servants and his doctor and when the shooting was over the executioners trampled on the bodies and smashed them with the butts of their rifles. No doubt if there had been no revolution and the Czarevich had become Czar, he would have been a bigot and a despot like his father. Also, no doubt, he would have died young, of hemophilia.

Of Lenin and Trotsky I had hoped for more than the mere sense of their presence. I think I was even looking for something that could be called "the face of revolution," and of course it wasn't there; only Eisenstein ever gives us anything like that, and what he gives is a falsehood. Yet one cannot pretend, either, to see these two figures "pure"; the revolution does envelop them like a cloud, and we look at them now through its thirty-eight-years' thickness of disaster. When Lenin poses informally for the camera in a sunny courtyard, smiling, relaxed, his hands in his pockets and a workingman's cap on the back of his head, it is easy enough to see that he must have been a man of grace and charm, only it is no longer easy to be interested in his grace and his charm. I

277

found him more "real" in his embattled postures: for instance when he harangues a crowd in the street, a black figure full of dangerous energy "explaining his purpose to the masses"; we do not hear his voice, of course, but the movements of his face are enough; we know in what language and what tones these "explanations" were offered. Trotsky's energy is less "elemental" than Lenin's, sharper and more nervous. We see him rushing around to his fourteen fronts, and the commentator reads us passages from his proclamation: "Without Czarist officers, bureaucrats, and capitalists, our country will live a peaceful and happy life. . . . Death to the hirelings of foreign capital!" Trotsky's little pedant's face is like the point of a weapon. His followers used to speak of him affectionately as "the Old Man," but that was when he was in exile and could no longer kill anybody.

They broke their eggs, and they made their omelette. But history was waiting for them too, just as if they were no better than the little spoiled Czarevich with his hemophilia. There is one very brief shot of the Great Muzhik who was to inherit: a heavy dark man standing at the very edge of a group, looking as if he is not quite sure where he fits in. Eastman says: "Nobody then dreamed. . . ." No, nobody did. Perhaps even Lenin and Trotsky were totally incapable of "understanding the situation."

What it means to break eggs we can perceive in the scene of the shooting of prisoners. That the victims are Communists and the executioners anti-Communist is of no importance. It could have been the other way around, or it could have been another war in another country: the firing squad is a leitmotif of modern history as the gallows was a leitmotif of the history of earlier times. Europe is covered with these graves where ten, twenty, or a thousand people lie dead together in pits that they themselves dug before they were shot.

The prisoners, twelve or fifteen of them, lie on their bellies on the ground under the guns of their captors; the land seems to stretch out flat and empty for limitless miles behind them. From what one can see of their faces, they are all quite young. Their shoes are collected from them, presumably for the use of Kolchak's soldiers. One of the prisoners raises his head and says something mocking to whoever is taking the picture. Max Eastman says in a tone of exaltation: "The Red soldier laughs!" Then the prisoners stand quietly, three at a time, at the edge of the grave. When they are shot, their hats fly ludicrously into the air and they fall backwards into the grave ungracefully and with astonishing speed; it is hard to believe, at first, that there is all there is to it. After each shooting the executioners walk up to the grave and look in to make sure the victims are dead; once or twice an additional shot is needed. Two of the prisoners wish to stand with their backs to the firing squad, but for some reason that is not proper and there is a pause while one of the executioners gently takes hold of their arms and turns them around. When it is the turn of the prisoner who had laughed, there is still something like a smile on his face, and Max Eastman again breaks the silence: "The Red soldier is *still* laughing!" But in a moment there are those little puffs of smoke from the rifles and the laughing soldier is in the grave with the rest of them.

To watch the suffering and death of real people in a movie is an ambiguous experience, and it would be a kind of moral outrage to make that experience an object of art criticism. All that must be said is that in this movie scene of the death of twelve or fifteen young men, nothing triumphs and nothing is "understood"; it is a record of something that happened. Even the one prisoner's laughter in the face of the firing squad, if it was a triumph at all, was his own triumph; it did not matter in the last moments of his life that the revolution was going to succeed, and as we watched the scene now it does not matter that the revolution failed. What is

279

offensive about Max Eastman's comments is that they are too ready to claim this man's death for something beyond itself; for the workers, or the revolution, or for the two great breakers of eggs, or simply for the human spirit—it doesn't matter what particular claim is made. I do not say that such claims may not be valid, but they are valid only at a distance, not *while* the man dies; the death we watch belongs to the man alone.

Yet it is not fair to complain of Max Eastman. One need only think of what one of the great Russian directors might have done with a scene like this in order to appreciate how utterly vulgar art and belief can be, sometimes, when measured against the purity of a real event. There are innumerable examples of such vulgarity in the Russian cinema, moments when the director, taken up with his role as an artist who controls and interprets—few artists have put a higher value on that role than the early Soviet film directors—forgets what is really at stake and commits an offense against humanity. I have already mentioned examples from the work of Eisenstein and Pudovkin. Let me offer another from Dovzhenko's *Earth*, a movie about the collectivization of agriculture.

Dovzhenko is celebrated as the great "lyricist" of the Soviet cinema, and to judge by this film—I have seen no others of his—the title is largely deserved. *Earth* is beautifully photographed and composed, full of dreamy evocations of the slow, patient life of the Russian peasantry skillfully contrasted with the more urgent movement of the "new life" of progress, optimism, and tractors. There are wonderful close-ups of peasant faces, at once appealing and frightening in their rigidity and incomprehension. One scene of a peasant household getting up in the morning could hardly be surpassed in its presentation of both the squalor of peasant life and its indestructibleness. And throughout the film there is

280

the sense of limitless land and limitless time, and of the constant possibility of violence. One begins to understand from this film the overheated and equivocal fascination which the peasants held for the Russian intelligentsia; if these dumb and alien figures were to be accepted as human at all, then the temptation was great to make of them something quintessentially human. I thought I could understand also, for the first time, what it must have meant to the Jews to live among these peasants in continual expectation of their rage. It must be added that Dovzhenko's picture of the peasants and the countryside is often grossly sentimental—the "beautiful" death of the old peasant Semyon at the beginning of the movie is the clearest example of this—and that the painfully restrained tempo of his direction produces long passages of almost unbearable tedium. Nevertheless Dovzhenko shows himself a serious artist responding sensitively to his material. Compared to this, Eisenstein's *The General Line*, another film about the collectivization of agriculture, is the work of a skilled hack and a philistine.

But Dovzhenko's virtues are all connected with a certain passivity. He is most successful in presenting the life of the peasants when he is willing to accept it as something irremediably "given" and devote himself to recording its meaningful appearances; even his sentimentality, though it is partly dishonest like all sentimentality, is not so much an active falsification of the material as a willfully excessive surrender to it. Whenever he assumes a more active posture—which is to say, whenever he becomes fully an "artist" in the sense in which the Soviet film directors understood that term —his work takes on as glassy and inhuman a brilliance as Eisenstein's. In *Earth*, this quality is to be seen most clearly in the funeral of the young peasant Vasili, the leader of the "progressive" peasants who has been murdered by a resentful "reactionary."

At the desire of Vasili's father, who has at last understood what his son was trying to do, the body is carried to its grave by a procession of energetic young people singing songs of the "new life." We have seen these young people often: strong forearms, open collars, "healthy" and rather empty faces lit up with purpose and conviction—every "movement" puts them on its posters to symbolize the "new life" that will make us all twenty again. They carry Vasili's body as if it were a banner. As the open coffin passes beneath the trees, branches laden with fruit brush the face of the corpse. While the procession moves on its way, a woman back in the village is taken with labor and goes indoors to have her baby: one man is dead, another is born. At the grave, one of the young men makes a speech in which he says that Vasili "gave his blood for the new life" and that Vasili's death has "sealed the death warrant of our enemies"; to the dead man's father he says: "Do not be sad and do not worry—Vasili was a hero!" In the meantime the murderer, seized with remorse, has been running across the field to catch up with the procession; at last he bursts out on a hill beyond the crowd and screams his confession: "I killed him! I am the murderer! I killed Vasili!" But not a head turns; they are all listening to the funeral oration. The murderer, like all enemies of the people, simply does not exist; he has become, in Orwell's word, an "unperson," and even his remorse is of no interest to anybody. Thus failing to attract attention to himself, the murderer continues his mad flight into the distance, diminishing to a tiny insect-like figure at the very bottom of the screen, dancing back and forth in a ridiculous frenzy, while above him rises the vast landscape of fruitful Russia.

(Left unfinished.)

Atheneum Paperbacks

THE WORLDS OF NATURE AND MAN

5 OF MEN AND MOUNTAINS *by William O. Douglas*

18 THE SUDDEN VIEW *by Sybille Bedford*

22 SPRING IN WASHINGTON *by Louis J. Halle*

33 LOST CITY OF THE INCAS *by Hiram Bingham*

45 THE SEA SHORE *by C. M. Yonge*

61 THE NEW YORK TIMES GUIDE TO DINING OUT IN NEW YORK
edited by Craig Claiborne

81 THE NEW YORK TIMES GUIDE TO HOME FURNISHING *edited by
Barbara Plumb and Elizabeth Sverbeyeff*

82 BIRDS AND MEN *by Robert H. Welker*

95 THE FIRMAMENT OF TIME *by Loren Eiseley*

LITERATURE AND THE ARTS

1 ROME AND A VILLA *by Eleanor Clark*

8 THE MUSICAL EXPERIENCE OF COMPOSER, PERFORMER, LISTENER
by Roger Sessions

11 THE GRANDMOTHERS *by Glenway Wescott*

12 i: SIX NONLECTURES *by e.e. cummings*

14 THE PRESENCE OF GRACE *by J. F. Powers*

18 THE SUDDEN VIEW *by Sybille Bedford*

25 THE ROBBER BRIDEGROOM *by Eudora Welty*

29 CONTEXTS OF CRITICISM *by Harry Levin*

36 GEORGE BERNARD SHAW *by Hesketh Pearson*

37 THE TERRITORY AHEAD *by Wright Morris*

39 THE LETTERS OF VINCENT VAN GOGH *edited by Mark Roskill*

42 THE GREEN MARE *by Marcel Aymé*

50 AMERICAN ARCHITECTURE AND OTHER WRITINGS *by Montgomery
Schuyler, edited by William H. Jordy and Ralph Coe;
abridged by William H. Jordy*

66 SELECTED POEMS INCLUDING THE WOMAN AT THE WASHINGTON ZOO
by Randall Jarrell

76 THE SINGER OF TALES *by Albert B. Lord*

96 CONRAD THE NOVELIST *by Albert J. Guerard*

99 MARK TWAIN *by Henry Nash Smith*

102 EMILY DICKINSON *by Thomas H. Johnson*

112 THE LIFE OF THE DRAMA *by Eric Bentley*

114 SELECTED MARK TWAIN-HOWELLS LETTERS *edited by Frederick
Anderson, William Gibson, and Henry Nash Smith*

122 REPORTING THE NEWS *edited by Louis M. Lyons*

131 WHAT IS THEATRE? *(incorporating* THE DRAMATIC EVENT*)
by Eric Bentley*

135 THE HERO OF THE WAVERLY NOVELS *by Alexander Welsh*

143 POETS OF REALITY *by J. Hillis Miller*

158 LANGUAGE AND SILENCE *by George Steiner*

159 THE IMMEDIATE EXPERIENCE *by Robert Warshow*

165 MOVIES: A PSYCHOLOGICAL STUDY *by Martha Wolfenstein and
Nathan Leites*

168 LITERARY DISSENT IN COMMUNIST CHINA *by Merle Goldman*

177 ALONE WITH AMERICA *by Richard Howard*

180 H. G. WELLS *by Lovat Dickson*

Atheneum Paperbacks

PSYCHOLOGY AND SOCIOLOGY

21 BIG BUSINESS LEADERS IN AMERICA *by W. Lloyd Warner and James Abegglen*

67 ON KNOWING *by Jerome S. Bruner*

100 AFRICAN HOMICIDE AND SUICIDE *edited by Paul Bohannan*

119 THE LAW OF PRIMITIVE MAN *by E. Adamson Hoebel*

120 THE SOVIET CITIZEN *by Alex Inkeles and Raymond Bauer*

133 THE FAMILY REVOLUTION IN MODERN CHINA *by Marion J. Levy, Jr.*

165 MOVIES: A PSYCHOLOGICAL STUDY *by Martha Wolfenstein and Nathan Leites*

182 THE CONSPIRACY AGAINST CHILDHOOD *by Eda J. LeShan*

LIFE SCIENCES AND ANTHROPOLOGY

9 MATTER, MIND AND MAN *by Edmund W. Sinnott*

16 THE HORMONES IN HUMAN REPRODUCTION *by George W. Corner*

26 THE OLD STONE AGE *by Miles C. Burkitt*

28 MORPHOGENESIS *by John Tyler Bonner*

33 LOST CITY OF THE INCAS *by Hiram Bingham*

35 GENETICS, PALEONTOLOGY, AND EVOLUTION *edited by Glenn L. Jepsen, Ernst Mayr and George Gaylord Simpson*

45 THE SEA SHORE *by C. M. Yonge*

48 TRISTES TROPIQUES *by Claude Lévi-Strauss*

62 TERRITORY IN BIRD LIFE *by Eliot Howard*

71 HEREDITY AND EVOLUTION IN HUMAN POPULATIONS *by L. C. Dunn*

85 THE INTEGRITY OF THE BODY *by F. M. Burnet, F.R.S.*

88 SPEECH AND BRAIN-MECHANISMS *by Wilder Penfield and Lamar Roberts*

91 CELLS AND SOCIETIES *by John Tyler Bonner*

95 THE FIRMAMENT OF TIME *by Loren Eiseley*

98 IDEAS ON HUMAN EVOLUTION *edited by William Howells*

101 COMMUNICATION AMONG SOCIAL BEES *by Martin Lindauer*

106 ON THE ORIGIN OF SPECIES *by Charles Darwin, a Facsimile of the First Edition, edited by Ernst Mayr*

109 AFRICAN HOMICIDE AND SUICIDE *edited by Paul Bohannon*

155 PEOPLE OF RIMROCK *edited by Evon Z. Vogt and Ethel M. Albert*

STUDIES IN HUMAN BEHAVIOR

Alfred M. Freedman, M.D., and Harold I. Kaplan, M.D., General Editors

HB1 DIAGNOSING MENTAL ILLNESS

HB2 INTERPRETING PERSONALITY

HB3 HUMAN BEHAVIOR

HB4 TREATING MENTAL ILLNESS

HB5 THE CHILD: NORMAL DEVELOPMENT AND PSYCHOLOGICAL ASSESSMENT, *Vol.*

HB6 THE CHILD: THE MAJOR PSYCHOLOGICAL DISORDERS AND THEIR TREATMENT, *Vol. 2*

Atheneum Paperbacks

TEMPLE BOOKS—*The Jewish Publication Society*

T1   JEWISH LIFE IN THE MIDDLE AGES *by Israel Abrahams*
T2   FOR THE SAKE OF HEAVEN *by Martin Buber*
T3   A HISTORY OF THE CONTEMPORARY JEWS *by Solomon Grayzel*
T4   THE ZIONIST IDEA *edited by Arthur Hertzberg*
T5   A HISTORY OF MEDIAEVAL JEWISH PHILOSOPHY *by Isaac Husik*
T6   THREE JEWISH PHILOSOPHERS *edited by Hans Lewy,*
       Alexander Altmann and Isaak Heinemann
T7   THE JEW IN THE MEDIEVAL WORLD *by Jacob R. Marcus*
T8   A HISTORY OF THE JEWISH PEOPLE *by Max L. Margolis and*
       Alexander Marx
T9   THE CONFLICT OF THE CHURCH AND THE SYNAGOGUE *by James Parkes*
T10   INTRODUCTION TO THE TALMUD AND MIDRASH *by Hermann L. Strack*
T11   AKIBA: SCHOLAR, SAINT AND MARTYR *by Louis Finkelstein*
T12   OF JEWISH LAW AND LORE *by Louis Ginzberg*
T13   JUDAISM AND MODERN MAN *by William Herberg*
T14   STUDIES IN JUDAISM *by Solomon Schechter*
T15   JEWISH MAGIC AND SUPERSTITION *by Joshua Trachtenberg*
T16   THE WILD GOATS OF EIN GEDI *by Herbert Weiner*
T17   JUDAISM AND CHRISTIANITY *by Leo Baeck*
T18   THEODORE HERZL *by Alex Bein*
T19   AMERICAN JEWRY AND THE CIVIL WAR *by Bertram W. Korn*
T20   SELECTED ESSAYS OF AHAD HA-'AM *by Leon Simon*
T21   NATIONALISM AND HISTORY *by Simon Dubnow*
T22   HELLENISTIC CIVILIZATION AND THE JEWS *by Victor Tcherikover*

PHILOSOPHY AND RELIGION

6   ROGER WILLIAMS *by Perry Miller*
9   MATTER, MIND AND MAN *by Edmund W. Sinnott*
19   BUDDHISM IN TRANSLATIONS *by Henry Clarke Warren*
31   PHILOSOPHY OF MATHEMATICS AND NATURAL SCIENCE
      by Hermann Weyl
38   TOWARD REUNION IN PHILOSOPHY *by Morton White*
52   RELIGION IN TWENTIETH CENTURY AMERICA *by Herbert W. Schneider*
60   HERACLITUS *by Philip Wheelwright*
69   ON THE USE OF PHILOSOPHY *by Jacques Maritain*
75   RELIGIOUS PHILOSOPHY *by Harry Austryn Wolfson*
97   THE EIGHTEENTH CENTURY CONFRONTS THE GODS *by Frank E. Manuel*
183   GENERALIZATION IN ETHICS *by Marcus Singer*

Atheneum Paperbacks

STUDIES IN AMERICAN NEGRO LIFE

NL1   THE NEGRO IN COLONIAL NEW ENGLAND *by Lorenzo Johnston Greene*

NL2   SEPARATE AND UNEQUAL *by Louis R. Harlan*

NL3   AFTER FREEDOM *by Hortense Powdermaker*

NL4   FREDERICK DOUGLASS *by Benjamin Quarles*

NL5   PREFACE TO PEASANTRY *by Arthur F. Raper*

NL6   W.E.B. DU BOIS: PROPAGANDIST OF THE NEGRO PROTEST
      by Elliott Rudwick

NL7   THE BLACK WORKER *by Sterling D. Spero and Abram L. Harris*

NL8   THE MAKING OF BLACK AMERICA *edited*

A&B   *by August Meier and Elliott Rudwick, 2 vols.*

NL9   BLACK MANHATTAN *by James Weldon Johnson*

NL10 THE NEW NEGRO *edited by Alain Locke*

NL11 THE NEGRO'S GOD AS REFLECTED IN HIS LITERATURE
      by Benjamin Mays

NL12 NEGRO POETRY AND DRAMA AND THE NEGRO IN AMERICAN FICTION
      by Sterling Brown

NL13 WHEN NEGROES MARCH *by Harbert Garfinkel*

NL14 PHILOSOPHY AND OPINIONS OF MARCUS GARVEY *by Marcus Garvey,*
      edited by Amy Jacques-Garvey

NL15 FREE NEGRO LABOR AND PROPERTY HOLDING IN VIRGINIA, 1830—1860
      by Luther Porter Jackson

NL16 SEA ISLAND TO CITY *by Clyde Vernon Kiser*

NL17 NEGRO EDUCATION IN ALABAMA *by Horace Mann Bond*

NL18 POLITICS, PRINCIPLE AND PREJUDICE, 1865—1866
      by LaWanda and John H. Cox

NL19 NEGRO POLITICAL LEADERSHIP IN THE SOUTH *by Everett Carll Ladd, Jr.*

NL20 BLACK RECONSTRUCTION IN AMERICA, 1860—1880 *by W. E. B. Du Bois*

NL21 NEGROES IN CITIES *by Karl E. and Alma F. Taeuber*

NL22 TWO JAMAICAS *by Philip De Armond Curtin*

NL23 VASSOURASS: A BRAZILIAN COFFEE COUNTY, 1850—1900 *by Stanley J. Stein*

NL24 THE ROYAL AFRICAN COMPANY *by K. G. Davies*

NL25 STRANGE ENTHUSIASM: A LIFE OF THOMAS WENTWORTH HIGGINSON
      by Tilden G. Edelstein

NL26 THE *Guardian* OF BOSTON: WILLIAM MONROE TROTTER
      by Stephen R. Fox

NL27 LEWIS TAPPAN AND THE EVANGELICAL WAR AGAINST SLAVERY
      by Bertram Wyatt-Brown

NL28 THE NEGRO IN BRAZILIAN SOCIETY *by Florestan Fernandes*

NL29 THE NEGRO AND THE COMMUNIST PARTY *by Wilson Record*

Atheneum Paperbacks

HISTORY—AMERICAN—1900 TO THE PRESENT

2   POWER AND DIPLOMACY *by Dean Acheson*

7   THE REPUBLICAN ROOSEVELT *by John Morton Blum*

40   THE UNITED STATES AND MEXICO *by Howard F. Cline*

43   HOLMES-LASKI LETTERS: THE CORRESPONDENCE OF JUSTICE OLIVER

A&B   WENDELL HOLMES AND HAROLD J. LASKI *1916–1935 edited by Mark De Wolfe Howe, abridged by Alger Hiss, 2 vols.*

51   TURMOIL AND TRADITION *by Elting E. Morison*

70   THE CHINA TANGLE *by Herbert Feis*

86   THE CORPORATION IN MODERN SOCIETY *edited by Edward S. Mason*

111   THE DECLINE OF AMERICAN LIBERALISM *by Arthur A. Ekirch, Jr.*

113   HARVARD GUIDE TO AMERICAN HISTORY *edited by Oscar Handlin, Arthur Meier Schlesinger, Samuel Eliot Morison, Frederick Merk, Arthur Meier Schlesinger, Jr., Paul Herman Buck*

115   THE ROOTS OF AMERICAN LOYALTY *by Merle Curti*

116   THE POLITICS OF PREJUDICE *by Roger Daniels*

117   CENTURY OF STRUGGLE *by Eleanor Flexner*

123   THE AMERICAN APPROACH TO FOREIGN POLICY *by Dexter Perkins*

126   THE AMERICAN AS REFORMER *by Arthur M. Schlesinger*

129   THE LEGEND OF HENRY FORD *by Keith Sward*

137   FREE SPEECH IN THE UNITED STATES *by Zechariah Chafee, Jr.*

140   MASSACHUSETTS PEOPLE AND POLITICS, 1919–1933 *by J. Joseph Huthmacher*

142   THE PROFESSIONAL ALTRUIST *by Roy Lubove*

149   THE COMMUNIST CONTROVERSY IN WASHINGTON *by Earl Latham*

150   THE DECLINE OF AGRARIAN DEMOCRACY *by Grant McConnell*

151   POLITICS AND POWER *by David J. Rothman*

160   UP AGAINST THE IVY WALL *by Jerry Avorn and members of the staff of the* Columbia Daily Spectator

161   QUANTIFICATION IN AMERICAN HISTORY *by Robert P. Swierenga*

162   PROHIBITION AND THE PROGRESSIVE MOVEMENT *by James H. Timberlake*

163   FARM POLICIES AND POLITICS IN THE TRUMAN YEARS *by Allen J. Matusow*

167   SENATOR ROBERT F. WAGNER AND THE RISE OF URBAN LIBERALISM *by J. Joseph Huthmacher*

173   THE IMAGE *by Daniel J. Boorstin*

175   SECOND CHANCE *by Robert A. Divine*

178   THE END OF THE AMERICAN ERA *by Andrew Hacker*

Atheneum Paperbacks

HISTORY

3   SIX MEDIEVAL MEN AND WOMEN *by H. S. Bennett*
10 TRAVEL AND DISCOVERY IN THE RENAISSANCE *by Boies Penrose*
30 GHANA IN TRANSITION *by David E. Apter*
58 TROTSKY'S DIARY IN EXILE—1935 *translated by Elena Zarudnaya*
63 THE SINO-SOVIET CONFLICT 1956–1961 *by Donald S. Zagoria*
83 KARAMZIN'S MEMOIR ON ANCIENT AND MODERN RUSSIA
    by Richard Pipes
97 THE EIGHTEENTH CENTURY CONFRONTS THE GODS *by Frank E. Manuel*
103 JACOBEAN PAGEANT *by G. P. V. Akrigg*
104 THE MAKING OF VICTORIAN ENGLAND *by G. Kitson Clark*
107 RUSSIA LEAVES THE WAR *by George F. Kennan*
108 THE DECISION TO INTERVENE *by George F. Kennan*
121 DRIVING FORCES IN HISTORY *by Halvdan Koht*
124 THE FORMATION OF THE SOVIET UNION *by Richard Pipes*
127 THE THREE LIVES OF CHARLES DE GAULLE *by David Schoenbrun*
128 AS FRANCE GOES *by David Schoenbrun*
141 SERGEI WITTE AND THE INDUSTRIALIZATION OF RUSSIA
    by Theodore Von Laue
152 A HISTORY OF THE WEIMAR REPUBLIC *by Erich Eyck,*
A&B *2 vols.*
161 QUANTIFICATION IN AMERICAN HISTORY *by Robert P. Swierenga*
181 THE COURT AND THE COUNTRY *by Perez Zagorin*

HISTORY—ASIA

44 CHINA'S RESPONSE TO THE WEST *by Ssu-Yü Teng and John K. Fairbank*
63 THE SINO-SOVIET CONFLICT 1956–1961 *by Donald S. Zagoria*
70 THE CHINA TANGLE *by Herbert Feis*
87 A DOCUMENTARY HISTORY OF CHINESE COMMUNISM
    by Conrad Brandt, Benjamin Schwartz and John K. Fairbank
92 THE LAST STAND OF CHINESE CONSERVATISM *by Mary Clabaugh Wright*
93 THE TRAGEDY OF THE CHINESE REVOLUTION *by Harold R. Isaacs*
147 AFTER IMPERIALISM *by Akira Iriye*
153 CHINA'S EARLY INDUSTRIALIZATION *by Albert Feuerwerker*
154 LI TA-CHAO AND THE ORIGINS OF CHINESE MARXISM *by Maurice Meisner*
164 COMMUNISM AND CHINA: IDEOLOGY IN FLUX *by Benjamin I. Schwartz*
168 LITERARY DISSENT IN COMMUNIST CHINA *by Merle Goldman*
176 THE COMMUNISTS AND THE CHINESE PEASANT REBELLIONS *by*
    James P. Harrison